TRAVEL TRADE
AND TRANSPORT

Also available:

Aronsson: *The Development of Sustainable Tourism*
Bray and Raitz: *Flight to the Sun*
Clift and Carter (eds): *Tourism and Sex*
Foley and Lennon: *Dark Tourism*
Godfrey and Clarke: *The Tourism Development Handbook*
Hudson: *Snow Business*
Julyan: *Sales and Service for the Wine Professional*
Law: *Urban Tourism*
Leask and Yeoman (eds): *Heritage Visitor Attractions*
Lee-Ross (eds): *HRM in Tourism and Hospitality*
Lumsdon and Swift: *Tourism in Latin America*
Tribe *et al.*: *Environmental Management for Rural Tourism and Recreation*
Van der Wagen and Davies: *Supervision and Leadership in Tourism and Hospitality*
Wright: *The Management of Service Operations*

Travel Trade and Transport

Lesley Pender

CONTINUUM
London and New York

Continuum

The Tower Building   370 Lexington Avenue
11 York Road   New York
London SE1 7NX   NY 10017–6503

www.continuumbooks.com

First published in 2001

British Library Cataloguing-in-Publication Data

A catalogue record for this book is available from the British Library.

ISBN   0–8264–5143–8 (hb)
      0–8264–5142–X (pb)

Typeset by Ben Cracknell Studios
Printed and bound in Great Britain, by the Cromwell Press, Trowbridge, Wilts

Contents

PART 1

1 Tour Operators

2 Holiday Packaging

CONTENTS

5 Travel Trade: Trends and Issues

PART 2

6 Rail Transport

7 Ferries and Cruising

CONTENTS

CONTENTS

List of Tables

List of Figures

Foreword

This book aims to provide comprehensive coverage of the travel trade and transport sectors. These are significant areas of economic activity within the overall field of tourism. A number of comprehensive texts cover each of the relevant areas in detail and many of these sources are referenced throughout this book.

The travel trade and transport sectors are involved in the organization and sale of travel and tourism services and in the movement of tourists to, from and within destinations. These organizations supply and distribute travel and tourism – activities for which demand is growing at a faster rate than most areas of economic activity – and have particular importance in respect of the outbound market.

This book is structured in two parts with the first dedicated to the travel trade and the second to transport for tourism. Despite the fact that this approach has been adopted for reasons of practicality it is important to note that often the organizations providing these services are integrated with one another. Indeed, reference is made in Part 1 to topics covered in Part 2 and vice versa. Arguably the chapter on travel trade and transport technology could have been placed in either part of the book.

The specific aims of this text are as follows:

- To provide the reader with an understanding of the role, function and operation of organizations in the travel trade and transport sectors.
- To provide the reader with an integrative view of the above sectors of the tourism industry.
- To emphasize the linkages between the different sectors of the industry.
- To examine key trends and issues impacting on the travel trade and transport sectors.

- To emphasize the dynamic nature of travel trade and transport.
- To examine the importance of technology to travel trade and transport operations and distribution.

Part 1 of the book examines the travel trade in detail, focusing heavily on retail travel and tour operations – two of the main components of travel distribution especially in the UK with its well-developed outbound tourism industry. Technology is also recognized as a significant aspect of the operation and distribution of travel and a chapter is therefore dedicated to discussion of this and technology used by transport providers. Part 1 concludes with a detailed look at many of the main trends and issues currently facing the travel trade and with some analysis of the strategies being adopted by organizations to cope with the business environment.

Part 2 of the book goes on to examine relevant forms of public sector transport involved in the transportation of tourists to, from and within resorts. This includes rail, sea and coach as well as airline transport forms. Public transport is a major aspect of the travel and tourism industry and represents a sector which has undergone great change during the past two decades. The end of the twentieth century were characterized by the processes of deregulation and privatization in transport subsectors operating both at national and international levels. These subsectors are now highly competitive.

There is much that this book does not do. It does not, for example, provide any coverage of private forms of transport. This may seem inappropriate given that the private car is the main form of transport for domestic travel in the UK but this form of transport does not involve the same type of organization as the public transport forms that are considered. The significant car hire business is also seen to fall outside the aims of this text. The aim here is not to cover all transport forms, merely those for whom a significant amount of business is derived from tourism.

The sectors covered are extremely dynamic in nature and whilst every effort has been made to examine this aspect, the approach taken has also considered the longevity of the book to be a priority. Indeed, many of the trends and issues of importance in today's travel trade and transport environment have been evolving over the past two decades. Care should however be taken when using any recent examples provided in the text as these quickly become outdated in an industry as dynamic as this. Whilst the travel and tourism industry as a whole is extremely fragmented, levels of concentration within the different sectors as discussed in this book are high and this proves to be a recurring theme throughout the text.

THE STRUCTURE OF THE BOOK

This book has been designed around a structure which comprises two parts as follows.

Part 1: The Travel Trade[1]

Part 2: Transport for Tourism.

Each chapter follows the same basic structure for ease of use. This structure is outlined below:

- Introduction
- Content
- Summary
- Discussion questions
- References and bibliography
- Further reading.

ACKNOWLEDGEMENTS

This book would have been impossible without the help of a great many people. I would particularly like to thank the following individuals and organizations for their help: BTA; Paul Beaumont, Sales Director, Greatdays Travel Group; Rachel Colquitt, JGPR; Caroline Rankin, Thomas Cook; Odile Triplet, Account Manager, ZFL Public Relations; Gwyneth Harkus, Virgin Holidays; Airtours International Plc.; Superbreak Golden Rail; and Nick Hayes.

NOTE

Technology is covered in Part 1 of the book although it could have been placed in either section as it relates to both the travel trade and transport sectors.

Abbreviations

AAC	Association of Airline Consolidators
AAIB	Air Accidents Investigation Branch
ABTA	Association of British Travel Agents
AEA	Association of European Airlines
AIT	Air Inclusive Tour
AITO	Association of Independent Tour Operators
ARTAC	Alliance of Retail Travel Agents Consortium
ASTA	American Society of Travel Agents
ATOL	Air Travel Organizers' Licence
AUC	Air Transport Users' Council
AV	Altan Velocidad
BA	British Airways
BAH	British Airways Holidays
BAWTA	British Association of Wholesale Tour Agents
BEA	British European Airways
BFF	Business Format Franchising
BITOA	British Incoming Tour Operators' Association
BNTS	British National Travel Survey
BOAC	British Overseas Airways Corporation
BTA	British Tourist Authority
CAA	Civil Aviation Authority
CAB	Civil Aeronautics Board
CARTA	Campaign for Real Travel Agents
CIT	Communication and information technologies
CPT	Confederation of Passenger Transport
CRS	Computerized Reservations System

CTC	Coach Tourism Council
DETR	Department of the Environment, Transport and the Regions
DTI	Department of Trade and Industry
EBA	EuroBelgian Airways
EC	European Community
ECAC	European Civil Aviation Conference
ERAA	European Regional Airlines Association
ERG	Economic Regulation Group
ETOA	European Tour Operators' Association
EU	European Union
FFP	Frequent Flyer Programme
FIT	Fully Inclusive Tour
FTO	Federation of Tour Operators
GBTA	Guild of Business Travel Agents
GDS	Global Distribution System
GHA	Ground Handling Agent
GSA	General Sales Agent
GS & WR	Great Scottish and Western Railway
GTG	Global Travel Group
GTO	Group Travel Organizer
GTOA	Group Travel Organizers' Association
HSE	Health and Safety Executive
IISS	High Speed Service
IATA	International Air Transport Association
ICAO	International Civil Aviation Organization
ICE	Inter-City Express
ILG	International Leisure Group
IPS	International Passenger Survey
IT	Inclusive Tour
ITC	Inclusive Tour by Charter
ITO	Incentive Travel Organizer
ITX	Inclusive Tour by Excursion
JEA	Jersey European Airways
LCC	Low Cost Carrier
LCR	London and Continental Railways
LTB	London Tourist Board
MMC	Monopolies and Mergers Commission
MOD	Ministry of Defence
MVC	Manchester Visitor and Convention Bureau
NAITA	National Association of Independent Travel Agents
NATS	National Air Traffic Services

NCL	Norwegian Cruise Line
NPD	New Product Development
OFT	Office of Fair Trading
OPRAF	Office for Passenger Rail Franchising
ORR	Office of the Rail Regulator
PPP	Public Private Partnership
PR	Public Relations
PSA	Passenger Shipping Association
RSC	Royal Shakespeare Company
RDA	German Travel Association for the Bus and Coach Industry
ROSCOS	Rolling Stock Leasing Companies
SRA	Strategic Rail Authority
TGV	Train à Grande Vitesse
TOC	Train Operating Company
TTG	Travel Trade Gazette
TTO	Thomson Tour Operations
UIC	International Union of Railways
UK	United Kingdom
UKTS	United Kingdom Tourism Survey
VDU	Visual Display Unit
VFR	Visiting Friends and Relatives
WWW	World Wide Web

PART 1

Introduction

This first part of the book introduces the travel trade, in other words tour operators and travel agents. Communication and information technology as applied to travel trade and transport sectors is also introduced. The travel trade, together with charter airlines (which are discussed in Part 2) are the most important suppliers and distributors to the outbound holiday market. The other principal suppliers to this market are ferry operators, Eurostar, Le Shuttle and scheduled airlines all of which are discussed in Part 2 of the book. The UK has one of the most developed outbound tour operating industries in the world – tour operators account for one-third of all outbound visits – and for this reason receives a lot of attention here.

CHAPTER 1

Tour Operators

INTRODUCTION

This introductory chapter describes the role and function of tour operators, the organizations at the heart of the travel trade. It also examines the structure of the tour operations sector. Chapter 2 goes on to examine the organization and operation of inclusive tours. This is followed by a detailed account of the intermediaries involved in distributing many tour operators' products, principally the travel agency sector. These three chapters compliment one another and should be viewed as this text's introductory coverage of the concept known as the travel trade. The remainder of Part 1 of the book looks at technology as applied to the travel trade and finally, in Chapter 5, at a number of strategic and current issues which characterize the industry.

Tour operators are commonly described as the creators of package holidays also known as inclusive tours (ITs) or, where the transportation element is by air, Air Inclusive Tours (AITs). This they do by packaging together the different components of tours and selling these on to the public with or without the help of an intermediary. This chapter first of all outlines the package holiday concept (which is discussed further in Chapter 3) and then examines the role of the tour operator in the provision of inclusive tours. Whilst the focus is on outbound tour operators the role of incoming and domestic tour operators is also examined.

Prior to more detailed discussion of the role and function of tour operators and the structure of the industry it is useful to clarify some of the terms used in this text. The following table which is adapted from Mintel (1998) is helpful in this respect. Tourism itself is defined, for our current purposes, as any travel which involves an overnight stay away from home.

Inclusive tours or package holidays

The simultaneous sale of at least two elements of a holiday to the traveller including fares on public transport (e.g. flights) and commercial accommodation (e.g. hotel accommodation). Other elements such as meals or excursions are not essential to the definition of a 'tour' but may be included.

Independent holidays
The traveller organizes and books the transport and accommodation from separate sources (e.g. a channel ferry crossing and a caravan site in France).

Seat-only
This is used to denote holidays in which travellers only purchase an airline ticket and thereafter book their own accommodation, car hire etc.

Fly-drive
A hybrid type of holiday (classified statistically as inclusive tours) which cross tours with independent holidays, to include a flight and car hire and possibly the first night's accommodation.

All-inclusive
A particular type of resort holiday in which food, drink, excursions and other services are provided as part of the total holiday cost.

Long holidays
Holidays of four nights or more away from home.

Short break holidays
Short breaks are holidays of one to three nights away from home.

Short haul
This normally refers to air holidays within Europe to particular destinations closer to the generating country. Spain, the Balearic Islands and Greece are typical short-haul destinations from the UK but holidays to Turkey, North Africa and the Canary Islands can also be classified in this way.

Long haul
Most air holidays outside Europe, other than the short-haul destinations described above, can be considered to be long-haul destinations. Chief long-haul destinations are the USA and Canada, the Caribbean, the Far East and Australasia.

Figure 1.1. Inclusive tours terminology. *Source*: Mintel, Leisure Intelligence (1998).

Tour operators combine the raw materials of a holiday including accommodation, the means of travel, facilities and possibly also food, excursions or activities. This package is then sold on to consumers, either direct or via a travel agent, at a price that is usually less than it would have cost the customer to purchase the various components themselves. That the tour operator is able to achieve this lower cost is partly due to the booking of blocks of the accommodation and transportation elements of the package. It is vital that the operator selects a successful combination of these elements and markets them appropriately. Where a package is sold through a middleman, a travel agent, then it is usual for the travel agent to earn commission on the sale. There has however been a slight shift towards fee based payments recently.

In addition to AITs, tour operators also meet demand for packages by sea, rail and coach. The latter sometimes also use the Channel Tunnel. Stena Line, Sally Line, P&O European Ferries and Brittany Ferries all market holidays involving sea crossings, transfers and European accommodation. Whilst rail, sea and coach based inclusive tours are covered in general terms in Part 1 of this text, they are covered in a great deal more detail by Chapters 6, 7 and 8 respectively. The focus of the current chapter is on AITs but the importance of non-air-based packages should not be forgotten when considering the total tour operations sector. Reference is therefore made to these suppliers of holidays throughout the text where appropriate.

In addition to making bookings tour operators undertake research and organization activities long in advance of a tour programme taking place or even being sold. This involves a degree of risk as well as which the company will incur the costs of designing, producing and distributing brochures as well as those of operating a reservations system. Further marketing expenses include a marketing communications programme. Discussion of these aspects of holiday packaging is provided in Chapter 2.

The package holiday market is subject to the vagaries of market forces including exchange rates and taxes as well as those elements over which tour operators have more control such as the final holiday prices. The total inclusive tour market is in excess of 15 million holidays. This overall market can be segmented in a number of ways including those shown in Figure 1.2.

- By mode of transport (i.e. air/rail/sea)
- By distance to destination (i.e. long haul/short haul)
- By length of holiday (i.e. short break/long holiday)
- By travel season (e.g. summer/winter)

Figure 1.2. Segmentation of the inclusive tour market.

MARKET DEMAND

Inclusive tours are attractive to particular market segments including the young (15–24) but less so to those in the 'young family' stage. Particular destinations also appeal to the package holiday market with France and Spain (including the Ballearic Islands) accounting for half of all outbound packages from the UK. The popularity of Greece, Turkey and Spain/Canaries as AIT destinations may alter as tourist demand changes. Demand for niche products has already started to alter destination choice with all-inclusives, skiing holidays and long haul exotic locations, amongst others, proving popular. The trend, seen in the 1990s, towards long haul holidays has helped the inclusive tour market as travellers are often less able or confident in terms of organizing independent travel to these destinations. One emerging feature is the provision of what Mintel (1998) terms 'quasi independent' holidays to destinations such as the USA. Special interest packages are seen to be increasingly important and in general terms outbound travellers are ever more sophisticated. Characteristic of today's market are not only independent travel bookings by these more sophisticated travellers but also bargain-hunting and consumer complaints. Key Note Ltd (1998) forecasts that the number of independent holidays will grow at a faster rate than package holidays.

Whilst there were 613 registered Association of British Travel Agent (ABTA) tour operators in July 1995 according to Key Note (1998), the tour operations sector is highly concentrated with the top five tour operators accounting for 58 per cent by volume of foreign package holiday sales in 1996. The majority of outbound tourism from the UK is however arranged independently as illustrated by Table 1.1.

Table 1.1. Estimated share of the UK tourism market accounted for by tour operators by value (%), 1997. *Source*: Key Note (1998).

	Tour operators
Domestic tourism	5
Outbound tourism	32
Total	37

There is a strong demand for independent travel to destinations such as the USA and so even the major tour operators, traditionally associated with 'packaged' tourism, are offering flexible options for separate flights and accommodation bookings.

Table 1.2. Number of holidays taken by the British, 1986–97 (figures in millions).
Source: British National Travel Survey (English Tourist Board, Northern Ireland Tourist Board, Scottish Tourist Board, Wales Tourist Board)/Mintel.

	1986	**1990**	**1995**	**1997**	**(% change) 1986–97**
Holidays in UK					
Independent	27.1	29.0	29.0	30.0	+11
Inclusive	4.4	3.5	4.0	3.8	−14
Total	31.5	32.5	33.0	33.8	+7
Holidays abroad					
Independent	6.5	9.0	11.0	11.5	+77
Inclusive	11.0	11.5	15.0	15.0	+36
Total	17.5	20.5	26.0	26.5	+51
All holidays					
Independent	33.6	38.0	40.0	41.5	+24
Inclusive	15.4	15.0	19.0	18.8	+22
Total	49.0	53.0	59.0	60.3	+23

Note: holidays in UK of 4+ nights, but of any length abroad.

THE DEVELOPMENT OF TOUR OPERATIONS

Thomas Cook, a printer from Market Harborough, is attributed by many with the introduction of package holidays in the nineteenth century. Holloway (1994) however informs that, contrary to popular belief, he was not in fact the first entrepreneur to organize tours for the public as there were excursion trains in operation by 1840. Holloway does however attribute Cook with having the greatest impact on the early travel industry. The company he founded is still a major force in the industry today as an integrated travel company.

1841	Thomas Cook organized his first excursion – a rail journey from Leicester to a temperance meeting in Loughborough. A special train carried 500 people a distance of 12 miles and back for one shilling.
1845	Thomas Cook conducted the first pleasure trip by railway to Liverpool from Leicester, Nottingham and Derby.
1936	The first of Butlin's holiday camps was founded at Skegness.
1950s	The group holiday concept grew in popularity although with only a small amount of the population as yet able to partake in such holidays due to post-war austerity including government restrictions on the export of sterling.

Figure 1.3. Some key aspects in the development of organized domestic travel and holidays. *Source*: based on Thomas Cook (2000), Laws (1997).

1855	Thomas Cook offered continental trips to The Paris Exhibition.
1878	Thomas Cook offered a round-the-world trip taking in Hong Kong, Singapore and India and lasting nearly a year.
1930s	Informal sources suggest that ad hoc charter-based overseas holidays to Europe were organized by British entrepreneurs.
WW2	Servicemen engaged in foreign military campaigns developed an appetite to return to these countries in peaceful times. The war provided people with the necessary training/experience in aircraft operations. Holiday destinations were developing at this time.
Post-WW2	Military equipment, including aircraft, became surplus to requirement and so could be purchased relatively cheaply.
1950s	Vladimir Raitz, who set up Horizon Holidays, organized what is said to be the first 'air inclusive tour' when seventeen professional people travelled to Corsica. Other companies were also promoting holidays by rail and air. Captain Ted Longton who became known as the father of today's inclusive tours formed Universal Skytours which later became Thomson Holidays.
1959	Airlines were allowed to undercut ordinary fares to produce charter rates (combined with accommodation charges).

Figure 1.4. The development of organized international holidays. *Source*: based on Holloway (1994), Horner (1996) and Laws (1997).

Since the end of the Second World War there has been significant movement of people between countries for leisure purposes. Indeed, organized groups of travellers have been paying professionals to make international travel arrangements on their behalf throughout this period. The development of such organized international travel is charted in Figure 1.4.

Cooper *et al.* (1998) also describe the British company Horizon (which was later acquired by Thomson in a well documented case) as having introduced the modern form of package holiday. In 1957 it marketed combined transport and accommodation arrangements for the holidays, mentioned above, in Corsica in order to circumvent exchange controls by paying the whole price in the country of origin. By the end of the 1960s package holidays were well developed in the UK and we shall now look at the way in which the industry developed. A main distinction that can be drawn is that between mass market and specialist operators.

MASS MARKET AND SPECIALIST TOUR OPERATORS

We shall consider the mass market tour operators who dominate the tour operating scene in the UK and some other countries first and then move on to look at specialist tour operators.

Mass market tour operators

Mass market tour operators arrange travel for the majority of holidaymakers travelling on inclusive tours. The focus of these companies is on high turnover with the aim being to maximize load factors on the travel portion and to negotiate very low rates with the accommodation supplier. This can be achieved through volume buying. Holidays can therefore be sold more cheaply which in turn may stimulate further demand. Mass market tour operators tend to produce holiday packages with wide public appeal usually visiting well-known, highly developed resorts. The larger tour operators or wholesalers usually offer a range of brochures to the market. Typically the selection of brochures might include the following:

- summer sun
- winter sun
- ski
- long haul
- short breaks
- popular destinations.

The example of Airtours Plc is introduced in Figure 1.5 and is continued in Chapters 3, 5 and 7 due to the highly integrated nature of the company's business.

Airtours is a multinational tour operating group employing 20,000 people worldwide and operating a fleet of 42 aircraft, 10 cruise ships and 46 resort properties. In 1999, the company had 10 million customers. Total turnover, including Airtours' share of the turnover of joint ventures, in the same year increased by 23 per cent to £3,771.3 million. Of this figure, 49 per cent was generated in the UK and 51 per cent was from overseas businesses.

Airtours has made no secret of its ambitions for further growth. The company's bid for the acquisition of First Choice Holidays plc was however finally blocked by the European Commission in September 1999.

Airtours is a vertically integrated, geographically diversified business with a broad portfolio of products and brands. In addition to the tour operations division there are distribution, accommodation and cruising divisions. The current profile of Airtours tour operating division is provided below.

United Kingdom

Airtours Holidays	Mainstream air-inclusive holidays
Tradewinds	Long-haul specialists to exotic destinations
Eurosites	Self-drive camping and mobile home based holidays
Panorama Holidays	Charter specialist: winter ski/sun, summer destinations
Direct Holidays	Direct booking tour operator
Cresta Holidays	Short break specialists with scheduled flight flexibility
Bridge Travel	Tailor-made holidays and short breaks

Scandinavia

Ving	Scandanavian direct brand
Spies	Air-inclusive high volume brand in Denmark
Saturn	Mainstream air-inclusive brands
Globetrotter	Specialist city breaks and long-haul operator to the Far East and the USA

Belgium, Holland and France

Sunair	Brand offering air-inclusive and land based holidays
Marysol	Tour operator to main Mediterranean destinations
Traveltrend	Long-haul specialist in The Netherlands
Voyage Conseil	French-based operations offering air-inclusive and land based holidays

Germany

FTI	Charter based air-inclusive sun and sea holidays
Berge & Meer	Package and distribute air-inclusive tours direct to the public

Sport Scheck	Specialist operator of sporting holidays
North America	
Vacation Express	Atlanta-based tour operator with destinations to Mexico and the Caribbean
Suntrips	Californian tour operator focusing on Mexico, Hawaii and the Caribbean
Sunquest	Canadian/USA brand offering charter holidays to the USA, Mexico and the Caribbean

The geographical diversification of the company is clearly evident. The company has equally expanded its products and services in all markets with increasing emphasis on differentiation to achieve strong brochure sales. For example, two new Airtours Holidays' products are Special Collection, offering small, tranquil hotels and villas and Prestige Collection, which is based on elite, four-star hotels. Airtours declared tour operating strategy is to build a critical mass of sustainable passenger volumes using a range of holiday brands offering a wide variety of products to generate brochure sales. Direct Holidays, which the company acquired in 1998, is the UK's fastest growing tour operator, having doubled its size in 1999.

Figure 1.5. Airtours Plc. *Source*: based on Airtours Plc (1999).

Specialist tour operators

Specialist tour operators tend to deal with niche products and markets. The focus might be on a particular activity, travel to a geographic area such as a continent or country or a certain type of holiday maker. Specialist camping holiday companies, for example, include Eurocamp, Key Camp and Canvas Holidays. There are a number of specialist long-haul operators with British Airways Holidays (BAH), Kuoni and Virgin Holidays all significant players. Both BAH and Virgin Holidays used their success in another travel sector, namely air transport, as the basis for moving into the long-haul tour operations business. Hayes and Jarvis and Abercrombie and Kent are specialists who operate in a niche position at the top end of this long haul market. The example of Abercrombie and Kent's Royal Scotsman rail packages is provided in Chapter 8 and the specialist tour operator Ski Esprit is discussed below. Another example of a specialist travel company is Chalfont Line, a company specializing in holidays for the disabled which arranges tours in the UK and Ireland.

Specialist chalet operator, Ski Esprit which was formed in 1983, pioneered the family skiing concept. Now entering the seventeenth year of running family chalet holidays, Esprit's whole programme is dedicated to and designed around the skiing family. The following are all provided;

- Six-day, in-chalet nurseries at all resorts
- An introduction to skiing for 3- and 4-year-olds
- Esprit's own ski schools for 5- to 10-year-olds
- An afternoon ski adventure programme for 8- to 12-year-olds
- An afternoon activity club for children who do not ski all day
- Evening clubs during adults' meal time
- Qualified British nannies
- Free baby-sitting
- Child care guarantee
- All no-smoking chalets

The company is a member of both IATA and ABTA.

Ski Esprit has a sister programme, Sun Esprit, in the summer which is also dedicated to the family market and is concentrated on the French Alps in the resorts of Morzine and Chamonix. Esprit offers a mix of child care alongside their usual chalet style service.

Figure 1.6. Ski Esprit. *Source*: Ski Esprit brochure, 2000.

Many apparently independent specialist tour operators are in fact owned by mass market operators. Cresta Holidays for example is part of the mass market tour operator Airtours which was introduced above. Cresta Holidays operation is outlined in Figure 1.7.

Cresta Holidays is a leading city break specialist, licensed to sell 154,000 air holidays but also using cross-Channel services in its programmes. Cresta offers over 100 destinations worldwide. Since the opening of the Channel Tunnel bookings have increased greatly to both France and Belgium. The company recently introduced London–Paris and London–Venice travel options with Orient Express as they believe this likely to be popular with its upmarket clientele. Cresta has a higher than normal share of AB clients. Around 90 per cent of Cresta's bookings are made through travel agents and it was voted Top City and Short Break specialist from 1992 to 1997 by the UK travel trade.

Figure 1.7. Cresta Holidays. *Source*: based on Mintel (2000).

Today, there is less distinction between mass market and specialist tour operators than there was in the past. Specialist products such as cruises, weekend city breaks and activity holidays are being marketed by tour operators who previously aimed to meet the needs of the mass market only. The trend, described above, towards the provision of long-haul packages is even being displayed by the mass market operators who are also now more willing to offer flexibility in their programmes. Stop-overs at destinations en route can be easily and cheaply arranged for customers particularly where the airline used operates a wide range of routes in the destination country. Activity holiday specialists are generally small operators and often focus on one particular activity or sport such as golf. Lotus Golf is an example of the latter. Figure 1.8 provides examples of specialist tour operators some of which are independent and some of which are part of larger integrated groups.

Golf	Lotus Golf
Adventure Holidays	Explore Worldwide
Ski Holidays	Bladon Lines
Family Ski Holidays	Ski Esprit
Short-breaks	Cresta
Cross-channel	Sally Line
Camping	Eurocamp

Figure 1.8.   Examples of specialist tour operators.

Figure 1.9 outlines some of the defining characteristics of mass market and specialist tour operators.

Mass Market	Specialist
Strong buying power	Specialists by type of holiday, destination or mode of transport for example
Holidays with wide public appeal	Relatively small (often providing holidays for only one or a few niche markets
Distribution is usually by travel agent	Flexible operators who can respond quickly to and direct changes in market demand
Destinations/hotels are often treated as substitutable	Distribution is usually direct as it can be difficult for small tour operators to achieve distribution via the travel agency sector
Standardized brochures are often used	Travel agents are often less familiar with their products
Linked often to a travel agency chain	

Figure 1.9.   Defining characteristics of mass market and specialist tour operators.

TRAVEL AGENTS AND TOUR OPERATIONS

Travel agents which are also licensed ATOL holders can create their own holiday packages for sale as do Thomas Cook. In September 1999 the company formed the UK's third largest tour operator, known as JMC, and its charter airline business, JMC Airlines Ltd. Further detail regarding the JMC operation is provided below. Thomas Cook itself is a leading global travel and financial services group, serving some 20 million customers each year and employing 20,000 people. In the UK and Ireland, Thomas Cook is a major vertically integrated travel company, owning its own travel shops, tour operators and airline. Use of the company as an example therefore continues in other relevant chapters of this book.

A twelve month market research and business strategy review at Thomas Cook, involving consumers who tested package holidays, focus groups seeking the views of holidaymakers throughout the country, competitor analysis and internal audience workshops led to the launch of a new mainstream holiday brand, JMC. A thorough review of the company's brand strategy was created with the acquisition of Flying Colours Leisure Group in June 1998, followed by the merger which saw Inspirations brought into Sunworld's tour operating portfolio. This offered an opportunity to create a new company bringing together three different philosophies and cultures into a single, unified and clearly focused unit.

JMC Holidays Ltd is now the third largest tour operator in the UK and its integrated airline, JMC Airlines Ltd, is the UK's second biggest charter airline. JMC combines the former operating brands Sunworld, Sunset, Inspirations, Flying Colours and Caledonian Airways. JMC operates nineteen brochures whilst JMC Airlines has a fleet of twenty-eight planes and aims to have one of the youngest charter airline fleets in the UK.

The new brand was launched in September, 1999, promoting a seamless link between its tour operating and airline divisions. The new identity also extended to the company's in-house airline. The somewhat unlikely name for a mass market tour operator stems from the initials of John Mason Cook, son of founder Thomas Cook.

JMC's launch was accompanied by an intensive package of activities to support the retail trade before the peak January booking period including significant investment in JMC's Agent Services team. A £6 million consumer advertising campaign ran on national television as well as in national newspapers and on outdoor posters.

Figure 1.10. JMC. *Source*: Thomas Cook and JGPR (2000).

OUTBOUND, DOMESTIC AND INBOUND TOUR OPERATORS

A main distinction in the tour operations sector is one drawn by market. Whilst some cross-over is evident, tour operators can usually be categorized as being outbound, inbound or domestic in focus. Each of these is now discussed in turn.

Outbound tour operators

Outbound tour operators are concerned with the organization, sale and operation of package holidays for travellers in the generating country going overseas. It is normal for outbound tour operators to offer complete packages. It is with outbound tour operators that this text is principally concerned due to the comparative size and complexity of their operations. We return to outbound tour operators later in this chapter.

Domestic tour operators

Domestic tour operators offer packaged travel to holidaymakers wanting to travel within their own country. In the UK a number of coach companies including Wallace Arnold and Shearings operate in this market as discussed in Chapter 8. Accommodation providers are also involved in the provision of domestic holiday packages as illustrated by the example of the Rank Group below. The domestic tour operators market is a highly fragmented one characterized by the following:

- A large number of relatively small companies.
- Smaller numbers of ABTA members.
- A number of 'direct marketers' who prefer not to use retail travel agents.

Whilst the larger mass market tour operators have traditionally had little involvement in domestic tourism, evidence of moves into this market is emerging. Thomson, for example, purchased Country Holidays (500 properties in the UK) and Blakes (around 1,700 properties) which was a departure from their usual concentration on the outbound market.

The largest domestic tour operator in the UK – the Rank Group – accommodates in excess of 3.5 million holiday-makers between its Butlins and Haven brands with 2 million and 1.5 million respectively. Further brands are Warner and Oasis. Butlin's has five holiday-worlds, five seaside hotels and the Grand Hotel whilst Haven sells static caravan holiday homes in addition to pitches for holiday home owners. The holiday division made profits of £72 million in 1997.

Figure 1.11. The Rank Group. *Source*: based on Key Note (1999).

Inbound tour operators

Inbound, or incoming, tour operators deal with tourists from overseas who are likely to have booked their travel at home possibly via a tour operator based in that country. They offer both full packages and tailor-made programmes. The commercial and political interests of incoming tour operators and other suppliers to the inbound tourism industry in the UK are represented by the British Incoming Tour Operators' Association (BITOA) described in Figure 1.12.

As outlined, the British Incoming Tour Operators' Association (BITOA), which was established in 1977, represents the commercial and political interests of incoming tour operators and suppliers to the inbound tourism industry in the UK. Both national and regional tourist boards as well as heritage sites, visitor attractions, hoteliers and transportation companies are members of the association alongside incoming tour operators. The association is involved in the promotion of tourism to Britain and the representation of the political interests of members in Whitehall, Westminster and Brussels. The association also aims to ensure that members adopt ethical 'best practice' procedures with clients and suppliers whilst encouraging the adoption of eco-friendly practice in their businesses together with improved educational and training programmes. Opportunities available to members include exhibiting at domestic and overseas exhibitions at reduced rates, free use of the BITOA legal hotline, subsidized educational, training and familiarization programmes, free listing in the BITOA handbook which is distributed worldwide and monthly updates on the travel industry through BITOA mailings.

Figure 1.12.   The British Incoming Tour Operators' Association. *Source*: BITOA (1998).

The incoming tour operator's business can form part of a lengthy distribution chain with a customer overseas, say in Spain, buying a package tour from a travel agent who books the holiday with the tour operator, who may have contracted for accommodation through a ground handling agent based in the destination country such as the UK. There are some operators specializing in both incoming and outgoing travel. Gulliver's Sports Travel for example organize group tours for both.

The inbound tourism market in both the UK and the rest of Europe has seen a demand shift in recent years characterized by the following:

• more sophisticated tourists; and
• more independent tourists.

Long-haul travellers on the sort of whistlestop tours traditionally associated with the North American market are still a feature of inbound tourism though. This requires the services of intermediaries to ensure that travellers' needs are met during their short visits. Tour providers have of necessity become more flexible. The US market itself now has more in common with the short-haul market as they have become more used to visiting Europe. Around a quarter of all inclusive tours to the UK are part of a broader European tour. This figure increases to around half when the American market alone is considered and around three-quarters when Japanese inclusive tour visitors are analysed (Key Note Ltd, 1999). These European tours are characterized by short durations (several days) in three or four European countries. Incoming tour operators need to research the changing needs of tourists from different generating countries in order to provide appropriate services.

Incoming tour operators in the UK identified the short breaks market as having similar growth potential to that seen in the domestic market in the 1980s and 1990s. They were not however alone in this and as evidenced by the proliferation of brochures offering international and increasingly longer-haul short breaks. A variety of types of firm deals with incoming tourists. Scotsell provides an example of a tour operator and incoming destination management company (receptive services agent) with over 25 years' experience of the Scottish hospitality and tourism business. The company sells itself as offering local knowledge having planned self-drive holidays to Scotland for individual travellers, couples, families and small groups.

GROUND HANDLING AGENTS

A similar service to that offered by incoming tour operators is provided by ground handling agents (GHA). They offer transfers from arrival points in the destination country to accommodation facilities. The different roles performed by incoming tour operators and GHAs are often blurred in practice with the latter sometimes even calling themselves incoming tour operators.

INCENTIVE TRAVEL ORGANIZERS

Travel is sometimes used by companies as a modern management tool aimed at motivating staff performance and thereby improving productivity. Incentive travel organizers (ITOs) are the middlemen who arrange this type of travel on behalf of companies, devising different programmes for their employees. This type of incentive has much in common with corporate hospitality. An example of the latter would be a 'day at the races' offered to employees and clients perhaps with a cocktail party thrown at the event. Davidson (1994) provides detailed coverage of the use, by companies, of incentive travel together with the role of ITOs. These are sometimes also referred to as 'incentive houses'. Brooke Green Travel for example is a business travel company specializing in ad hoc and incentive groups. The company undertakes incentive tour planning.

GROUP TRAVEL ORGANIZERS

Group outings and holidays may be arranged for members of clubs, societies and organizations such as retirement and social clubs. A group travel organizer (GTO) undertakes to make the necessary arrangements often on a voluntary basis. A significant amount of business for the travel trade can be generated by these unpaid intermediaries. Educational institutions including schools also organize group travel in this way and specialist tour operators, such as Jac Travel, exist to meet the needs of these travelling groups.

The remainder of this chapter is concerned with the outbound tour operations market.

THE UK OUTBOUND TOUR OPERATIONS MARKET

As described above, the concept of tour operations was pioneered in the UK. The UK remains one of the largest producers of package holidays worldwide with a highly competitive industry. The tour operations market in the UK is often described as a mature one having reached a degree of saturation. Overseas expansion has therefore been a recent strategic focus for many of the larger UK based tour operators.

Europe's main market for package tours is Germany where numerous large commercial companies, including banks and retailers, have subsidiary tour operators. In common with some UK firms, German tour operators are seeking to expand internationally. At the time of writing, Europe's largest tour operator, the German company Preussag, had just announced a takeover of the UK's largest tour operator, Thomson. There may be objections to this move on competitive grounds and indeed other attempted takeovers in the industry have failed as discussed in Chapter 5. At the time of the Preussag announcement another major

UK operator, Airtours, has attracted speculation that it is contemplating an approach to C & N Touristic, another of Germany's large tour operators. A very different picture of European tour operators could therefore be emerging.

At the UK level, the market is greatly polarized with a few large dominant companies at one end of the spectrum and a proliferation of smaller players at the other. Operators have traditionally competed on the basis of market share, often at the expense of profit. Market share is usually measured by licensed capacity (see discussion of ATOL on pp. 25–6) or by audited sales of ITs via the travel trade. This has, in part, accounted for the development of a highly concentrated market as the top tour operators stole a lead over the rest of the competition through increased capacity and sales. The market has become even more concentrated in recent years as a result of take-over and merger activity. The ten largest tour operators account for more than 80 per cent of the market. The key players however are the top three tour operators – Thomson, Airtours and First Choice – who between them have approximately 60 per cent of the market. Other important tour operators are JMC (formerly Thomas Cook) and Carlson Leisure. Table 1.3 examines the market shares of the top five ATOL holders by passengers carried between 1995 and 1997.

Table 1.3. Market share of the top five AIT tour operators by volume, 1995–7. *Source*: Key Note (1999) (based on Thomson Tour Operations/Key Note).

	1995	**1996**	**1997**
Top five			
Thomson Tour Operations	24	22	21
Airtours/Aspro	15	15	15
First Choice	12	12	10
Cosmos/Avro	6	6	6
Sunworld/Thomas Cook	4	4	5
Total top five	61	59	57
Other operators	39	41	43
Total	100.0	100.0	100.0

The issues surrounding market concentration, including that of competition driving down both the price and quality of package holidays, are examined in Chapter 5.

The leading brand in AITs from the UK has been the 'Thomson' brand for some time with Thomson Tour Operations (TTO) having held the largest share of this market since the 1970s. In the late 1990s however this market became even more competitive than previously and, as mentioned earlier, was characterized by a degree of saturation. In the late 1990s we witnessed a good period for the inclusive holiday market partly accounted for by a good exchange rate and a buoyant economy.

THE INTERNATIONAL PICTURE

The French company, Club Méditerranée, is a well-known travel firm overseas but in general terms tour operators in France do not share the higher profile image of their German and British counterparts. Vellas and Becherel (1995) group together Switzerland, the Netherlands and Scandanavia, describing tour operators in each as having very high penetration in their respective markets. They further describe the package tour market in these areas as very concentrated. In North America domestic travel arrangements account for far more of the tour operators' business than is the case in Europe.

PRODUCT DEVELOPMENTS

Tour operators' products are constantly being developed and market gaps filled. Thomson's *Just* brand for example is a new low cost, no frills operation aimed at the cost conscious part of the market.

Having considered the role and function of tour operators and having touched on the international expansion strategies of some tour operators it is worth noting also another of the strategic moves that some operators have involved themselves in, namely diversification.

DIVERSIFICATION

Tour operators have often chosen to diversify into other areas of business with mixed results. The case study of Saga (Figure 1.13) illustrates a move away from the firm's core holiday business into other areas.

Saga was founded in 1951 as a domestic travel operator, to sell off-season breaks in a family-run hotel in Folkstone, for the over-50s. The group was floated in 1978 and diversified heavily in the 1980s and now offers everything from insurance to Home Shopping to the over-50s.

After inheriting Saga as a recently-floated travel operator for retired people in the 1970s, Roger de Haan launched a strategic review of the company. This concluded that Saga would have to become a diversified product supplier in order to survive. The travel industry was, at the time, becoming increasingly competitive and the consolidation that characterizes the industry today had already begun. Saga therefore moved into the home and motor insurance markets in 1987 following tests. The division, which was set up as a separate subsidiary, now has one million customers, contributes 72 per cent of group profits and is growing at 20 per cent per annum. The range of services offered has also grown and includes telephone services, investment products and a glossy magazine.

The diversification strategy helped to offset volatile profits in the travel division which suffered as a result of both the Gulf War in 1991 and an earlier wave of terrorist activity. The company generated a pre-tax profit of £20.7 million in 1998. Despite being the largest division in turnover terms, the travel division now only accounts for a quarter of the company's profit. One of the most valuable assets that Saga has is its database which covers 32 per cent of the over-50 population. This enables the group to engage in excessive cross-selling and to charge advertisers premium rates in its magazine. Turnover of Saga Holidays has increased from £75 million in 1994 to £113.4 million in 1996.

Figure 1.13. Saga. *Source*: *Financial Times*, 23 November, 1999, p. 30 and Mintel, Inclusive Tours, Leisure Intelligence, March 1998.

CUSTOMER CARE

Researching customer care typically involves holding interviews and focus groups as well as analysis of customer correspondence. Travel agents might employ *mystery shoppers* to research their levels of customer care whilst *mystery guests* at an all-inclusive holiday resort used by a tour operator might provide valuable feedback for the operator.

Laws (1997) reviews the theories underpinning service industry management practices, considering the meaning and nature of quality and customer satisfaction as applied to inclusive holidays. He examines service 'blueprinting' in detail.

TRADE ASSOCIATIONS

The role of one of the main trade associations relevant to tour operators – the Association of British Travel Agents (ABTA) is discussed in Figure 1.14. This organization is also relevant to travel agents. The role and function of travel agents is examined in Chapter 2. The role of the British Incoming Tour Operators' Association (BITOA) was outlined in Figure 1.12.

The Association of British Travel Agents (ABTA) was formed in 1950 with both a commercial and regulatory role. Reflecting this ABTA's original objectives were 'to promote and develop the general interests of all Members of the Association' and 'to do all such things as may be deemed necessary or expedient to raise the prestige and status of Members of the Association'. The Association sets comprehensive guidelines for members via separate Codes of Conduct for both tour operator and travel agent members. Financial checks of members are applied and financial protection of consumers provided. The association is concerned by the damage that financial failure or inadequate performance on the part of tour operators or travel agents can do to the travel trade as a whole. It has therefore become an independent, self-regulatory body. Individual company bonds and members' contributions provide financial protection for consumers. Complaints resolution is a further role offered by ABTA to members' clients. The low-cost independent arbitration scheme is administered by the Chartered Institute of Arbitrators. The role that ABTA performs in the industry is likely to change in the future.

Figure 1.14. The Association of British Travel Agents. *Source*: ABTA (1998).

A further relevant association is an alliance of smaller specialist tour operators known as the Association of Independent Tour Operators (AITO). The association was established in 1976 mainly in response to the problems posed for smaller travel companies by a sudden sharp increase in bonding requirements following a couple of major collapses. Further details of the association are provided in Figure 1.15.

Aims

- To ensure that the public can book AITO members' holidays with every confidence.
- To inform members of the issues of the day and to encourage higher standards and greater professionalism amongst members.

- To encourage members and their clients to be aware of environmental issues and to promote environmentally sustainable tourism.
- To help members market their wares more effectively to customers.
- To ensure that the views and problems of the smaller, specialist tour operator are understood and that the interests of their clients are protected.

AITO primarily provides a forum for specialist tour operators whilst acting as an information source for the public and offering a marketing service to members. The organization is often regarded as the official voice of smaller specialist tour operators.

Membership

AITO has in excess of 150 members and in 1996 the membership as a whole carried 1.6 million passengers. Individual passenger carryings range from several hundred to around 200,000 per annum. The majority of members are responsible for between 10,000 and 20,000 passengers per annum. The number of passengers carried by association members gives them the benefit of bulk buying power.

Bonding scheme

AITO has its own bonding scheme, administered by AITO Trust Limited, which has approved status under Regulation 18 of the Package Travel, Package Holidays and Package Tour Regulations 1992. This offers full financial security, including repatriation if needed, to the customers of companies bonded via the system. AITO is responsible for monitoring the financial performance of member companies within the scheme as well as for setting bond levels and collecting premiums. Bonding via AITO Trust is only available to members of AITO and it is intended to bond non-licensable turnover including self-drive, train or coach-based holidays.

Legal hotline

Since 1997 members have had the additional service, for a fee of £100 per annum, of a legal hotline. Members are kept up-to-date on all issues which may affect them.

Insurance

The association arranges favourable rates for members covering a variety of insurance policies including travel insurance for clients, cover for member's representatives, public liability and credit insurance.

In addition to the above, the association runs seminars and training courses for members and their staff.

Principal requirements for membership

AITO companies and applicants for membership are required to satisfy certain criteria including the following:

1. They should be bona fide tour operators engaged first and foremost in the sale of inclusive holidays (departing from the UK) involving both transport and accommodation.
2. They should be able to demonstrate independence from mainstream tour operating companies.
3. They should conduct a minimum of 50 per cent overseas business.
4. They should have been trading as a tour operator for a minimum of two years.
5. They should be UK-based and all literature/brochures should be in English.
6. They should have a proper, creative brochure rather than an overprinted shell or photocopied leaflets (i.e. a good standard of presentation is required).
7. They should match the profile of AITO members, i.e. should be specialist companies at the smaller end of the spectrum, with hands-on management as far as the day-to-day running of the company is concerned.
8. They should be fully bonded for financial protection of clients.
9. They should have public liability insurance. (Cover of £2 million is required.)
10. They should be prepared to abide by the terms of the AITO Quality Charter and Code of Business Practice.
11. Their booking conditions and methods of operation should meet all the requirements of the EC Directive on Package Travel and other applicable laws.

Figure 1.15. The Association of Independent Tour Operators. *Source*: AITO (1997 and 1999).

Whilst ABTA is the main body representing tour operators, a less formally organized group containing many AIT providers is the exclusive Federation of Tour Operators (FTO). AITO, as seen above, mainly represents smaller and usually more specialist tour operators although it does accept larger companies which meet the stated criteria for membership.

REGULATION

Regulation of the industry comes in a number of different formats, the most important being those described below.

The Civil Aviation Authority (CAA) has a role in the package holiday industry in that they issue licences to sell holidays by air. These licences, known as Air Travel Organizers' Licences (ATOLs) aim to protect the 28 million people in the UK who take air holidays each year from financial loss resulting from the failure of a tour operator and are examined in detail in Figure 1.16. They are a legal requirement for travel organizers selling most air inclusive holidays and some air seats to the public.

The Air Travel organizer's licence (ATOL) scheme, introduced in 1972, is a statutory one, managed by the CAA, which exists to protect the public from losing money or being stranded abroad due to the failure of a firm selling flights or package holidays by air. Under the Civil Aviation (Air Travel Organizers' Licensing) Regulations 1995, it is a legal requirement for most travel firms to hold an ATOL to sell flights and package holidays by air. The main exceptions are airlines and agents of licensed firms. Airlines do not need to hold ATOLs themselves to sell their seats directly, or through agents, but are required not to supply tickets to any firm which needs an ATOL and does not hold one.

The system usually requires each applicant to provide a bond (a financial guarantee provided by a bank or an insurance company) for a specified amount before a licence is granted. These bonds are irrevocable undertakings from third parties giving the CAA the right to obtain a specified amount of money in the event that the licence holder is unable to meet its obligations to its customers. This money can be used by the CAA, in the case of insolvency, to fly customers home at the end of their holiday and to repay those booking who have not had a holiday. Bonds may be replaced by guarantees, from airlines, to honour bookings if an ATOL holder selling scheduled air tickets at discounted prices fails. If the bond is not sufficient, any shortfall is met by the Air Travel Reserve Fund which is managed by the CAA and backs up the individual bonds.

The minimum bond level for all forms of licence is £10,000 although more than one company in a group may provide a joint bond for the same minimum.

The CAA, prior to granting a licence, has to be satisfied that the applicant is a fit person to hold a licence and (for most licences) has sufficient funds for its business. The ATOL holder will be given a unique ATOL number which it must use in any advertising and brochures as well as on documents such as booking forms and confirmation letters. This enables the public to recognize that a booking is financially protected.

It is a legal requirement to hold an ATOL to sell flights and package holidays by air except in certain circumstances as well as which the ATOL satisfies the requirement under the Package Travel, Package Holidays and Package Tours Regulations 1992 as discussed above for a package tour organizer to provide financial security for customers' money. Separate arrangements do however need to be made for non-air packages. Each ATOL contains specific terms such as the number of passengers that may be carried under it and standard terms.

Each travel organizer holding an ATOL is examined by the CAA annually to ensure that it is properly managed and financially sound. The CAA also publishes Guidance Notes on the Internet and in leaflet form for the benefit of interpretation of the Air Travel Organizers' Licensing Regulations 1995. These contain information that is useful to tour operators and travel agents as well as auditors, accountants and solicitors who work with the travel industry. The CAA also monitors advertising in the press, television/teletext and Internet, follows up information from the general public and trade and prosecutes firms who breach the Regulations.

Figure 1.16. Air Travel organizers' licences. *Source*: CAA (1999) and www.atol.org.uk*
Note: * Permission required for public use.

An example of the CAA's Consumer Protection Group calling in the ATOL bond of a travel firm is provided in the press release shown in Figure 1.17.

Ski package operator fails

31 March 2000
The CAA's Consumer Protection Group has called in the ATOL bond of a travel firm operating ski holiday packages to Italy and Switzerland, which ceased trading today.

Winterski Holidays Ltd, based in Milton Keynes, traded as Vita Holidays, Fare Savers and Snowbreaks.

The company held an Air Travel Organizers' Licence (number ATOL 2504) and all customers will be protected under the ATOL scheme.

The CAA has issued the following advice to customers:

The CAA will arrange for people currently abroad to continue their holidays, and they will be brought back to the UK as planned.

* For people booked on future packages there will be no further holidays after today, 31 March, and anyone due to travel from 01 April onwards should not go to their departure airport. They will be able to claim a refund from the CAA.
* Claim forms will be sent out shortly to those customers unable to travel.

For further information, customers can contact the CAA on 020 7832 5600 during office hours.

Note to Editors:

The Air Travel Organizers' Licensing Scheme, introduced in 1972, gives comprehensive consumer protection to the 28 million people in the UK who take air holidays each year. The ATOL system protects them from losing their money or being stranded abroad, if their travel organizer fails.

An ATOL is a legal requirement for travel organizers selling most air holidays and some air seats to the public. Each travel organizer holding an ATOL is examined every year by the CAA to ensure it is properly managed and financially sound. Before it gets a licence, the travel organizer has to lodge a bond – a financial guarantee provided by a bank or insurance company. If it then fails, the CAA uses the money to pay for people abroad to continue their holidays and to travel home as planned, and to make refunds to those who have paid, but not yet travelled. If the bond is not enough, any shortfall is met by the Air Travel Reserve Fund which is managed by the CAA and backs up the individual bonds.

Figure 1.17. CAA press release. *Source*: www.caa.co.uk

We have already seen that tour operators and travel agents who are members of ABTA are regulated by a voluntary Code of Conduct. This Code imposes duties on tour operators in connection with booking conditions and minimum standards of brochures. In addition the law provides consumer protection. Downes and Paton (1993) explain that clients contract for holidays with the tour operator and under that contract have a right to performance, in other words, a right to the holiday they have paid for. If performance is unsatisfactory, the client has a right to sue for damages. The client must pay the full price for their holiday and take the holidays they have paid for in accordance with the rules set out in the booking conditions.

Regulation of the relationship between 'organizers', 'retailers' and 'consumers' in respect of 'packages' is provided by the EC Directive on Package Travel, Package Holidays and Package Tours. The Directive was adopted in 1990 aiming to harmonize the rules governing packages throughout the whole community. Member states had until 31 December 1992 to implement the Directive. In the UK these are implemented within The Package Travel, Package Holidays and Package Tours Regulations 1992, generally referred to as 'The Package Travel Regulations'. Advice on how to comply with the Package Travel Regulations 1992 can be obtained from local Trading Standards Officers.

Despite the above there are still many unregulated and unbonded tour operators operating in the marketplace with no association membership. Chapter 3 discusses the legal status of the tour operator and travel agent. The law of agency provides the legal basis for the relationship between a tour operator and a travel agent. This and the other legal aspects relating to the tour operator, including the Package Travel, Package Holidays and Package Tours Regulations are discussed fully by Downes and Paton (1993).

A FRIENDLY INDUSTRY?

Tour operators are often criticized for a number of reasons. Package tours can provide exactly that which tourists are attempting to escape by going on holiday as evidenced by hectic airports, crowded hotels and busy roads. Krippendorf (1987) examines this paradoxical situation in more detail. Further reasons for criticism of package tours are outlined in Figure 1.18.

- The allegiance of tour operators to particular destinations are tenuous with destinations often suffering greatly when a tour operator changes its programme and moves away from a particular resort or even an entire region or country.
- The economic buying power of the larger tour operators is a concern expressed by destinations, particularly those in less developed countries.
- Package holidays can be detrimental to the environment bringing mass tourism to particular areas.
- The production and marketing of homogeneous products often meets with disapproval.

Figure 1.18. Indicative criticisms of tour operations.

Tour operators however, do bring a regular flow of tourists to destinations which can be seen to have the advantages shown in Figure 1.19.

- Regular flows of tourists to destinations.
- The role of destination marketing is simplified by the attraction of tour operators to destination marketers to overcome the problem of reaching a diverse market.
- By bringing tourists in groups to particular 'hot spots' environmental destruction to other areas can be curtailed.

Figure 1.19. Indicative benefits of tour operations.

From the consumer point of view tour operators' packages also have advantages and disadvantages. A particular advantage as far as some clients are concerned is the ease of booking all the components of a package holiday when travelling to remote and unfamiliar destinations. Furthermore, packages provide apparent additional security. The main disadvantages relate to the lack of flexibility these programmes offer.

TOUR OPERATORS AND THE TOURISM VALUE-CHAIN

Poon (1993) describes the tourism industry value-chain drawing upon the work of Porter (1987) in relation to this analytical tool developed to trace the process of value-creation in an industry. This concept is concerned with understanding the role of each player in an industry through understanding of how the industry creates value. The position of these players are not static particularly in an industry as dynamic as tourism. The value-chain was developed in the 1980s in relation to the manufacturing sector and Poon has applied this to the travel and tourism industry through identification of six primary activities and five support services. These are shown in Figure 1.20.

Primary activities	Support services
Transportation	Firm infrastructure
On-site services	Human resource development
Wholesale/packaging	Product and service development
Marketing and sales	Technology and systems development
Retail distribution	Procurement of goods and services
Customer service	

Figure 1.20. Primary and support services in the tourism industry value-chain. *Source*: based on Poon (1993).

Both the primary and support activities of the value-chain create value. Tour operators can be seen to contribute to the value-chain in a variety of ways. Principally they do this by selecting and combining the elements of a package holiday, distributing and promoting them and organizing excursions and entertainment and so on. Those tour operators involved in vertical integration control more activities along the value-chain. Control also of information can be seen to be important and as the tour operations sector becomes more technology driven achievements may be made in this area as they have in the scheduled airline sector.

SUMMARY

This introductory chapter outlined the package holiday concept prior to examining the role and function of tour operators. Whilst principally concerned with outbound tour operators, other organizations involved in the packaging and sale of inclusive tours were discussed. An introduction is provided to the structure of the tour operations sector in the UK. As mentioned at the beginning this chapter complements Chapters 2 and 3. Together these three chapters describe the concept known as the travel trade.

DISCUSSION QUESTIONS

1. Compare and contrast the different roles performed by incoming and outbound tour operators.
2. Discuss the means by which providers of air inclusive tours are regulated.
3. Outline the structure of the tour operations market in the UK.

REFERENCES

Airtours Plc (1999) Annual Report and Accounts.

Airtours, The story so far...

Cooper, C., Fletcher, J., Gilbert, D., Wanhill, S. (Edited by Shepherd, R.) (1998) *Tourism Principles and Practice* (2nd edn), Longman.

Davidson, R. (1994) *Business Travel*, Pitman.

The Department of Trade & Industry (1995) *Looking into The Package Travel Regulations; a guide for organisers and retailers*, January.

Downes, J. and Paton, T. (1993) *Travel Agency Law*, Pitman Publishing.

EIU Travel and Tourism Analyst (1991) *No. 1, The European Inbound Tour Operators' Market*.

Holloway, J.C. (1994) *The Business of Tourism*, (4th edn) Pitman Publishing.

Horner, P. (1996) *Travel Agency Practice*, Addison-Wesley Longman.

Key Note (1998) *Market Review, Travel Agents and Overseas Tour Operators*.

Key Note Ltd. (1999) *UK Travel and Tourism*.

Krippendorf, J. (1987) *The Holidaymakers*, Heinemann.

Laws, E. (1997) *Managing Packaged Tourism – relationships, responsibilities and service quality in the inclusive holiday industry*, International Thomson Business Press.

Lickorish, L.J. and Jenkins, C.L. (eds) (1997) *An Introduction to Tourism*, Butterworth Heinemann.

Mintel, City Breaks, *Leisure Intelligence*, March 1998; March 2000.

Mintel, Travel Agents, *Retail Intelligence*, January 2000.

Pender, L. (1999) Marketing Management for Travel and Tourism, Stanley Thornes (Publishers) Ltd.
Poon, A. (1993) Tourism, Technology and Competitive Strategies, CAB International.
Vellas, F. and Becherel, L. (1995) *International Tourism*, Macmillan Business.
www.atol.org.uk
www.caa.co.uk

CHAPTER 2

Holiday Packaging

INTRODUCTION

As described in Chapter 1, package holidays are organized trips of predetermined activities involving several tourism services. These holidays are sold in advance at a fixed price (Vellas and Becherel, 1995). This chapter outlines the means by which such packages are put together and sold. The different stages involved in planning and creating package holidays are introduced first together with consideration of the risks and costs attached to the preparation of inclusive tours. The chapter then examines each of the relevant stages in detail before going on to discuss other areas of tour marketing including pricing, distribution and promotion.

Tour operators are involved in the purchase of the different elements that contribute to the eventual 'package' and in combining these for sale either directly or indirectly to consumers. By buying in bulk tour operators can negotiate discounts. At the same time though they both carry risks and incur costs in the preparation of inclusive tours. Ways in which they do each are indicated in Figure 2.1.

Risks	Costs
Researching holiday programmes months or years ahead of sale	Brochure design, production and distribution
Organization of holiday programmes months or years ahead of sale	Installation and staffing of a reservations system
	Investment in a marketing communications programme

Figure 2.1. Tour operator risks and costs in the preparation of inclusive tours. *Source*: based on Laws (1997).

THE TOUR PRODUCT

At the heart of the package tour are the transport and accommodation elements of the package. These can be enhanced by elements such as entertainment, and further augmented by additional aspects such as information provision, insurance and service guarantees. The extent to which a tour operator enhances its core product to make it more attractive to consumers varies greatly.

The role and function of the tour operator revolves around making block bookings of the transport and accommodation elements of the overall package holiday and in feeding passengers into the different aspects of the holiday. Of paramount importance is the combination of elements chosen to create a suitable package to meet consumer demand and both preparation and presentation of this in an appropriate manner to make sufficient sales.

The tour operations cycle requires careful planning and preparation involving a variety of different departments with different aspects. Some tour operators contract out the organization of trips to wholesalers and pass on the bookings as they are received. Travel clubs and professional associations, known as affinity groups, often do this. The role of coach tour wholesalers is described in Chapter 8.

PLANNING AND CREATING PACKAGE TOURS

Tour operators typically follow a set pattern in terms of the planning and creation of package holidays. The steps undertaken are outlined in Figure 2.2.

We will now look at each of these different stages in turn. First we will examine the role of market research.

THE ROLE OF MARKET RESEARCH

It is essential that tour operators undertake market research prior to implementation of any holiday programme. This will enable the company to make a decision as to whether or not to go ahead with the launch of a new product or indeed to continue with an established programme. The role of market research will vary between established programmes and the introduction of new programmes. Keeping abreast of changing consumer tastes is a prerequisite of business success. One of the main responsibilties of those conducting market research often is to determine the correct capacity to offer to the market, usually for an entire season. Market forecasts can

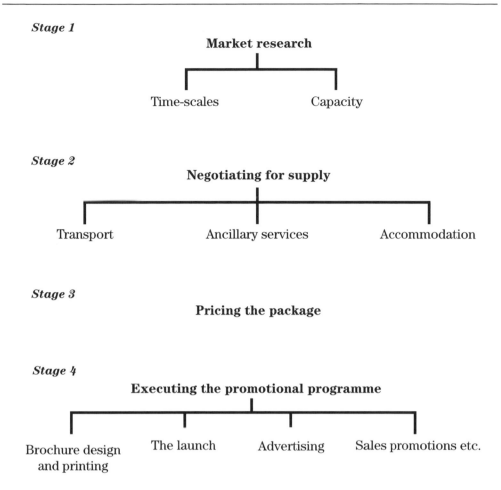

Stage 1

Market research

Time-scales   Capacity

Stage 2

Negotiating for supply

Transport   Ancillary services   Accommodation

Stage 3

Pricing the package

Stage 4

Executing the promotional programme

Brochure design and printing   The launch   Advertising   Sales promotions etc.

Figure 2.2. Holiday packaging

help with capacity planning. This is an important area as situations of over- and under capacity can result:

Over capacity: this situation occurs when the tour operator contracts for too much capacity for the season and cannot sell it.

Under capacity: this situation occurs when the tour operator contracts for too little capacity for the season and could have sold more.

Both of these situations can lead to problems which can affect profit levels for the season. Forecasting the overall market size is clearly important in terms of capacity. Forecasting changes in holiday patterns is equally important. It is generally the case that smaller tour operators can respond more quickly to changes in market conditions due to their flexibility.

COMPETITOR RESEARCH

As is true in any industry it is important for tour operators to research their competitive environment. The extent to which the mass market operators research one another's moves is evidenced by the speed with which they react to developments.

Qualitative research techniques, including group discussions and individual depth interviews, are particularly useful to tour operators as part of the new product development (NPD) process for idea screening and to help identify market gaps. At a more detailed level tour operators considering a new programme need to research all of the factors in both the home and the host countries that are outlined in Figure 2.3 at least.

Home country research	Host country research
Market demand for the destination/ holiday type planned	Infrastructure provision
	Political environment
Currency/exchange rate factors	Currency/exchange rate factors
Appropriate marketing mix elements	Availability of suitable suppliers
Relationship with host country	Relationship with home country
Competitors' activities	Competitors' activities

Figure 2.3. Market research and tour programme development.

ASSESSING CONDITIONS IN THE HOST COUNTRY

Market research helps to assist companies with the assessment of conditions within the host country. It may be, for example, that a hostile native community would be less than welcoming to overseas travellers. Planners need to take into account whether it is therefore wise to bring such tourists to the destination. A body of literature exists in relation to the impacts that tourists can have on destinations. In some cases local residents have reacted in extreme ways to the influx of mass market tourists from overseas. Such reactions might be in relation to the volume of tourists or indeed to the behaviour of tourists. It is often the case that customs will be very different in the home and host countries and this too can lead to conflict. A further possibility is that residents in very poor countries will be confronted by very wealthy foreign visitors. In some destinations tour operators accommodate tourists within enclosed resorts to avoid hostility often advising them to remain within the confines of the complex. A further source of aggravation can be a political situation between the home and host countries. A war between the two would be an extreme example of a situation that could influence tour operator planning. Decisions against operating in a country tend to be easier when the situations are extreme. What is far more difficult is making a judgement, often considerably in advance of a potential programme's implementation, in respect of a more subtle problem that could potentially develop in the intervening time. Tour operators have in the past pulled out of certain countries on political grounds. For example, where a tour operator is opposed to the regime operating in a country they may select not to operate in that country as do other types of organization.

Product development research is usually undertaken by staff who travel to the company's destinations or potential new destinations. For smaller tour operators this is likely to be the owner/manager whereas larger tour operators have entire departments involved in this aspect. Accessibility to countries, resorts and accommodation units has to be assessed. Tourist infrastructure also has to be assessed *in situ*. Due to the requirement for brochure descriptions to be accurate it is no longer sufficient for operators to rely on previous information. Photographs also need to be updated regularly. Tour operators cannot afford to be complacent in this respect.

There is a difference, as mentioned above, between the planning of programmes to new destinations and accommodation units to that concerning resorts where a tour operator already has an established programme and accommodation units they have used previously. Whilst the latter is still extremely important it tends to involve less work than the former. Staff in resorts for example can greatly help with the research process as can other established contacts. Where a new programme is being developed, the tour operator concerned may have to start by selecting a destination country. Normally this process will involve consideration of a selection of likely destinations. A process of rejection through general research of all possible countries will then take place followed by detailed comparison of the remaining alternatives.

NEGOTIATING

In negotiating contracts, the tour operator is concerned to establish the availability of elements of the package and to obtain a price that will be attractive to customers yet profitable to the company. The negotiation process and supplier contract details vary with the type of supplier.

SUPPLIER CONTRACTS

The arrangement of contracts for bulk purchases of transportation and accommodation was described in Chapter 1 as a key role performed by tour operators. We will now look at this often repeated aspect of the tour operator's function in more detail. Laws (1997) correctly examines this in the context of the theory of organizational buying. This activity is significantly different from purchasing by final consumers as shown below:

- Organizational buyers are more expert than final buyers
- Organizational buyers tend to buy in bulk
- Organizational buyers have increased negotiatory power
- Organizational buyers are more likely to have long-standing relationships with suppliers
- Organizations may use teams of purchasers
- Organizational buyers face a more complex situation than do individual buyers.

We will now look at contracts with the main suppliers to tour operators in turn.

ACCOMMODATION

Contracts for accommodation vary in terms of the level of commitment required. The least flexible contracts are those which commit the tour operator to paying for an agreed number of beds regardless of whether or not they can actually be filled. This can ensure a good price but could mean that unsold beds have to be paid for. Contracting accommodation 'by allocation' allows the tour operator to keep a number of beds until a release date. Reasonable prices can be negotiated and tour operator risk reduced with this method. Finally, tour operators can contract accommodation on an ad hoc basis which has no risk for the tour operator but has the disadvantage of being more expensive.

The accommodation contract, whatever form it takes, should be detailed as shown in Figure 2.4.

Room type (single, double etc.)
Meal arrangements (half board, full board etc.)
Reservations procedures

Accommodation details for the representative (desk space, noticeboard etc.)
Fire and safety procedures
Special arrangements or facilities (for disabled guests etc.)

Figure 2.4.   The accommodation contract.

AIR

As discussed in Chapters one and five, the larger tour operators have their own charter airline. Some airlines have their own tour operating division. For those tour operators without an airline there are several options for contracting a supply of aircraft seats. These are outlined below and discussed more fully in Chapter nine.

Time charter	contract of an aircraft for a whole season
Whole plane charter	a contract for specified flights
Part charter	purchase of a block of seats on a scheduled service or a chartered airline

Whilst charter flights are traditionally associated with tour operating, scheduled carriers are often happy to offer inclusive tour by excursion (ITX) fares to increase their load factors. Scheduled airlines often make a number of seats available to tour operators agreeing a cut-off date after which the airline can sell the seats itself if the tour operator has not already done so. Charter airlines normally require a deposit of around 10 per cent with the balance payable once the flight has taken place. Contracting for aircraft seats can be a lengthy and formal process in comparison to the other areas that tour operators need to negotiate. A high degree of commitment is often required.

Involved in the negotiation process for aircraft capacity is the production of what is known as the tour operating flight plan which shows the dates and times of flights, arrival and departure airports and such like. This will form the basis of a condensed version for inclusion in the tour brochure.

TRANSFERS

Tour operators make arrangements for clients to be transferred from the airport to their accommodation be this by taxi or, more commonly, by coach. A courier usually accompanies coach transfer passengers introducing them to the area and possibly also to the particular company or tour programme they have selected.

ANCILLARY SERVICES

In addition to the organization of transfers for package tourists, tour operators will often operate additional excursions and entertainment for visitors. As was mentioned above this can be a lucrative source of additional revenue for the company and resort representative alike. Involved in the organization of these additional services is a process of negotiation with any transport providers, attraction or restaurant managers or entertainers. Factors such as service levels and language abilities of staff are typically discussed at the planning stage together with rates for the tour operator.

TIME-SCALES IN THE PLANNING PROCESS

Time-scales involved in the planning of tour programmes vary with the type of programme (e.g. short break as against a main holiday) and also with the size of tour operator. The time-scales shown in Figure 2.5 would not be unusual in the industry for an overseas summer holiday programme.

Activity	Typical start date
Market research	Around two years ahead of programme start
Capacity decisions	Around 18 months ahead of programme start
Accommodation contracts	Around 18 months ahead of programme start
Brochure design	Around 12 months ahead of programme start
Contracts for transfers	Around 12 months ahead of programme start
Brochure printing and distribution	Around 6 months ahead of programme start
Reservations	Around 6 months ahead of programme start
Brochure launch	Around 3 months ahead of programme start
Advertising	Around 3 months ahead of programme start

Figure 2.5. Time-scales in tour planning. *Source*: adapted from Horner (1996).

Cooper *et al.* (1998) provide a detailed account of the tour operating cycle of an abroad summer programme.

Tour operators provide their own staff in resorts and are not solely dependent on suppliers to look after their customers' needs once at the destination. We will now look at the role of the resort representative.

THE ROLE OF THE RESORT REPRESENTATIVE

It is common for tour operators to have representatives at the different destinations they offer. These representatives provide ground arrangements and other support for clients. Their role usually involves meeting clients on arrival, providing accommodation providers with rooming lists, assisting with general enquiries and providing local information and dealing with any problems. They might possibly also provide entertainment for their holidaymakers. A typical larger tour operator might have a number of resort representatives supervised by an area office. In this situation the area office staff may be involved in the following:

- supervision of resort representatives;
- dealing with flight details;
- arranging transfers;
- maintaining contact with accommodation providers;
- maintaining contact with the home country office; and
- organization of excursions (paid-for excursions are often used as a means of generating additional income by tour operators with representatives receiving commission on the sale of these).

Cost pressures have forced some tour operators to reduce the amount of representation they provide in resorts and this has in some cases led to complaints from consumers. Having one representative travelling between resorts clearly reduces their level of availability. Some smaller specialist ski companies will have a member of staff acting as both manager of a chalet or small hotel and resort representative at the same time.

MARKETING PACKAGE HOLIDAYS

As consumers have become more used to travelling and the options available to them have increased, somewhat inevitably the job of the marketer of package holidays has become all the more difficult. Whilst there is insufficient room in this chapter to discuss the marketing of package tours in detail, the key areas of this are discussed below. Pender (1999) covers marketing management for travel and tourism in more depth.

Pricing package tours

Pricing

Supply and demand play a major role in the pricing of tour operators' products as indicated by the issue of seasonality. Seasons form the basis of many tour operators' pricing strategies. The following seasons are usually identified in brochures:

High season   The most popular dates, typically those during the school holidays for the family market, are often priced more expensively than other times. High seasons can vary between different holiday types. Ski holidays for example tend to show peak demand at different times to other types of holiday.

Low season   The cheapest dates are usually those when demand is poor as might be the case during the rainy season in some countries.

Shoulder season   Those dates not referred to as high or low season are often referred to as the shoulder season.

It used to be the case that the government set a price below which package tours could not be sold. This price covered the standard airfare plus a supplement. The subsequent removal of this floor price led to an increase in the sale of inclusive tours. This is not surprising given the highly price elastic nature of much tourism demand. This sensitivity to price which is evident in the mass market leisure sector creates a dilemma for tour operators. There is a clear need to balance an attractive price to the market against the requirement to cover all cost elements of the holiday. These elements will vary with different holidays and their distribution but typically might include research, marketing, (including brochure production and distribution), CRS, telecommunications, sales representatives, agency commission and other incentives, all transport (flights and transfers etc.), accommodation, resort staff, administration, and currency exchange. All of this is before the tour operator builds any profit into the package. Mass market tour operators tend to operate on the basis of small profits (this can be as little as a few per cent of the selling cost) but large volume. Smaller tour operators may work to larger profit margins as they do not have the capacity to achieve the high sales figures of the mass market operators' sales.

Discounting

Discounting of published tour prices has been widely accepted practice since the 1980s originally done in respect of late bookings in an attempt to remove excess stock. A later development was the use of discounts to try to manipulate demand by encouraging early bookings. A further method of doing this involved the use of price guarantees. Discounts for last minute sales have been used extensively by tour operators due to the highly perishable nature of the product. Sometimes this is for unnamed accommodation and consumers really do not know what they are buying.

That the tour operations market is highly competitive has already been discussed and one aspect to stem from this has been that the sector is heavily price-led. Price cuts, aimed at maintenance of booking volumes or increasing market share, are therefore an industry feature. Price panels are often the very last thing to be inserted into holiday brochures with some operators analysing the competitors' prices before making a commitment on price. A degree of undercutting takes place with 'lead offers' a significant tool for many operators.

The image and quality of package holidays have undoubtedly suffered as a result of the above. Indeed, much criticism has been levelled at the pricing policies of the package holiday industry. Price wars in particular have affected the industry with the resulting emphasis on low price as versus quality or even value for money. This has led many more discerning consumers to turn to independent and long haul travel options instead. There have been attempts to improve the image of the sector following consumer dissatisfaction with the reduction in quality that accompanied price cuts. Much of this dissatisfaction however related to extremely cheap packages yet there was little recognition of the fact that, in common with many other industries, to an extent, you often get what you pay for.

Exchange rates

Exchange rates greatly influence package holiday prices. Sterling has been strong against key foreign currencies in the latter part of the 1990s leading to improved prices for holidays to these destinations.

Surcharges

Surcharges were for some considerable time a contentious issue in relation to holiday pricing. Tour operators have tried to justify these on the basis that aspects such as exchange rates, fuel prices and the rate of inflation can greatly alter between the time of the brochure going to print and the commencement of a holiday promoted within it. They further claim that anticipating these changes and building them into the cost of a holiday can result in the programme becoming uncompetitive. Charging less could mean that they will lose profit when costs later increase. The difficulty for consumers was knowing when a surcharge was fair and when a tour operator was abusing their use. Guaranteed prices are far more common today than in the mid-1980s.

Fluid pricing

The emergence, towards the end of the 1990s, of the term 'fluid pricing' brought with it much confusion. The concept which rewards early bookers, was introduced by Thomson Holidays and quickly followed by other operators adopting similar policies.

The published brochure price has a variety of potential discounts available enabling tour operators to alter prices to match demand. Brochure prices therefore become merely a guide and are subject to change. Prices can be adjusted on viewdata according to demand. Reductions are on a sliding scale and the closer to the departure date, the higher the price. This is not a surprising development given that tour operators have often lost money through heavy discounts aimed at removing excess capacity. A great deal of confusion surrounded the introduction of fluid pricing, stemming from the fact that both prices can come from the brochure and consumers could think that the tour operator has increased the price of the holiday.

Distributing package tours

Essentially tour operators choose between direct and indirect distribution or a combination of both. Increasingly direct distribution methods are of a technical nature. Indirect distribution continues to mean the travel agent although developments in this area are likely in the near future.

Direct marketing

Marketing directly to consumers, in their home, office or some social environment, without the use of a middleman, has become increasingly popular in recent years. A popular example of a direct marketer of holiday products is Tjaerborg, a company that introduced this outstanding concept to the market in the 1970s. Tour operators use direct mail, telemarketing, computerized home selling and direct response advertising to communicate directly with potential customers. Indeed, the largest tour operators today often have a direct marketing arm to their organization as does Thomson with Portland. Many of the smaller tour operators do not ever use middlemen preferring to rely solely on direct marketing methods. Pender (1999) provides more detailed discussion of the different forms of direct marketing favoured by travel and tourism organizations. Technological developments including CRS and the internet as discussed in Chapter 4 have enabled tour operators to increase the scale of their direct marketing activities.

Reservations systems

It is possible for tour operators to use manual reservations systems, including wallcharts or cards showing the availability of units of stock for flights, beds and so on. For anything other than the smallest tour operators this basic system becomes inadequate. Computerized reservations systems (CRS) are discussed in Chapter 4.

Travel agents are involved in the distribution of package holidays as discussed in Chapter 3. A further method of distribution is that which takes place through newspapers and is referred to as reader holidays.

Promoting package tours

Tour operators face fierce competition from within the sector as well as outside, where the growth of direct sales has provided additional impetus for the use of promotions by those companies supplying package holidays. Traditionally promotional methods used by the industry have been categorized as being aimed at either the middleman (what is known as a push strategy) or aimed at the end consumer (a pull strategy). We will consider first those methods used when a push strategy is being employed. Familiarization trips offered to travel company staff as a means of increasing product knowledge and motivating active selling have proved popular in the industry over the years. These have not however been without their problems and more recently have become less popular partly due to their cost. Many companies do however continue to offer incentives of varying types to travel agents for selling their products.

In common with many industries, marketing today in the tour operations sector is highly characterized by activities aimed at creating strong brand images. The larger tour operators have the resources available to develop clear brand recognition. The trend at present appears to be towards maintenance of individual brands within a tour operator's overall portfolio when mergers occur. Some acquisitions however have led to the dissolution of smaller, relatively less well-known brands.

The Founders' Club

The Thomson Group was floated on the Stock Exchange in 1998 with all successful applicants allocated shares entitling them to membership of Founders' Club. Honorary membership, valid until the end of 1998, was also given to anyone who registered an interest in buying shares but did not receive them.

Thomson Superfamily

This new brochure offers dedicated family services and facilities at particular properties highlighting the free kids' club and the introduction of Breakfast and Evening Clubs and Crèches.

The loyalty card

Thomson, together with MasterCard, launched a credit card loyalty scheme in 1999 allowing customers to earn holiday points when using the card to make purchases. One point is received for every £10 spent and points can be redeemed as a discount on a Thomson holiday.

Figure 2.6. Thomson's travel incentives. *Source*: Mintel (1999).

45

We will now turn our attention to promotions used to help these brands reach the end consumer.

Figure 2.6 outlines some of the travel incentives offered to customers by Thomson.

Holiday brochures are often seen to be the visible face of the package tour industry. In a service business characterized by intangibility, the brochure offers not only a means of communication with potential customers but also a tangible representation of the product on offer. Arguably the brochure retains a higher profile as a promotional method for tour operators than could be expected given the many alternatives available in the twenty-first century. Despite the emergence of video, CD-Rom, teletext, interactive TV and virtual reality, it is still brochures that those visiting travel agents or contacting tour operators directly are likely to be provided with. The brochure accounts for a significant proportion of most mass market tour operators' marketing budgets. It is therefore worth looking briefly at the design, production and distribution of travel brochures.

Brochure design and production

The process of designing and producing holiday brochures can be carried out either in-house or by contracting an agency. This process may begin anything up to two years before the package tour is to take place. Typically the process involves graphic designers, photographers and copy-writers. A great deal of research will need to be undertaken prior to the design of the brochure and as discussed above some of this will be concerned with the development of the product itself. Consumer reactions to different brochure designs may also be researched possibly using qualitative research methods. Figure 2.7 highlights some of the decision areas facing those responsible for brochure design and production.

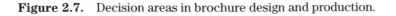

Typeface to be used
The copy to be included
The layout of the text
The use of colour, maps and photographs
The overall quality of the brochure
The design of the front cover (considering 'racking' issues if using middlemen)
The amount of information to provide
The launch date

Figure 2.7.   Decision areas in brochure design and production.

The resultant brochures are often highly standardized. This is partly caused by the requirement for brochures to fit travel agents' display racks and partly due to the requirement to include sufficient relevant information. Brochures take a long time from conception to production. Typically a brochure will be launched up to a year before the tour programme commences with production starting a season ahead of this. The market leaders usually launch their brochures for a season ahead of the competition amid a large promotional campaign and doing as much as possible to attract positive publicity. There has been a move towards earlier launch dates for brochures and this can mean that a tour operator may have several seasons' brochures on the market at any one time.

Brochure distribution

The larger mass market tour operators may select to undertake their own brochure distribution but specialist organizations also exist for this purpose. BP Travel Trade Services is one such organization distributing 140 million brochures a year on behalf of the industry (TTG, 1997). Due to the costs of producing and distributing brochures many tour operators now analyse sales figures in relation to the number of brochures sent for different travel agencies and use this *conversion rate* to help them become more selective in their distribution.

Public relations activities

Whilst often seen to be broader than promotions, successful management of a tour operator's public relations is of great importance to communications success. Unlike other promotional elements, tour operators do not select to use public relations (PR). Rather, public relations exist and the discretionary aspect is how to manage these. A variety of activities can be used in a variety of situations to manage a tour operator's public relations. A tour operator might, for example, need to manage their PR during a crisis at a resort in their portfolio. This would involve setting up an information line, dedicating a spokesperson to deal with the media and providing some kind of reaction to the disaster. A good relationship with the media can reward a company at times such as these. Alternatively, PR activities may be concerned with creating goodwill with the travel agents selling the tour operator's programmes. In the past agency educationals, whereby agents are sent to resorts to experience the product first hand, were a popular and informative means of doing this. Sadly educationals are becoming less frequently used tools. Tour operators also run competitions for travel agents and often do so through the trade press. Involvement with consumer competitions is also undertaken.

The importance of good relations with the media has already been introduced above and a strategy many tour operators choose is to provide travel journalists with free travel in the hope that this will lead to positive publicity. Not all journalists accept free travel in the interests of objectivity although most do.

Finally, most larger tour operators employ sales representatives in the home country to promote their products to the agency sector. These important members of the marketing team will visit travel agents ensuring that they receive sufficient publicity materials and brochures. Strong relationships can develop between the representatives, many of whom will have been travel agents in the past, and agency staff.

Clearly the above discussion of promotional methods used by the tour operations sector is limited by the availability of space and requirements of a chapter such as this. Chapter 4 examines some of the technological developments that have influenced the promotion of tourism products. A more detailed discussion of travel and tourism promotion is provided by Pender (1999).

It can be seen therefore that the roles performed by outbound tour operators can be split into those conducted in the home country (usually at the company's main headquarters) and those conducted overseas. Figure 2.8 summarizes these different roles. Poynter (1993) provides a 'hands-on' practical approach to learning tour development, design and marketing.

Home office	Overseas offices
Research	Research
Customer services	Customer services[*]
Accommodation contracts	Accommodation contracts[*]
Flight contracts	Transfers
Marketing including	Excursions
Distribution	Car hire
Pricing	Couriers
Agency sales support	Complaints
Promotion	Repatriation

*Note: These aspects can be the responsibility of either office or may be a joint responsibility.

Figure 2.8. Roles and responsibilities in the provision of tour operators' programmes. *Source*: adapted from Horner (1996).

Tour operators' product portfolios

Larger tour operators need to manage their overall portfolio of products. This is an important mix to get right and includes the following aspects:

- destinations served;
- modes of travel;
- quality/type of accommodation; and
- activities offered.

Portfolio decisions will be influenced greatly by factors such as market segmentation and competitor's product portfolios.

DOMESTIC TOUR OPERATORS

It was mentioned in Chapter 1 that there is far less 'packaging' of domestic tourism products than there is of outbound travel products mainly stemming from a lack of demand for this. It is however worth noting here that a variety of organizations are involved in tour operations for the domestic market. Coach holiday operators are for example heavily involved in the domestic market and are examined in Chapter 8. There are also domestic packages by train as discussed in Chapter 6. Other operators, particularly accommodation providers are involved in the provision of packages of accommodation and entertainment often without the transport element.

INCOMING TOUR OPERATORS

Incoming tour operators, as discussed in Chapter 1, vary in the degree to which they offer packaged services. Some incoming companies will be full service tour operators, based often in the generating country and taking care of all aspects of the overseas holiday. Others operating in this sector offer less complete packages and many are flexible enough to be able to react to the particular needs of the traveller or travelling group.

CUSTOMER COMPLAINTS

Whether dealing with outbound, incoming or domestic clients, most tour operators will at some time have to deal with customer complaints and it is not unusual for larger tour operators to have a department dedicated to dealing with this aspect of business. Negative publicity has often resulted from customer complaints and this is something that many tour operators are now keen to avoid. Customer services departments respond to complaints aiming to placate disappointed clients with an apology, compensation or *ex gratia* payment. Some complaints may be more serious and once again this department would be likely to be involved with any case that goes to court.

MARKET RESEARCH REVISITED

The importance of market research in the context of planning package tours has already been introduced. It should also be pointed out that market research ideally continues beyond the planning stage. In the interests of good marketing tour operators will at the very least want to receive feedback from both customers and resort-based staff as to the success of the programme. Resort-based staff may also be able to update information in relation to the host country. Staff from the home country may also visit the resort to conduct ongoing research. It is usual for customers to be asked to complete a questionnaire at the end of their holiday. These tourist satisfaction surveys should be used as a means of identifying any problem areas and as a basis for product improvements.

SUMMARY

This chapter has attempted to illustrate the many steps involved in planning and putting together tour operators' programmes. In doing so, we outlined the different steps involved including market research, supplier negotiations, pricing and promotion, before going on to consider each of these in detail. The chapter concluded with a discussion of the packaging of both domestic and incoming tour operations.

DISCUSSION QUESTIONS

1. Examine the value, for tour operators, of undertaking market research prior to the design and implementation of a new tour programme.
2. Outline factors that need to be taken into account in relation to the holiday brochure.
3. Discuss reasons why the pricing of package holidays has attracted criticism.

REFERENCES

Cooper, C., Fletcher, J., Gilbert, D. and Wanhill, S. (1998), in R. Shepherd (ed.) *Tourism: Principles and Practice*, Pitman Publishing.

Davidson, R. (1994) *Business Travel*, Pitman.

Downes, J. and Paton, T. (1993) *Travel Agency Law*, Pitman Publishing.

Holloway, J.C. (1994) *The Business of Tourism*, (4th edn), Pitman Publishing.

Horner, P. (1996) *Travel Agency Practice*, Addison-Wesley Longman.

Key Note Market Review (1998) *Travel Agents and Overseas Tour Operators*.

Key Note Ltd. (1999) *UK Travel and Tourism*.

Laws, E. (1997) *Managing Packaged Tourism – relationships, responsibilities and service quality in the inclusive holiday industry*, International Thomson Business Press.

Lickorish, L.J. and Jenkins, C.L. (eds) (1998) *An Introduction to Tourism*, Butterworth Heinemann.

Mintel, Inclusive Tours (1998), *Leisure Intelligence*, March.

Mintel, Travel Incentives and Promotions (1999) *Leisure Intelligence*, November.

Pender, L. (1999) *Marketing Management for Travel and Tourism*, Stanley Thornes (Publishers) Ltd.

Poon, A. (1993) *Tourism, Technology and Competitive Strategy*, CAB International.

Poynter, J.M. (1993) *Tour Design, Marketing and Management*, Prentice Hall.

Renshaw, M.B. (1997) *The Travel Agent*, (2nd edn), Business Education Publishers Ltd.

Vellas, F. and Becherel, L. (1995) International Tourism, MacMillan Business.

CHAPTER 3

Travel Intermediaries

INTRODUCTION

This chapter is concerned with the role and function of intermediaries in the context of travel and tourism distribution. The importance of the travel agent in the travel industry today is examined together with some of the threats the sector faces due to developments in travel distribution. Travel and tourism intermediaries, other than travel agents, are also discussed including air brokers and consolidators. An introduction to the role of technology in the distribution of travel is provided although more comprehensive coverage of this aspect can be found in Chapter 4.

Successful distribution is vitally important in travel and tourism. This is an area of increasing choice stemming mainly from the many technological developments that are taking place. Choice of distribution alternatives is complicated further by the service nature of tourism products. Intangibility in particular increases the importance of information provision as discussed in Chapter 4. Perishability, similarly, heightens the importance of communications methods in order to remove excess stock. Once an aircraft, ferry, train or other transport form has departed, so too has the opportunity to sell any unsold stock. The same theory can be applied to hotel accommodation and other tourism services.

AN OUTLINE OF TRAVEL AND TOURISM DISTRIBUTION

An important distinction is often drawn between direct and indirect, or mediated, travel distribution. Selling to the consumer without making use of a *middleman* is known as direct distribution and might include direct mail or telesales as well as sales via a principal's owned retail outlet. British Airways shops are an example of the latter. Where indirect distribution, or mediated sales, take place in the travel industry this usually involves a travel agent. There is little competition in terms of travel distribution from other types of retailer although this situation looks likely to change in future. We are currently seeing a move towards supermarkets retailing holiday insurance and post offices offering foreign exchange. Tesco's travel insurance for example is underwritten by Direct Line who deal with all customers by telephone. Direct Line provide all quotes and their claims department deals with any claims. Promotion is by flyers in Tesco's stores. Direct marketing methods are growing in popularity in general and the holiday industry is no exception to this. Indeed, the nature of the holiday and business travel product lends itself to direct distribution in many respects. We shall explore this concept in more detail later in this chapter and Pender (1999) provides further discussion of direct versus indirect travel distribution.

DISTRIBUTION CHANNELS

Marketing or distribution channels are used to move services, like products, from their original source to the end consumer. In the case of physical products this usually involves the physical transportation of the goods accompanied by the transfer of title for them. It is not therefore uncommon, in many industries, for intermediaries to hold stock and share financial risk at the same time as helping the product to reach end consumers.

Choice of marketing channel or channels is a difficult one for many marketers. Where more than one channel is used, the precise mix of methods needs to be carefully selected. In the case of service organizations, whilst a sequence of firms may still be involved in the movement of the service from producer to consumer, so providing a distribution channel, there are often differences in the way that these function. Service intermediaries tend not to hold stock and so are less likely to share any of the financial risk with the provider.

Renshaw (1997) has compared travel distribution to the distribution of other products as shown in Figure 3.1.

A striking difference between the two models is that manufacturers are replaced by principals in the travel and tourism model. Principals are service suppliers (airlines, hotels etc.) and as such do not perform a manufacturing function. Indeed, tour operators, represented at a later stage in Renshaw's model, combine different elements of the holiday package for resale and so could more accurately be described as performing a role similar to that of manufacturers. Tour operators are

Other Industries   *Travel Industry*

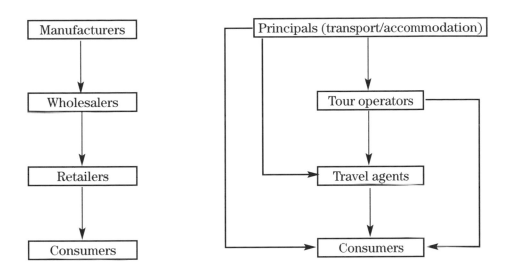

Figure 3.1.   A comparison of distribution channels. *Source*: Renshaw (1997).

sometimes also referred to as both principals and wholesalers. Use of these terms is not however universally accepted in relation to tour operators.

Renshaw (1997) further provides comprehensive coverage of the slightly different set of distribution alternatives facing each different sector of the industry. In this text distribution is discussed in relation to the different sectors of the industry in the relevant chapter in addition to the discussion in this chapter. Approximately two-thirds of package holidays and half of all independent holidays by air are booked through travel agents. Of the remainder, some are booked directly with the tour operator or principals, some via teletext and some through newspapers, clubs and loyalty schemes. Technology is a crucial aspect of distribution policy in most travel and tourism organizations. We shall start here by examining the travel agency sector.

Retail travel agents

Key Note (1998) describes the travel agency sector as highly concentrated with the top four travel agents increasing their share of the AIT market from 48 per cent to 54 per cent between 1991 and 1994. There are around 7000 travel agent branches in the UK owned by some 2000 companies. Figure 3.2 illustrates that the total number of travel agent branches has changed little in the last five years.

Behind this picture however lies a highly dynamic sector characterized by regular changes to ownership profiles.

1995	6938
1996	6844
1997	6833
1998	6930
1999	7000

Figure 3.2. Total number of travel agency outlets, 1995–9. *Source*: Mintel (2000).

THE ROLE AND FUNCTION OF TRAVEL AGENTS

Travel agents distribute the products of principals and tour operators as well as which some travel agents will package their own tour programmes for sale. This form of mediation not only offers consumers a convenient location to purchase travel products but also a whole host of other benefits including the sale of ancillary products as shown in Figure 3.3. At the same time travel agents offer the principals a network of outlets through which they can sell their products. Travel agents are distinct from other retailers in a number of respects including that they hold no stock and have no financial stake in the products they are selling. Travel agents therefore tend not to carry a great deal of risk. Whilst travel agents are mainly involved in the distribution of products created by principals and tour operators, some also create and sell their own package holidays. A similar, albeit more narrowly defined, service is provided by specialist reservations and booking agents for products such as hotels.

For customers

Multiple locations nationwide
Ancillary services (foreign exchange, insurance, airport transport service)

Additional perceived benefits of using a travel agent

A choice of principals' products to choose from*
Unbiased advice*

For principals

A network of outlets nationwide (wide reach)

Joint marketing opportunities (point of sale materials and suchlike)

Note: * whilst in reality many travel agents are linked to tour operators this is something that consumers are often unaware of. The operators concerned argue that this does not necessarily mean that they will engage in directional selling although others have disputed this.

Figure 3.3. Indicative services provided by travel agents.

The role of ABTA was discussed in Chapter 1.

Table 3.1. Estimated share of the UK tourism market accounted for by travel agents by value (%), 1997. *Source*: Key Note (1998).

	Travel agents
Domestic tourism	11
Outbound tourism	38
Total	49

THE DEVELOPMENT OF TRAVEL RETAILING

The march of the multiples

Renshaw (1997) describes a phenomenon known as the 'March of the Multiples' (MOM) which occurred in the retail travel sector throughout the 1980s and into the 1990s and consisted of both agency mergers and spectacular takeovers. Motivations for the march of the multiples are outlined in Figure 3.4. The multiples expanded in this way and in some cases also through new openings on 'green field' sites. The top five multiples controlled nearly one quarter of all travel agency outlets by 1990.

Economies of scale (cost efficiencies i.e. spread of advertising costs)

Increased assets (offices)

Addition of expertise (staff)

Reduction in competition (by buying it up)

More bargaining power with principals (possibly leading to lower prices and
more support)

Enhanced public awareness (through branding opportunities, common shop-fronts etc.)

Geographical spread (increased distribution)

Figure 3.4. Motivations for MOM. *Source*: based on Renshaw (1997).

The 'March of the Multiples' inevitably left those smaller chains and independents who had not themselves been absorbed by a larger multiple feeling vulnerable and facing difficulties competing in terms of discounting, technology and bargaining power with suppliers.

THE STRUCTURE OF THE INDUSTRY

Travel agents can be categorized in several ways with the usual distinction being drawn on the basis of size. Renshaw (1997) describes the following categories (by size) of travel agent.

- multinationals (with offices worldwide);
- national multiples (with offices throughout a country);
- regional multiples or miniples (with a number of offices but concentrated in one region of a country); and
- independents (with anything from one to a handful of branches).

A further way of categorizing travel agents is by the type of business conducted. Figure 3.5 identifies different types of travel agent.

Holiday shops

Sometimes referred to as leisure agents, these are usually based in busy shopping areas and deal mainly with the sale of package holidays.

Business travel agents

Sometimes referred to as 'business houses' they deal with travel for reasons connected with work. Business travel agents meet quite different needs to holiday shops yet they may be linked to a holiday shop owned by a multiple or a well-known independent.

Implant agents

These are usually a version of the above specialized business travel agent category which is established at a client's premises

General agents

General agents deal with both leisure and business travel.

Figure 3.5. Types of travel agent.

Thomas Cook is discussed below as an example of a multiple travel agency chain. Thomas Cook is an international travel and financial services group employing 20,000 people worldwide. The group has 1800 wholly-owned operations in 25 countries worldwide including tour operations, retail travel, a charter airline and global and financial services. The company's tour operator business was discussed in Chapter 1 and we return to the company as an example in Chapter 5 due to the integrated nature of its services. The discussion in Figure 3.6 relates only to Thomas Cook's retail and call centre business however.

Thomas Cook is, at the time of writing, the second largest retail network in the UK with 750 Thomas Cook high street shops and five Thomas Cook Plus travel warehouses. The company also has 870 bureaux de change, 750 of which are in travel shops, 109 in branches of HSBC banks and eleven of which are standalone. The company operates the world's largest network of retail foreign exchange bureaux with over 1000 locations worldwide. There are four Thomas Cook call centres.

The company's retail and call-centre operations are not solely based in the UK as they operate major retail businesses in Canada, Australia, New Zealand, Hong Kong, Mexico and Egypt and run direct telephone sales centres in Australia and Canada.

In July 1997, Thomas Cook's Travel business in Canada signed a licensing agreement with Wal Mart Canada to open travel branches in Wal Mart stores across Canada. Wal Mart is North America's leading retail department store, and this deal has added 60 franchised travel branches.

Figure 3.6. Thomas Cook. *Source*: Thomas Cook (2000).

Lunn Poly (owned by Thomson TO) has 800 'holiday shops' in the chain, selling 20–25 per cent of the AITs bought in the UK (Mintel, 1998). Thomas Cook has a network of High Street branches totalling 385 Travelshops as well as 215 implants in other retail outlets and exchange bureaux. The company also operates through a network of other, associated companies and has built up a total of 5,000 outlets in 120 countries worldwide. (Mintel, 1998).

The example of the tour operator Airtours Plc was given in Chapter 1 and as this is a vertically integrated company, it can also be used to illustrate the operation of retail travel agents. This aspect of Airtours distribution strategy is outlined in Figure 3.7. The company's Going Places chain of travel agents opened its first 'Holidayworld' – a 3000 square metre (10,000 square foot) holiday hypermarket – in 1999. In common with the other mass market tour operators, Airtours does not rely on retail distribution alone. Other aspects of the distribution strategy include call centres, teletext, the Internet and interactive television.

Going Places	728 outlets
Travelworld	123 outlets
Ving	67 shops; 9 franchises
Allkauf	90 shops; 63 franchises
FTI	9 outlets
Flugborse	147 franchises
5vF	22 franchises
Maretours	21 outlets

Figure 3.7.   Airtours Plc's retail travel agents. *Source*: adapted from Airtours (1999) Annual Report and Accounts.

In common with the tour operations sector, the travel agent business is a polarized one with just a few large multiples at one end of the spectrum and thousands of independents at the other. The largest multiple travel agents by outlets, 1993–7 are shown in Table 3.2.

Table 3.2.   The largest multiple travel agents by outlets, 1993–7. *Source*: Mintel (1998).

Chain brand and parent	1993	1995	1997	1993–7
			(% change)	
Lunn Poly (Thomson Travel Group, Canada)	530	795	800	+51
Going Places (Airtours)	340	725	715	+110
Thomas Cook (Westdeutsche Landesbank)*	331	385	385	+16
Worldchoice**	–	–	1100	–
Co-op Travelcare	350	460	475	+36

Notes: * 385 Travelshops; excludes 215 implants in other retail outlets and exchange bureaux
      ** approximate number, made up of a consortium of around 400 outlets owned by Carlson Leisure Group and 600 independent, voluntary members of the Worldchoice consortium.

It is worth noting that despite the above description of a sector dominated by large integrated companies a survey of travel agents conducted for the MMC's report on 'Foreign package holidays', published in December 1997 found that 71 per cent of travel agencies had one outlet. The average turnover for these independent agencies is however far less than that for branch outlets of multiple chains and so the latter achieve far higher market shares overall (Key Note, 1999). Small miniple agencies are however far less prominent than they were in the past.

RELATIONSHIPS WITH PRINCIPALS

The fact that many tour operators' brochure distribution strategies have become more selective in recent years was mentioned in Chapter 2. It is also worth noting here that travel agencies have, at the same time, become more discerning in respect of which brochures they choose to display on their shelves and of those which they display most prominently. A number of factors influence corporate policy in this regard. The larger, vertically integrated companies may position their own company's brochures most favourably whilst a specialist agency is more likely to give priority to brochures featuring holidays offering their particular specialism. Another common method of selecting brochures to display is to examine past success. This is not however as straightforward a choice as it may appear and there have been significant *racking rows* between agents and operators in the past. The trend towards earlier bookings has created even more difficult decision-making for agents who may have as many as three different seasons' brochures to rack at any one time.

TRAVEL AGENCY APPOINTMENTS

Travel agents generally seek appointments which are recognized by the public. Consumers are often advised to ensure that agents have an ATOL. ABTA appointments are also widely recognized by the general public. Both of these were discussed in Chapter 1.

TRAVEL AGENCY SKILLS

Travel agents have the great advantage of knowing where to find relevant information. Whilst for the more complex journey or travel itinerary most consumers will be unaware of what options exist, a good travel agent will know how to access the appropriate travel and accommodation suppliers. A number of recognized qualifications are offered to agents including ticketing and CRS courses.

TRAVEL AGENCY PAYMENT SYSTEMS

Traditionally travel agents have earned commission payment – a percentage of the value of the sale – on any booking made with a principal on behalf of a client. Whilst commission payments vary by type of product and by company it is not unusual for a figure of between 8 and 10 per cent to be paid as commission. Travel agents can derive additional earnings from the sources outlined in Figure 3.8. There has, however, been a fairly recent move towards fee based payments for travel agents.

Overrides

These represent an increase in the level of commission not linked to sales performance

Incentive payments

These represent an increase paid for the achievement of a certain level of sales

Ancillary services

These include the sale of such things as holiday insurance and transport to airports

Referral vouchers

These are issued by principals (hotels, car hire firms etc.) in exchange for a travel agent's recommendation to clients. The agent receives commission or a standard payment once the client presents the voucher, makes a booking and pays directly

Interest on money held

Money received by an agent from a client but not yet passed on to the principal, sometimes known as 'pipeline money' can be used to earn interest for the agent

Service charges

Service charges are a means of recouping money on a transaction (telephone booking or visa application for example) that it might otherwise cost the travel agent to carry out rather than a main source of income for an agency

---

Figure 3.8. Additional sources of travel agency earnings.

The majority of retail travel agents concentrate on the leisure sector of the outbound holiday market and the sale of AITs in particular. Reductions in travel agency commissions by scheduled airlines may reinforce this.

THE AGENCY EDUCATIONAL

A further aspect that characterizes the relationship between travel agents and principals, including tour operators, is the provision of agency 'educationals' sometimes also referred to as 'familiarization trips'. These are aimed at increasing agents' knowledge of a tour operator's, principal's or even a destination's product(s) at the same time as which it is hoped they will help to put the sponsor's product to the forefront of the agent's mind when selling. Often a variety of sponsors come together with one another to offer an educational. It is not uncommon for an airline, a destination tourist board and a hotel chain to offer an educational. These can be a useful way of courting positive public relations with the middleman when used appropriately. The use of educationals is sadly on the decline partly due to the high cost of hosting them. There have also been problems with these in the past and they have sometimes been seen to be 'freebies' as opposed to study tours.

This chapter now considers another facet of the business of travel distribution which is the growing area of call centres.

CONSORTIA OF TRAVEL AGENCIES

Consortia membership benefits can include marketing support (such as advertising, public relations activities and field sales teams), commission overrides and an all-important national identity. Clearly membership of consortia enables the independents to operate on a level playing field with the multiples particularly due to the strength of their commercial negotiations. Given the squeeze on independents described above, the benefits of consortia membership become even more attractive especially as consortia are prepared to fight for the independent sector.

One of the largest grouping of independent travel agents in the UK is the Alliance of Retail Travel Agents Consortia (ARTAC) which has over 700 members. Advantage Travel Centres is the brand name used by members of the National Association of Independent Travel Agents (NAITA). Until recently the Association had franchise members set up in association with Airtours as discussed in the next section. Other significant groupings of this type include The Campaign for Real Travel Agents (CARTA) and Global Travel Group (GTG).

FRANCHISED TRAVEL AGENCIES

The travel agency sector has, in common with some airlines, relatively recently become involved in franchising. Franchising is a system under which a business known as a franchisor allows other organizations known as frachisees to use their name and market their products for a 'royalty' or fee. In the case of retail travel the franchisor is likely to be an established distributor and the franchisee an existing independent agency or a new outlet. There have been examples of consortia members becoming franchisees.

Holloway (1994) describes earlier failed attempts by travel agents to involve themselves in this form of partnership, highlighting reasons for their failure. Among these were; the lack of a strong name or unique product, the lack of price and product advantages, the inability to guarantee principals' approval and IATA appointments, the inadequacy of staff training, problems with standards and quality, legal problems affecting the payment of royalties (as commission could not then be split between an agent and another organization) and a lack of marketing back-up. In addition to these problems were exaggerated claims in relation to potential profits and broken promises in relation to exclusivity. More recent attempts at travel agency franchising have met with mixed results.

Examples of franchising arrangements established in the sector during the latter half of the 1990s included Bonanza Travel which specializes in independent travellers and Airtours with Advantage Travel Centres. The Bonanza arrangement is operational at the time of writing but the Advantage arrangement has been withdrawn. This latter arrangement was however an interesting example as Airtours held a minority stake in a new franchise company within Advantage Travel. Advantage had previously been operated solely as a consortium of independent travel agents. Not all Advantage members chose to sign up to the franchise arrangement however.

The Canadian travel agency chain, Uniglobe, illustrates a franchised operation which has been used as a successful means of entry into the UK market. The company has over 1000 franchises in eighteen country locations worldwide. There are 25 in the UK with many more planned. The Uniglobe Master Franchise for the UK is owned by one of the company's co-founders and his wife. Aspects of the Uniglobe franchising arrangement are outlined in Figure 3.9.

Selection

A lengthy selection process is implemented at Uniglobe to ensure that any potential franchisee is suited to the company

Support

Support is provided for Uniglobe franchisees in the following areas:

Sales and marketing
Accounting
Technology
Training

Exclusivity

Franchisees are guaranteed an exclusive geographical territory

Negotiated supplies

Uniglobe has negotiated deals with suppliers but leaves the purchase decision to franchisees

Control of service quality

A variety of methods are used to ensure the maintenance of standards including the following:

Visits to agencies
Written manual
Awards dinners
'Star' agencies
Quality control cards (these rate agencies and are sent to customers to be
   returned to Uniglobe's UK headquarters)
Robotics software (purchased with the Galileo system, this checks every booking made)

Figure 3.9. Franchising at Uniglobe. *Source*: Uniglobe (2000) and Pender (2000).

There are clear advantages to franchising for both franchisors and franchisees but despite this survival of this type of arrangement in the travel agency sector cannot be guaranteed. Pender (2000) discusses franchising in the retail travel sector in more detail.

BUSINESS TRAVEL AGENTS

The Guild of Business Travel Agents (GBTA) represents the business sector. The membership includes all leading multiples as well as smaller, more specialist companies.

GLOBALIZATION

Particularly in the growing area of business travel, a global presence is important for specialist business agents. The needs of large corporate clients are increasingly for global business travel agents as business travel becomes more multinational. This could make it more difficult for smaller companies to compete effectively.

CUSTOMER SERVICE

Customers are becoming more discerning about the quality and level of service they demand which has implications for staff training and such like. The future of the independents, in particular, is likely to depend greatly on them providing excellent customer service.

TRAVEL AGENTS IN THE TOURISM INDUSTRY VALUE-CHAIN

The concept of the tourism value-chain was introduced in Chapter 1 and the position of tour operators within the chain was discussed. Travel agents can also be seen to create value through activities such as counselling travellers, processing information, preparing itineraries and other customer services.

REGULATION

Voluntary regulation has traditionally been a feature of the travel agency business and this has stemmed in part from the introduction, in the 1960s, of *operation stabilizer*. The travel industry, at the time, faced a number of difficulties including some poor quality holiday products and the failure of some companies. ABTA had, as we saw in Chapter 1, been created in the 1950s by leading tour operators and the organization implemented a code of ethics which was later to become known as their code of conduct. Activities instigated for members included those shown in Figure 3.10.

The common fund

This was aimed at helping package tourists stranded abroad due to the failure of a member

The arbitration scheme

This was aimed at helping to settle disputes between operators and the public

---

Figure 3.10.   ABTA-instigated member activities.

Despite the above self-regulatory role that the government were happy to leave ABTA to manage, failures of non-ABTA companies continued to harm the industry. ABTA found themselves in the position of having to use funds to repatriate tourists stranded abroad who had not travelled with an ABTA tour operator but who had booked through an ABTA travel agency. This problem was resolved by the introduction of Operation Stabilizer, a virtual closed shop, which meant that ABTA member travel agents could only sell ABTA member tour operators' products and ABTA member tour operators' products could only be sold through ABTA member travel agencies. In addition to this the association developed a bonding scheme (a financial guarantee provided by a third party) as the common fund could not cope with too many collapses. All new ABTA travel agencies had to be bonded from the early 1970s. Further financial protection was provided in 1975 by the establishment in the UK of the air travel reserve fund. This involved 1 per cent of all inclusive tour departures being used to build reserves and repay a government loan.

Operation Stabilizer was limited to ABTA members and major company collapses continued into the early 1990s signalling a need for further regulation and protection. The UK was not alone in having these concerns over the industry. Indeed European commissioners were, at the time, also examining consumer protection issues in other countries. This was to lead to the instigation of the EC Package Travel Regulations. Indeed, the European Directive was adopted in 1990 and the individual countries concerned had until 31 December 1992 to implement it. The Directive had been designed to extend responsibility to all sectors of the industry and covered non-air based holidays. Further details regarding the EC Package Travel Regulations are provided by Downes and Paton (1993).

ABTA itself has an uncertain future at present. How the Association will evolve remains to be seen and certainly meeting the needs of an ever-changing industry is not easy. Confounding this problem is ABTA's diverse membership of large, small, independent and integrated companies. Despite that ABTA's role is undoubtedly ripe for change, it has in the past held a powerful position in the industry with over 3000 members at its peak.

The distribution of package holidays has attracted a great deal of scrutiny in recent times as evidenced by the referral of the industry to the Monopolies and Mergers Commission (MMC) by the Office of Fair Trading (OFT) in 1996. The MMC report in 1997 concluded that vertical integration of tour operators, travel agents and airlines (as discussed in Chapter 5) did not adversely affect consumer choice. Using British National Travel Survey (BNTS) data, the MMC concluded that, in 1996, about 80 per cent of inclusive tours were booked through visits to travel agents whilst the remaining 20 per cent were booked by telesales to travel agents, including teletext, and by direct sales.

Vertical integration has increased since the publication of the monopolies and mergers commission (now competition commission) report. Ownership of travel agents by tour operators remains something that many travellers are unaware of.

The main regulation for air based holidays is via the Civil Aviation Authority (CAA) which license companies organizing air inclusive tours (AITs) and issue Air Travel Organizers' Licences (ATOLs) in return for bonds to cover any failure. This clearly affects those travel agents organizing their own air based packages. The ATOL scheme is discussed more fully in Chapter 1.

BUSINESS INCENTIVE TRAVEL AGENCIES

The concept of incentive travel was introduced in Chapter 1 and Mintel (1999) describes business incentive travel agents including the IATA and ATOL bonded agent Page & Moy Marketing Group. This organization which is involved in staff motivation, communications, incentives and event management in 1998 had a turnover estimated at around £8 million for its incentive travel. Others include Meritz Ltd and World Event Marketing.

CALL CENTRES

The retail sector has developed a number of call centres in response to the expansion of the direct bookings market. This is exemplified by Thomas Cook's call centres at Peterborough and Falkirk. The latter deals with over 1000 calls a day. In 1999 Lunn Poly announced plans for 1000 call centre jobs in Glasgow within five years. The company was attracted by the city's 'great telephone accent'. (*Financial Times*, 1999). Airtours opened a new retail telephone centre in Newcastle which significantly increased the call handling capacity for Late Escapes and other Group tour operators. New technology in Scandanavia enabled Airtours to create a 'virtual call centre' whereby telephone calls are automatically routed to available staff in any of the outlets.

TECHNOLOGY, TRAVEL AGENTS AND THE FUTURE

The increasing use of technological and other direct means of selling places a question mark over the future need for travel agency shops.

Technology is indeed having an impact at two levels in terms of the distribution of travel and tourism products. Firstly it is providing opportunities for organizations outside the travel and tourism field, including telecommunications and other technology based companies as well as start-up businesses to enter the field. Secondly, technology offers opportunities to those already operating in the travel and tourism arena (travel agents, tour operators and principals) to embrace new means of reaching consumers. Some of the technological developments adopted by the industry are now discussed.

Viewdata

Viewdata achieved quick success in the UK retail leisure sector and filtered into some areas of the accommodation and transport sectors. The launch of 'Top,' Thomson's system, in 1982 was significant in terms of package holiday distribution. Viewdata is still used in the leisure sector today despite the more recent technologies.

Computer reservations systems (CRS)

Like viewdata, CRS are used as online booking systems in travel agents. They have been more readily accepted by the business travel agents who are dealing with more complex itineraries and where speed is often of the essence. As costs fall leisure agents are now also purchasing these systems in greater numbers. They are used to update availability information, make bookings and perform back-office functions such as accounting. Four systems have become dominant worldwide. These are Worldspan, Galileo, Sabre and Amadeus.

Internet travel agencies

As is discussed in Chapter 4 we are currently witnessing the emergence of the *Internet* travel agency concept. This development has potential to have great impact on travel distribution. These Internet companies do not necessarily bear any relationship to the traditional high street agencies although there are some established travel companies which recognize this new threat and have made moves to confront this. The profile of online travel agencies includes start-up companies and partnership ventures with technology based organizations. Some of these companies also have involvement with other emerging technological channels of distribution, such as interactive television, leading some observers to conclude that the future of travel distribution will have significant input from companies that have not necessarily had any previous involvement in travel. It is not therefore only the independents that are vulnerable to the advantages of supplier/customer links that the Internet can offer. Technology for the travel trade is discussed more fully in Chapter 4.

Air brokers and consolidators

A further intermediary role in travel distribution is that of specialists in the provision of airline seats in bulk to other tour operators, in other words air brokers and consolidators. The latter are principally concerned with the consolidation of seats on behalf of operators who have achieved insufficient load factors for their charters. They have a different customer base to brokers.

Brokers negotiate with airlines for capacity which they then sell on, usually in smaller blocks but also individually, to tour operators and travel agents. When fulfilling a distribution role for airlines that have been unable to fill their seats these intermediaries can negotiate low rates. A mark-up is then added by the broker in return for the risk carried as they assume responsibility for marketing the seats.

The seat-only market has developed as a way for tour operators with their own charter airlines, to sell flights without accommodation to independent travellers. Surrounding these tour operator divisions has developed a more fluid pattern of buying flights. Consolidators traditionally sold seats on scheduled flights at discount through travel agents. Some of the larger consolidators now have their own high street premises and travel agents take out ATOL licences to enable them to sell flights. Tour operators quickly met the demand for flights without accommodation themselves, rather than rely on broking companies. (Mintel, 2000).

A main development in the consolidator market occurred when they were drawn into the ATOL scheme and so became licensed by the CAA. The traditional image of consolidators as 'bucket shops' has been replaced by these recognized intermediaries. There is even an Association of Airline Consolidators (AAC) which represents the sector and has over 50 members. The Association, which includes companies such as Unijet Group Plc and The Airline Seat Company Ltd amongst its membership is discussed in more detail in Figure 3.11.

AAC is an organization which was formed to represent the interests of consolidators and the wider travel industry. The organization works closely with other important trade bodies such as ABTA and government departments including CAA. Recent figures suggest that members account for 80 per cent of discounted airline tickets sold in the UK accounting for around £1.8 billion of annual revenue. Further details of the Association are provided below:

Mission statement

To foster greater understanding of the role of the consolidator, a provider of airline seats at a discount to regular published fares
To cultivate meaningful relations with government and its agencies, other industry bodies, the press and media
To effectively represent members and to act and advise without bias towards size and profile
To encourage formal and informal contact between members
To endorse consumer protection offered by members to its consumers and retail partners

Benefits to members

Regular communications (e-mail/fax) regarding important/urgent industry issues
Legal advice on problems relating to the consolidation and travel industry
Continuing dialogue with government and other industry bodies
Monthly meetings of the Executive Council, representing members' interests
The opportunity to meet and discuss critical issues
Exclusive discounted rates for bonding and scheduled airline failure insurance

Membership fees

AAC requires all members to hold a current ATOL
The yearly subscription for 2000/2001 will be £475 plus a joining fee of £100 plus VAT for new members

---

Figure 3.11. The Association of Airline Consolidators (AAC). *Source*: AAC (2000) and www.aac-UK.org

The CAA conducted research into the discount fares market in 1994. These discounted fares are not available from the airline direct but usually via a consolidator (wholesaler) which may deal with a number of airlines. This may be a tour operator which also deals in the seat-only market although some airlines prefer to confine their dealings to their own General Sales Agent (GSA). Fares can therefore be far less than those published by the airline but it is the latter that are shown on discounted tickets rather than that actually paid. For the airline's accounting purposes special codings are used on the ticket to show the actual rate at which the ticket was sold. Some consolidators deal with particular geographical areas whilst others deal with numerous airlines. (Civil Aviation Authority, 1994). Trailfinders is an airline ticket broker which had expanded to a turnover of over £200 million by 1997 with ATOL capacity of nearly 450,000 for 1998 (Mintel, 1998). The same source informs that Gold Medal Travel claims to be the largest distributor of consolidated air tickets through the trade. The group has links with the expanding travel agent multiple, Travelworld, which has nearly 100 branches in the North of England.

SUMMARY

This chapter has discussed the role and function of intermediaries in the distribution of travel and tourism products. The focus was on the retail travel agency sector – the main intermediaries currently used by travel principals. Air brokers and consolidators were also discussed due to their importance in the distribution of air seats. Reference was also made to the growing use of direct methods of travel distribution. This aspect is discussed further in Chapter 4 which focuses on technology in travel distribution whilst also considering other direct methods of distribution. Clearly taken together these two chapters account for the majority of mediated and non-mediated methods of travel distribution.

DISCUSSION QUESTIONS

1. Discuss threats facing the traditional travel agency sector. You may wish to make reference to Chapter 4 in order to provide a more thorough answer to this question.
2. What, if anything, can travel agencies do to combat the threats identified in answer to Question 1 (above)?
3. Compare and contrast the use of direct as against indirect methods of travel distribution.

REFERENCES

ABTA Members Handbook (1994)

Beaver, A. (1993) *Mind Your Own Travel Business: a manual of retail travel practice* (3rd edn).

Brendon, P. (1990) *Thomas Cook, 150 Years of Popular Tourism*, Secker & Warburg.

Civil Aviation Authority (1994) *Airline Competition on European Long-Haul Routes*, CAP 639, November.

Downes, J. and Paton, T. (1993) *Travel Agency Law*, Pitman Publishing.

Financial Times, 30 November 1999, Scotland II.

Holloway, J.C. (1994) *The Business of Tourism*, (4th edn), Pitman Publishing.

Horner, P. (1996) *Travel Agency Practice*, Addison-Wesley Longman.

Key Note Market Review (1998) *Travel Agents and Overseas Tour Operators.*

Key Note Ltd. (1999) *UK Travel and Tourism.*

Mintel, Inclusive Tours, Leisure Intelligence, March 1998.

Mintel, Independent Travel, Leisure Intelligence, April 2000.

Mintel, Travel Incentives and Promotions, Leisure Intelligence, November 1999.

Pender, L. (1999) *Marketing Management for Travel and Tourism*, Stanley Thornes.

Pender, L. (2000) Travel trade and transport, in C. Lashley, and A. Morrison *Franchising Hospitality Services*, Butterworth Heinemann.

Poon, A. (1993) *Tourism, Technology and Competitive Strategy?*, CAB International.

Renshaw, M.B. (1997) *The Travel Agent* (2nd edn), Business Education Publishers Ltd.

Thomas Cook (2000) Company Information.

Uniglobe (2000) Company Information.

www.aac-UK.org

CHAPTER 4

Travel Trade and Transport Technology

INTRODUCTION

The previous three chapters introduced the structure of the travel trade and Part 2 of the book goes on to examine the transport sectors. Something that is common to each of these and to many of the other types of organization (tourist boards and such like) is the extent to which technology can, or at least has the potential to, help them. Technology is a broad term with a range of applications. What we are concerned with here is principally technology as a means of distribution of the travel product, be that an airline seat or a fully inclusive tour. Technology as it affects the design of transport forms, is therefore seen to be outside the scope of this chapter.

Technology offers important means of information provision to both middlemen and consumers for travel trade and transport operators. A problem traditionally associated with service firms in general has been that of providing information in relation to intangible products. The role of the brochure was, in the past, paramount partly as a result of this need to inform travellers as to what it was that an organization was offering for sale. The use of technology has greatly helped some such companies and the emerging technologies are offering further opportunities for them. This chapter outlines both the early technological developments to affect the industry as well as the newer and emergent forms. Prior to doing so, consideration is given to the reasons why the travel trade and transport areas are so suited to technological means of distribution.

BACKGROUND

The term 'communication and information technologies' (CITs) is used to describe particular modes and mechanisms used to manage information. According to Poon (1993) this involves computer and communications technologies used to acquire, process, analyse, store, retrieve, disseminate and apply information. Such technologies can reduce costs whilst at the same time also improving efficiency, productivity and competitiveness.

The strategic implications of new and emerging technologies are great for all of the travel trade and transport sectors. Various types of technology-based system are involved in the production and distribution of tourism products and no serious travel trade or transport business can afford to ignore these. Equally though, it cannot be assumed that the adoption of information technologies leads to guaranteed success. These need to be part of a long-term strategic plan. Implementation needs to be both well managed and supported. Indeed, significant change may be required within organizations to accommodate the implementation of information technologies.

TECHNOLOGY AND TRAVEL TRADE AND TRANSPORT

Much of the technological development taking place in the travel trade and transport sectors is, surprisingly, still at the embryonic stage. The extent to which the subsectors utilize the technology will undoubtedly grow substantially in future. This may have the effect of increasing the market or alternatively it may merely displace business by changing channels of distribution.

Difficulties traditionally experienced by service firms in reaching consumers were introduced above and reasons why technology benefits the travel trade and transport sectors in particular are outlined in Figure 4.1.

Reason	Explanation
Information intensity	Information is central to distribution success in the complex and global tourism industry. Tourism itself is an information intensive business. The intangible nature of tourism products necessitates the provision of information to middlemen and consumers. Technology can be used to transmit, store, retrieve and update information both speedily and effectively

Image and perception	Linked to the above point is the importance of information to the formation of images and perceptions held by tourists
Product complexity	Holidays are expensive and infrequent purchases often bought for more than one 'user' and will possibly involve an element of risk for the consumer. This complexity is added to by the fact that a variety of organizations are likely to be involved in the supply of an overall holiday experience. Once again this makes the role of information paramount. Technology can be used to market 'as one' the different products and services that constitute the tourism product. This eases the purchasing process for the consumer
Perishability of product	Having the means to distribute unsold services at the last minute becomes vital due to the inability to store travel and tourism services for future sale
Demand management	Reservations systems are used by most travel trade and transport firms as an important means of controlling demand. The high seasonality that is characteristic of the industry can make it difficult to balance supply and demand. Reservations systems and sophisticated yield management systems, such as those used by the larger airlines, can help companies to maximize their revenue. Technology has greatly aided the development of reservations systems
Cost control	Driving down the costs of distribution is a main priority for tour operators, transport and accommodation providers. Technology can help to reduce these costs
Competitive marketplace	The competitive nature of the travel and tourism marketplace makes information all the more necessary to meet consumer needs

Figure 4.1. Reasons why technology benefits the travel trade and transport sectors.

RESERVATIONS SYSTEMS

Reservations systems are popular amongst both principals and intermediaries. Advance bookings enable suppliers to control demand, especially where seasonality is high. This can be an expensive area but at the same time one that can help organizations to maximize their revenue. Both manual and computerized reservations systems are available.

FROM VIEWDATA TO CRS

Viewdata

One of the earliest technologies available to the travel trade and transport sectors and which is still very much in evidence today is that based on information transmission by telecommunications lines. In the UK the term *viewdata* is, according to Inkpen (1998), used to describe the technology referred to internationally as *videotext*. The two terms are used interchangeably here. These systems use a telephone line, a modem, a keyboard and a VDU to enable communication between leisure travel agents and tour operators or other companies' reservations systems. The popularity of videotext networks in the leisure market stems in part from the fact that they are relatively inexpensive, relatively easy to use and reasonably reliable. Furthermore, viewdata equipment already has an established presence in travel agents and many tour operators have invested in their own system or in access to one. Renshaw (1997) provides more detailed discussion of the development of viewdata.

Computerized reservations systems

First introduced in the USA in the 1980s as a means of helping American Airlines to control their inventory, computerized reservations systems (CRS) are essentially databases that enable improved accessibility to information within and between partners. This became necessary, in the airline industry, following deregulation when a vast array of services and fare types became available. The potential of these new systems as 'sales tools' was quickly recognized. Among the many benefits of these systems for airlines were the worldwide distribution possibilities and the revenue earning opportunities created due to third party services. Buhalis (1998) describes these CRS as strategic business units (SBU) in their own right.

It was not only the airlines who were involved in the ownership of CRS. Tour operators first entered the market in 1976 when Thomson's Open-line programme (TOP) – a real time, computer-based reservations system – was introduced. By 1982 the system was capable of enabling direct communication between agents and operators. TOP has been attributed by many (Holloway, 1994; Renshaw, 1997) with helping to make Thomson the major player in the UK's tour operations sector. Other tour operators however soon followed this lead. Tour operators became used to CRS as a means of distribution, a means of monitoring and a means of control of 'back office' operations. Sabre was a classic case of how technology can drive business strategy.

FROM CRS TO GDS

Suppliers, utilizing CRS, recognized the opportunities that these offered for product display and sales worldwide. This had clear implications for the competitiveness of firms and so the all-encompassing global distribution systems (GDS), with which the travel industry is familiar today, developed out of the early CRS. This has also partly resulted from the growth of air traffic. There are now four dominant GDS – Amadeus, Sabre, Worldspan and Galileo. GDS were initially used by business travel agents but now have wider applicability and are also attracting leisure based products.

Taken together, videotext networks and GDS technologies have a number of advantages for travel agents. Some of these are outlined in Figure 4.2.

There are a number of advantages that all travel agencies using these systems can benefit from including those listed below:

- Instant information provision
- Complete reservations facilities
- Organizational improvements including:
    Integration of 'back-office' functions e.g. accountancy/personnel
    Integration of 'front-office' functions e.g. customer records/itinerary
        construction/ticketing/communication with suppliers
- Financial and operational control
- Market research and strategic planning

Benefits that the larger travel agents experience in addition to the above:

- Better coordination and control between remote branches and headquarters.

Figure 4.2. Advantages of GDS and videotext for the travel agent. *Source*: based on Buhalis (1998).

Despite the importance of GDS to travel and tourism distribution, an array of technologies exist and can be used in place of GDS or in combination with them. We will now discuss one option that is much discussed in the mainstream media today; the Internet.

THE INTERNET, INTRANETS AND EXTRANETS

Buhalis (1998) describes the development of networks that can be used to help multilevel integration within the industry, identifying three types of network:

1. Internet facilitates the interactivity of the enterprise and individuals with the entire range of external world through multimedia representations.
2. Intranets are closed, secured or 'firewalled' networks within organisations, which harness the needs of internal business users, by using a single controlled, user-friendly interface to demonstrate all company data.
3. Extranets utilise the same principle with external computer networks to enhance the interactivity and transparency between organisations and trusted partners. This works by linking the shared data and processes to format a low cost and user-friendly electronic commerce arrangement, similar to the electronic data interchange (EDI) attempted in the previous ITs eras.

(Buhalis, 1998; pp. 424–5)

Many of the larger travel trade and transport organizations are using intranets whilst their use of extranets is also on the increase. British Airways has developed an extranet for the trade which aimed to offer online bookings before the end of 2000. There will be one version for business travel and one for retail agents. Both will offer news on BA brands, fares and services as well as promotions and a directory of useful numbers. Use of the Internet in the travel trade and transport sectors is discussed below.

THE INTERNET

The Internet is a diverse series of networks owned and operated by Internet service providers (ISPs). According to Mintel (2000a), the name stemmed from the fact that a number of backbone providers, phone, cable and other communications companies all become inter-connected to provide this technology. Internet developments first began in the 1960s and by the 1970s had grown to support a number of organizations in the US Defense Department and other government agencies. Universities also began to use the Internet. Access has increased greatly since the mid-1990s.

Unlike both viewdata and CRS, with their travel related focus, the Internet has both a far wider audience and application. The general aspects of Internet usage are widely covered in the literature and so shall not be repeated here. Instead we shall discuss some of the ways in which the travel trade and transport sectors are using this technology. The travel business was one of the first to embrace online technology. Whilst many sites sell flights, hotel accommodation and car hire, the sophistication and capabilities of the sites are often not as advanced as those in other business areas.

The Internet is still relatively young and changing constantly. The US domestic Internet market has been growing at a phenomenal rate since the mid-1990s. Growth on a large scale has only more recently begun elsewhere in the world. In March 1999 Mintel commissioned research through NOP which found 13 per cent of adults to have a personal computer with Internet connection in their home. Some other adults were expecting to become connected and yet others will have access to the Internet at their place of work. Clearly any increase in the number of adults able to access the Internet has implications regarding how many are able to use this as a method for booking holidays. Only around a third of those with access had made a purchase online yet selecting holidays/flights from travel agents/tour operators was the second most popular use of the Internet.

There is a lack of accurate data in relation to the size of this market sector. Estimates suggest that the UK market for online holiday and travel sales was worth between £350–400 million in 1999 (Mintel, 2000b). The future size of the market is equally difficult to estimate although it is generally recognized that the market sector is growing rapidly. Internet sales are expected to grow as consumers become more familiar with this distribution channel. The medium is highly suited to the sale of late availability products. It is however argued that consumers still like face-to-face contact, particularly when booking a costly main holiday.

To date, the vast majority of travel booked online has been airline tickets and whilst this is likely to continue to dominate, other travel products including car hire and package holidays may account for a greater percentage of total sales in future. There are both advantages and disadvantages to this method of booking as illustrated in Figure 4.3. There is some overlap with factors mentioned presented as both pros and cons. This reflects not only differences between countries (some have more advanced technology than others) but also differences in consumer perceptions – what appears easy to use to one consumer may appear complex to another. Generally, younger consumers are more comfortable with the Internet than are older consumers.

Pros	Cons
Access 24 hours/day	Problems with speed in some countries
Available from the comfort of one's own home	Customer service requirements not always met
Speed	Problems with access in some countries
Simple to use	Telephone charges high in some countries
Comparison of different principals' sites is possible	The complexities of the industry may not be fully appreciated by the consumer
A variety of online travel agencies exist	Complicated/confusing
Useful tool to research options	Problems with cost in some countries
Cost reduction	

Figure 4.3. Pros and cons of the Internet for travel and tourism consumers.

The low-cost airline, easyJet, has shown a strong preference for the Internet in its distribution strategy. Indeed the company had at the time of writing changed its policy regarding the way in which customers can book flights. Any booking for flights departing more than two months ahead can now only be made on the Internet. easyJet claims that this offers the easiest and most cost-effective way of buying seats. As fares generally increase as the departure date gets closer, the airline further claims that this means the lowest fares will always be available on the Internet. The gap between booking and departure is also getting smaller for some types of traveller. Advertisements have also been used to urge agents to make bookings for clients over the Internet and obtain a £1 discount for each one-way flight. Customers booking directly through the company's Internet site receive a £5 discount. The same company offers customers the chance to buy flights, holidays and other goods on-line in its easyEverything Internet cafés, the first of which was opened in June 1999 in London's Victoria. By the end of April, 2000 there were five outlets in London with a further six European cities to have outlets later in the year. Aimed at members of the public who do not have regular Internet access, the cafés are based on the same low price, high volume product as the airline. Each cybercafé has between 4–600 computer terminals. Cybercafés open up access to the Internet to a wider audience and some of these users may use the facilities to research and book travel related products.

A variety of organizations and systems have evolved around Internet technology. 'The Corporate Team' for example operates an online booking service providing corporate travellers with access to more than 500,000 hotels worldwide. This service completely bypasses the conventional GDS and therefore also GDS fees.

The Corporate Team promotes itself as enabling companies to enforce travel policies by controlling which hotels are made available to business travellers based on employee status and suchlike. It is accessible online via the company intranet or the Internet.

Buhalis (1998) describes the Internet as also providing unique opportunities for multimedia presentations, transforming uninspiring, text-based screens of GDSs into interactive electronic brochures.

Specialist online airline and travel agency sites are being continuously developed at present. Whilst many of the established high street travel agents have been slow to develop their online offerings, other so-called .com organizations have established web-based travel intermediaries. Figure 4.4 below outlines some of the main specialist online travel services currently available and their contents. According to Tyler (2000) it was the online travel agents who took an early lead in terms of online market share with some 80 per cent of online travel sales made via these sites in 1996 whilst only 20 per cent were made direct to the airlines. This Tyler partly attributes to the fact that most airlines were slow to develop effective, fast and easy-to-use websites. This is easily understandable in the case of the smaller airlines as the costs of a good online site can be prohibitive. More recently, major airlines have been upgrading their sites with some offering non-air-based travel products alongside their own products. Customers also like to have a choice of both fares and routeings which of course favours online agencies over airline websites. In order to pursue the right combination of airline sites consumers may need a high degree of knowledge regarding which carriers operate on which routes (depending on the complexity of the journey). Added to this, time searching the different airlines' sites can be extremely time-consuming.

Company	Description of Online Service
British Airways.com	Launched in 1995, BA's Internet website was one of the first airline websites to go live. At the time of writing it operated in 79 countries, receiving 2.5 million visits/month. Almost continual change has been necessary in response to both developing markets and customer demands. The site includes Fodor's detailed data on 99 destinations, specific information on Heathrow and Gatwick airports and an online virtual facility to fly with Concorde. Development of extranet business links with companies is one of the newer initiatives.

Bargainhols.com	Part of the Internet media group, Emap Plc, which includes the UK's (Emap Online) largest radio group, Emap Online was set up to exploit the interactive digital market with an emphasis on travel. The company now claims to be the largest online package holiday supplier via Bargainhols.com. It has partnerships with different companies yet maintains independent status as a holiday intermediary. The company also has specialist ski and snowboarding offerings as well as sites offering all modes of travel and one providing a guide to UK airports
Deckchair.com	This company, established in 1998 by Bob Geldof and James Page, aims to simplify the process of accessing destination information. In excess of 100,000 flights, hotels and destinations are accessible
ebookers.com	Previously known as flightbookers.com, ebookers.com was launched in 1999. Flightbookers.com claimed to be the first fully interactive travel booking website in 1996. The company offers worldwide flights and hotel booking, car hire and travel insurance as well as package holidays. Additional services include information from Lonely Planet and Timeout guides, and Flightwatch which provides updated flight status information straight to consumers' mobile phones
Expedia.com	A leading provider of branded online travel services for leisure and small business travellers, Expedia Inc has information available on over 450 airlines, 40,000 hotels and all major car rental companies. The company, which is owned by Microsoft, uses the latest encryption technology to increase security of payment and licenses key components of its technology to selected airlines
Lastminute.com	Set up as an Internet travel company selling late holiday deals online, moving unsold capacity for operators. The company has expanded into other areas such as last minute theatre tickets, child minders and gifts. The majority of their business is however still travel related.
Travelocity.com	An active online travel agent in the UK, Travelocity.com is owned by Sabre Holdings in the USA. The online offering includes reservation capabilities for air, car, hotel and holiday products as well as access to a vast database of destination and other travel information. Having merged with Preview Travel, this is now the largest company in the field. The company has also announced deals with leading Internet

portals including America Online (AOL). Travelocity has a five year deal to be the exclusive provider of travel booking sites on all AOL properties. In the UK it has a deal with Emap Online to show its holiday and travel range.

Figure 4.4. Some major specialist online travel services. *Source*: adapted from Mintel (2000a).

In addition to the major online specialist travel service providers outlined above, there are numerous other specialist companies. Indeed, it can be argued that the medium lends itself to the needs of specialist operators and the travellers they aim to attract. There are specialist online travel companies for women-only travel organizations such as www.adventurewomen.com and www.arcticladies.com. A specialist online Winter sports site is being created as two specialist online travel sports sites merge into an online business called IfYouTravel.com as illustrated in Figure 4.5.

Background

IfYouTravel.com is being created through merger of the following two companies:

Complete-skier.com: a ski holiday online company launched two years ago by Michael Liebreich (a former member of the British Olympic ski team). The average age of users of the site is 36 and around 60 per cent of users are in professional or management positions with an average spend/head of £450

Skiin.com: a specialist online travel sports site launched by Jean-Marc Holden (an Olympic sailor)

The new venture

Backed with £3m of funding by Europ@web, the new venture will create Europe's largest Internet winter sports site. A Danish online ski site, skiguide.dk, has already been purchased to add to the business

Planned developments

A specialist golf holiday site, IfYouGolf.com is to be launched with further sites focusing on diving and adventure holidays to follow by the end of the year

---

Figure 4.5. IfYouTravel.com *Source*: based on *Financial Times* (2000).

CLEARING INVENTORY

We have already seen that a useful way of employing online technology is to use this to remove unsold stock at the last minute in order to overcome some of the difficulties caused by the perishability of the travel product. One means of doing this is to hold online seat auctions as pioneered by Cathay Pacific USA in 1995. According to Tyler (2000), these have the added advantage of drawing attention to new destinations or website improvements and so are used also for promotional purposes. He describes a further way of clearing inventory, used by Priceline.com, whereby prospective customers 'bid' for tickets. This involves the prospective traveller in filling out a ticket request form on the company's website, stating where and when they wish to travel and the price that they are willing to pay. Priceline then examines the seats at its disposal from participating airlines and informs the traveller within 24 hours as to whether or not their bid has been accepted. Bids that are too low will be rejected and the consumer then has the opportunity to submit additional bids using different airports or dates. The downside to use of the system includes that tickets are non-refundable, non-exchangeable and non-endorsable as well as which flexibility is required in terms of flight times, stops or connections en route may be necessary and no choice of airline is offered.

ROBOTIC SEARCH ENGINES

A further, price-sensitive technological aid to travel booking, also described by Tyler, consists of robotic search engines. These are designed to search a range of participating airline and GDS websites for the lowest fares on specified routes and dates. intelliTRIP, developed by TRIP.com is an example of such a system currently dealing with flights originating in the USA on particular carriers.

THE INTERNET AND GDS COMPANIES

All four major GDS companies view the Internet as providing a focus for advances in travel technology. Competition is based on the fight to become the booking engine behind the Internet companies which will have increased exposure through interactive TV. According to Mintel (2000a), Worldspan has links with Microsoft in the USA and Europe as the booking engine behind Expedia, Sabre has Travelocity in the USA and Amadeus has Compuserve in the UK.

CD-ROM TECHNOLOGY

This technology enables travel and tourism providers to promote their services in a less traditional manner than the ever-popular holiday brochure. Despite its potential, this technology has not been used extensively by the travel and tourism industry to date. Virgin is one of the companies to use this though having introduced a Ski-D-Rom brochure in 1996 to guide viewers through a range of holidays. The 1998 disk, which was offered to customers for £10 (refundable if they booked a Virgin holiday), featured the following:

- Visual graphics
- Videos of all resort areas
- Virtual tours of three areas by helicopter
- Nine interactive ski trail maps
- Interactive street maps
- Photo galleries with full screen pictures of the resorts
- On-screen prices for all holidays.

VIRTUAL REALITY

Like CD-Rom technology, virtual reality offers great opportunities to aid the promotion of travel and tourism products by enabling potential consumers to experience a 'virtual tour' and make a more informed choice as to whether or not to visit a region, resort or even a particular hotel. This technology could help with even more specific decisions such as choice of cabin on a cruise.

SMART CARDS

In common with other commercial areas, travel and tourism could benefit from smart card technologies. These cards contain a miniature computer processor chip with memory. Amongst other applications, smart cards could be used to record frequent flyer programme (FFP) points and for accommodation check-in.

ELECTRONIC TICKETING

In common with most of the main developments in the airline industry that are discussed in this book, this form of 'paperless travel' originated in the USA and has since moved into Europe and Asia. Whilst not yet the norm, the use of electronic tickets, or e-tickets, has expanded rapidly. Their use offers a number of advantages for both airlines and consumers as summarized below in Figure 4.6.

For airlines
- Savings in ticket distribution costs
- Savings in revenue accounting and billing processes
- Reduction in handling costs associated with paper tickets

For consumers
- Ease of use
- Impossibility of ticket loss
- Flexibility
- Time-saving
- Faster check-in

Figure 4.6. Advantages of e-ticketing. *Source*: based on Tyler (2000).

E-tickets can be purchased by telephone, through the Internet, at airline counters or travel agents. Typically consumers pay with a credit card and receive a confirmation number at the time of booking. Once at the airport, the passenger simply needs to give their name and show some identification or the credit card used to make the booking. They will usually receive a boarding pass in return. This form of 'paperless travel' is not however without its problems as outlined in Figure 4.7.

- Government regulations require various 'notices' to be provided to passengers on international flights and in Europe the onus is on travel agents to inform passengers of their travel rights under the Warsaw Convention. This may involve sending a letter or fax to the traveller
- E-tickets cannot be used by passengers on journeys with more than four flight sectors or those involving more than four different carriers
- If a passenger, with an e-ticket, misses a flight or needs to make a schedule change it is difficult for other carriers to honour tickets without proof.*

Note: *interline e-tickets are now emerging.

Figure 4.7. Problems encountered with the use of e-tickets. *Source*: based on Tyler (2000).

The idea behind e-ticketing is to remove the paperwork from ticketing although in reality airlines often send written confirmation of the booking. Expedia introduced e-ticketing for customers booking BA flights. Users get an e-mail confirmation of the booking and then simply turn up at check-in with their credit card (Hodson, 2000).

MULTI-MEDIA KIOSKS

Electronic systems enable customers to research and book travel products through networks of self-service kiosks. Whilst these systems are still emerging and not yet widespread, they offer considerable scope for the future of travel distribution. Non-travel retailers wanting to develop travel-related sales yet without the expertise to do so easily could employ these as a means of establishing a travel sales interest.

TELETEXT

Teletext is a popular consumer method of researching package holiday options, especially late availability products. Thomson acquired two leading Teletext agencies, Team Lincoln and Manchester Flights. Travel House is one of the UK's largest Teletext agents.

INTERACTIVE MEDIA INITIATIVES

Emap online which was introduced above in relation to their Internet offering, also has eight interactive TV services with cable company networks. This offers a further means by which consumers can access information from home. The company are also trialling hand held devices including WAP (wireless application protocol) phones with Nokia 7110. WAP is discussed below.

INTERACTIVE TV

The number of households subscribing to digital TV services will influence the extent to which shopping for travel and holidays via interactive TV will take place. NTL, the cable company, for example, has launched digital cable

TV which provides an interactive channel. Whilst it is not certain what proportion of subscribers will wish to buy travel and holidays in this way, Mintel (1999b) describes household penetration of digital TV as set to reach 31 per cent by 2002.

Some leading travel companies are already developing a presence on interactive TV. Going Places is a content provider for the interactive television service OPEN. The system enables customers to access a mixture of information, including video clips, on destinations, resorts, flights and hotels. This is in addition to the company's presence on Teletext. Similarly, Thomas Cook has signed an interactive TV deal with Telewest. The UK's first home shopping TV channel, TV Travel Shop, is discussed in Figure 4.8.

> TV Travel Shop describes itself as providing a travel agency service in the comfort of your own home. The UK's first home shopping TV channel has grown substantially since it was launched as Europe's first transactional travel channel in 1998. It is carried on satellite, cable and digital TV presenting studio reports and interviews, destination 'brochure' films, special programmes featuring exclusive offers and newsroom-style bulletins with up-to-the-minute special offers. TV Travelshop is fully bonded with ABTA and works in conjunction with leading tour operators including Airtours, First Choice, Kuoni and Virgin Holidays. Sales in the first year reached £72 million and TV Travelshop is now available in more than 7 million homes across the UK. Further development is planned with new digital TV channels, a website and interactive television. International development commenced in 2000.

Figure 4.8. TV Travel Shop. *Source*: tvtravelshop.co.uk

WIRELESS APPLICATION PROTOCOL (WAP) PHONES

At the time of writing wireless application protocol phones are an emerging technology. WAP gives Internet access, via a mobile phone or palmtop, delivering information via the Internet to consumers on the move or away from their usual access site. Competition for the third generation (3G) phones is likely to be fierce given the fact that a single global standard could emerge reasonably quickly. Early versions are mobile phones that comply with the wireless applications protocol (WAP) standard way of transmitting real time content. This allows mobile phones to browse the Internet. According to Martin (2000), successful contents businesses will take advantage of the inherent characteristics of these little devices. One area Martin suggests in this respect is geography. Whilst handheld devices are mobile, their position is instantly identifiable. Identification of 'content' that knows where the user is and offers content tailored to that geography might therefore be appropriate. The potential for relevant application of this technology to tourists could exist for example through provision of weather forecasts, restaurant locations and even bookings. The integration of computers and wireless technologies will undoubtedly impact on the travel market.

FREQUENT FLYER PROGRAMMES AND TECHNOLOGY

Major carriers usually offer bonus miles for bookings made directly through the airline's website. In 1999, United Airlines offered 4000 frequent flier miles to each customer for the first United ticket they bought directly through United's website in order to promote this method of booking.

RELATIONSHIPS WITH INTERMEDIARIES

According to Tyler (2000), discounts linked to bookings made via airlines' own websites have met with opposition from the American Society of Travel Agents (ASTA). The US Department of Transportation was asked to investigate airline Internet 'fare wars'. The investigation aimed to determine whether or not these were unfair and deceptive practices under the Federal Aviation Act by discriminating against customers without Internet access. The airlines argued that there were sufficient public Internet access points.

TECHNOLOGY AND THE LARGE OPERATOR

E-commerce is a major expansion area for most of the large tour operators. Some showed reluctance towards the adoption of key technologies in the past yet most now have realized that they cannot afford to be without it. Airtours provides an example of how these companies are embracing relevant technologies.

Airtours has a £100 million e-commerce strategy, designed to cover all areas including interactive television and mobile phone technology. The company launched a new global cyber-brand, mytravelco, in 2000. This development is to involve branding on Airtours aircraft and brochures as well as the conversion of some

Going Places and Travelworld shops into cybercafé agencies. Airtours do however claim that this development does not signal that they will be closing all of their shops.

Figure 4.9. Airtours and technology. *Source*: adapted from TTG (2000).

Large airlines are equally keen to keep abreast of technological developments and to implement these appropriately. Indeed, Mintel (2000b) informs that British Airways set up a special airline taskforce in 1999 to ensure that the company stays at the forefront of e-commerce.

TECHNOLOGY AND THE SMALL OPERATOR

ITs can help smaller operators to conduct business on a level footing with their larger counterparts. The Internet for example enables smaller tour operators to compete with the promotional reach and distribution strategies of the mass market players. This has clear implications for an industry characterized by a polarization between a handful of extremely large, dominant companies and a proliferation of small, specialist firms.

The Association of Independent Tour Operators (AITO) is currently helping smaller tour operators to offer their services on-line. The traditional Viewdata systems are prohibitively expensive for these organizations.

TECHNOLOGY AND THE FUTURE

Whilst technology has been rapidly diffused within some sectors of travel trade and transport, other sectors have shown less willingness to embrace the technology and are likely to suffer for this. Debate surrounding the future of the retail travel sector in an age characterized by both established and emerging technological means of reaching the travelling public appears likely to continue for some time to come. The need for technology and technological expertise is increasing the number of barriers for both travel agents and tour operators according to Key Note (1998). It could equally be argued however that this is decreasing the number of barriers as the falling costs of technology and telecommunications could however help to offset the barriers in the longer term.

Technological developments are likely to continue apace in travel and tourism. Martin (2000) suggests the emerging market for wireless portable appliances and especially Internet-enabled mobile phones will result in a boom similar to that caused by the emergence of the Internet. Whilst the early versions which are appearing at the time of writing are restricted in both form and content, they could point the way to the future. Indeed, mobile electronic commerce (m-commerce) applications for small mobile phones are still limited but market researchers suggest a rosy future for it. It is however still extremely early days to comment on this.

SUMMARY

The application of communication and information technology in travel and tourism is highly relevant given the information-intensity of the industry and the implications of this are far-reaching. There are many obvious benefits to the assimilation of new technologies, including increased competitiveness and profitability. These should not however be adopted in blind faith without consideration being given to their context and how they can best be integrated into this. Following on from the early development of videotext, CRS and then GDS, the Internet is becoming a popular method of researching and increasingly also of booking travel products. Emerging technologies that could become significant once refined include WAP. Whilst many in the travel and tourism industry recognize the potential of technology in terms of distribution, others do not yet appreciate the effect that this is having.

DISCUSSION QUESTIONS

1. Outline reasons why the travel trade and transport sectors are ideally suited to technological means of distribution.
2. Critically evaluate the Internet as an alternative to retail distribution for a small, specialist tour operator.
3. Discuss the view that, in the light of technological developments, the days of the travel agent are numbered.

REFERENCES

Buhalis, D. (1998) Information technology, in C. Cooper, R. Shepherd, S. Wanhill, *Tourism: Principles and Practice*, Pitman.

Daneshkhu, S. (2000) Olympic sportsmen hit off IfYouTravel.com, *Financial Times*, Monday 5 June, p. 30.

Hodson, M. (ed.) (2000) A week on the web, *Sunday Times*, 11 June, p. 6.4.

Holloway, J.C. (1994) *The Business of Tourism*, Pitman.

Inkpen, G. (1998) *Information Technology for Travel and Tourism*, (2nd edn), Longman.

Key Note (1998) *Travel Agents and Overseas Tour Operators*.

Martin, P. (2000) The next Internet boom, Understanding WAP, *Financial Times*, Summer.

Mintel (1999a) Online shopping, *Retail Intelligence*, July.

Mintel (1999b) *Special Report, Digital TV*.

Mintel (2000a) Leisure on the Internet, *Leisure Intelligence*, May.

Mintel (2000b) Travel agents, *Retail Intelligence*, January.

Pender. L.J. (1999) *Marketing Management for Travel and Tourism*, Stanley Thornes Ltd.

Poon, A. (1993) *Tourism, Technology and Competitive Strategies*, CAB International.

Renshaw, M.B. (1997) *The Travel Agent*, (2nd edn), Business Education Publishers Ltd.

Travel Trade Gazette (2000) Airtours vows not to scrap agencies, 15 May, p. 1.

Tyler, C. (2000) Ticketing and distribution in the airline industry, *Travel and Tourism Intelligence*, *Travel and Tourism Analyst*, No. 2.

www.tvtravelshop.co.uk

CHAPTER 5

Travel Trade: Trends and Issues

INTRODUCTION

This chapter expands on a number of trends and issues that were identified earlier in this section of the book and in Chapters 1 to 3 in particular. The chapter starts off by considering the somewhat turbulent history of the travel trade, charting some of the many problems that the travel agency and tour operations sectors experienced during the last four decades of the twentieth century. There is detailed consideration of pricing issues, the effects of discounting and the issue of quality. The extent of integration between different travel companies is such that this forms the main focus of the current chapter. Horizontal and vertical integration are considered in turn. Discussions of internationalization and diversification then follow. The use of both franchising and consortia formation by the sector is also analysed. The chapter concludes with an examination of the possibility of disintermediation.

BACKGROUND

The travel trade has, as introduced above, experienced a number of difficulties during its comparatively short history as a main area of commerce. Holloway (1995) describes some of the defining characteristics of the sectors together with a number of problems encountered by the industry by decade and these are summarized in Figure 5.1.

1960s	Problems began to be associated with the tour operations sector as early as this, partly stemming from the fact that the sector had no barriers to entry. There were particular problems in relation to airlines leaving tour operators to repatriate stranded tourists. A lot of outdated airlines were flying outdated aircraft.
1970s	Competition intensified around this time. This, combined with a lack of control over the ways in which operators conducted their business led to further problems for the industry. Misleading brochure descriptions and poor quality products were helping to create image problems. Bargain holidays were available although the oil crisis increased prices despite the recession. A government inquiry following the collapse of a tour operator prompted the establishment of the Air Travel Reserve Fund.
1980s	Competition had become even more intense by the 1980s. The leading tour operators were concerned with their market share although they were making large profits and so price wars began. These could not however be sustained in the long run. Integration also led to investigations of the industry. Thomson's take-over of Horizon for example was referred to the MMC.
1990s	The collapse of ILG (and its tour operator division Intasun), occurred in 1991, increasing the market share of the other largest tour operator even more. This was also a period characterized by recession, extreme competition, price wars and market share wars. Rapid concentration market share among the major companies led to yet more price cutting.

Figure 5.1. Intensity in the travel trade and associated problems. *Source*: based on Holloway (1994).

PRICING

It is the case that the British have long had competitively priced package holidays as evidenced by comparison to the prices paid by travellers to certain resorts from other Northern European countries. This has the effect, in some countries, of making it difficult for UK operators to negotiate accommodation at suitable rates with suppliers. Despite this there has been a suggestion that inclusive tours in the UK are over-priced. This, together with other complaints against the industry, led to a lengthy investigation for the government being undertaken by the MMC. Exchange rates are an important factor in the pricing of package holidays.

The traditional UK tour operations sector competed on the basis of market share by volume often at the expense of both profit and long-term planning. This fight for market share had numerous repercussions in addition to the availability of 'cheap' package holidays. The companies involved often suffered from poor margins, a lack of funds to invest in the company and overcapacity all of which left them at risk of financial collapse in many cases. Indeed, some notable failures can be cited including the International Leisure Group (ILG) with its tour operations arm Intasun which collapsed in 1991 as discussed above. The tour operations market is a volatile market.

Market share is still considered highly important by the industry. The latest battle is one for shares in niche markets such as cruises and all-inclusive holidays. The major tour operators are actively pursuing their interests in these fields. Similarly shares in packaged versions of travel types that were traditionally arranged independently are being fought over by tour operators. There have long been allegations that monopolistic practices keep prices high in this market.

One problem to result from the competitive situation in relation to market share was that operators increased their capacity to such an extent that they could not sell it at profit. Indeed, holidays often ended up being sold at cost or even at a loss close to their departure date. Indeed, damaging price wars often occurred late in the season. Keen for this situation not to recur, tour operators cut their summer season capacity in 1996 instigating a system whereby prices actually increased in many cases to improve profitability. Further to this, *fluid pricing* was introduced to reward customers for booking early. Under these controversial 'fluid pricing' systems, holiday prices are cheapest when first published, increasing the longer they are in the market. Earlier brochure production has therefore accompanied this change with some being produced up to 18 months prior to departure. Fluid pricing is discussed in more detail below.

Thomson led the AIT sector by reducing capacity in 1996 in order to produce profitability and fund product diversification. The chase for volume market share at all costs is reducing in importance. Market conditions allowed Thomson to increase capacity again for 1998 from 2.75 million to 3 million. A change to a fluid pricing policy and Earlybird Savers has enabled Thomson to reduce from 20 per cent to less than 10 per cent the proportion of its holidays sold at last minute discounts (Mintel, 1998).

Early booking discounts

The last few seasons have been characterized by tour operators offering discounts for early bookings. Added to this more recently has been the early brochure publications which have resulted in travel agents having to take a number of different seasons' brochures at once. The potential for customer confusion is therefore great in addition to which there could be a shift in the main booking period which was traditionally in the immediate aftermath of the Christmas holidays. A further likely outcome would be year-round brochures linked to year round bookings. Mintel (1998) suggests that this would change the structure of tour operations as companies would be able to purchase more rooms on a permanent, long term basis. They further suggest that different editions of the brochures would still be re-published during the year to reflect price changes based on exchange rates or other changes in the marketing environment.

INTEGRATION

Integration is an economic concept to describe formal linking arrangements between one organization and another. This can be seen to include linkages both across and down the chain of distribution. Each of these types of integration, namely horizontal and vertical, is now discussed in turn.

Horizontal integration

Horizontal integration takes place at any one level in the chain of travel distribution. A travel agent may therefore integrate with another travel agent or a tour operator with another tour operator.

Horizontal integration can take a number of different forms as shown below:

- *Take-over:* one company takes over another, usually smaller, company.
- *Merger:* this can be a more equal arrangement of a voluntary nature.
- *Consortia formation:* independent organizations can retain more independence with this form of affiliation whilst still obtaining advantages, e.g. joint brochures, joint purchasing and increased bargaining power.

Complementarity is often the reason for horizontal integration taking place. During the march of the multiples for instance Thomas Cook bought out travel agents in areas where the company had no presence and so expanded rapidly in a short space of time. This march of the multiples, discussed more fully in Chapter 3, provides an extreme example of organizations at the same stage in the production process integrating with one another. This process led to greatly increased levels of concentration in the travel agency sector by the end of the 1980s and indeed has continued to have an effect throughout the 1990s. Further outcomes of the march of the multiples are provided in Figure 5.2.

Recipient	Effect
Travel agency Sector	Increased use of market segmentation
	Development of corporate images
	More staff development
	Increased use of customer incentives (low deposits, discounts and free insurance etc.)
	Investment in new technology
	Product discrimination (the operation of 'preferred operator' schemes etc.)
	Development of call centres
Independents	Excessive competition
	Extreme pressure on profits
	Reduction in market share
	Formation of consortia
	Involvement in franchising schemes*
Customers	Changed industry structure
	Many independents squeezed out (this could be seen to represent a reduction in consumer choice)
	Parent companies were often non-travel companies
	Discounting and price cuts resulted from intense competition

Note: * These franchising schemes were not always successful as discussed later in this chapter.

Figure 5.2. Outcomes of the march of the multiples. *Source*: based on Renshaw (1997).

A similar effect can be seen in the tour operations sector where significant integration also took place in the 1980s. Increased concentration in the tour operations sector led to domination of the outbound market by just a handful of tour operators. There are around 650 companies operating in this sector with three-quarters of the market revenue shared amongst only a few of the largest. The growth of these larger companies has resulted from developments in the industry since the 1960s. Leisure holidays in particular were seen as a future growth area leading to company expansions in attempts to ensure market domination.

Thomson's take-over of Horizon in 1988 was extremely public as the Monopolies and Mergers Commission (MMC) investigated it as they believed it could be against the public interest. Thomson's overall share of the outbound tourism market, however, was considered not too great despite their share of the package holiday market, and so the ruling was in the company's favour. Shortly after this decision had been made the collapse of the International Leisure Group (ILG), including its tour operator Intasun, in 1991, led to a redistribution of market share particularly among the leaders so altering the position yet again. This collapse was blamed on a number of factors including recession, competition, price wars and the weak pound as well as on expansion of the company. A further well documented case in the early 1990s was the attempt by Airtours to take-over the tour operator Owners Abroad (now First Choice) in 1993. This particular attempted take-over was not however successful. Indeed, a second attempt by Airtours, to acquire First Choice in 1999 faced the same outcome.

Despite this rapid concentration of market share amongst the key players in the industry price-cutting continued into the 1990s. This price competition inevitably led to concerns for the smaller tour operators. The incredible power in the marketplace displayed by the dominant mass market operators enabled them to obtain large discounts on their bulk purchases of transport and accommodation. Their size also enables them to gain enhanced exposure for their products through deals with retailers. There is little room for product differentiation in the price led and competitive mass market sector.

The market for tour operations continues to be dominated by just a handful of mass market players. The 'top' tour operators account for the majority of business. Below these companies there is a levelling out of capacity with medium sized firms remaining largely static. There have been exceptions to this with some companies displaying fairly rapid development including Inspirations and Flying Colours.

Horizontal integration is likely to continue if allowed to but this is more likely to take place across national boundaries in future with tour operators and travel agents following the example of airlines as discussed in Chapter 11. Once again, Thomson and Airtours provide early examples of this having both moved into overseas markets building business in, for example, North America and Scandinavia. This internationalization of tour operations is examined further below as an aspect of the diversification of the traditional tour operators' programmes.

Lateral expansion at both Thomson and Airtours is evidenced by moves into the cruise, skiing and cottage holidays markets in addition to continued domination of the mainstream summer sun market.

A further method of horizontal integration has occurred in a less 'involving' manner through the creation of consortia. An example of consortia formation in the travel agency sector is provided by ARTAC Worldchoice although these agencies are now being rebranded as Thomas Cook following yet another merger.

As seen above and in Chapter 3, the distribution of package holidays has recently attracted a great deal of scrutiny.

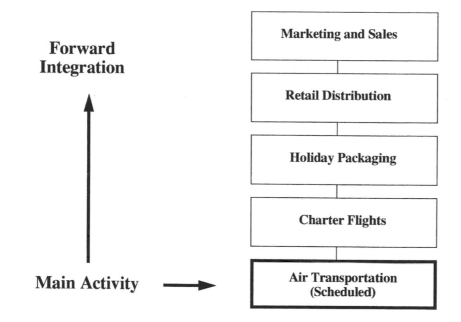

Figure 5.3. Vertical integration in the tourism industry: airlines. *Source*: Poon, 1993.

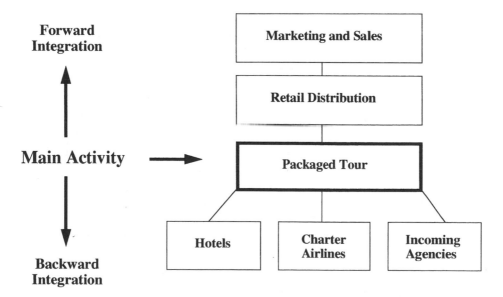

Figure 5.4. Vertical integration in the tourism industry: tour operators. *Source*: Poon, 1993.

Vertical integration

Vertical integration occurs where organizations at different levels in the chain of distribution link together. This integration can be either forward or backward along the chain of distribution as the following industry example illustrates:

- Forward integration: a tour operator purchases a travel agency.
- Backward integration: a travel agent purchases a tour operator.

Vertical integration is described by Burns and Holden (1995, p. 26) as: 'the business phenomenon whereby firms seek to control various stages of production, delivery and marketing of their products'.

The same authors go on to explain that, in the production of mass tourism, this has been something of an established practice giving the example that airlines can own hotels, travel agencies, and tour operators. Firms integrate vertically in order to control the different stages of production.

Poon (1993) has examined vertical integration in the tourism industry as compared to manufacturing where this has been a common practice. This form of integration is becoming more pervasive in the tourism industry. Clearly this takes place between different sectors but it has also been driven by different sectors, often at different periods during the development of the industry. Tour operators are, according to Poon, the most vertically integrated of all industry players. The evidence of this amongst the mass market tour operators in particular is strong. The ways in which tour operators vertically integrate, both backwards and forwards, is illustrated in Figure 5.3.

A further example, provided by Poon, is of forward vertical integration by the scheduled air transport sector and this is shown diagrammatically in Figure 5.4. Figure 5.5 summarizes some potential motivations for vertical integration.

Possible motivation	Explanation
Control	By integrating vertically organizations can gain control over all aspects of the product so leading, in theory at least, to quality improvements
Continuity of supply	Vertical integration can help organizations to source goods and services more easily. Tour operators for example can benefit from integration with hotels and airlines which then supply them with bedrooms and airline seats

Guaranteed sales outlet(s)	Problems associated with selective selling on the part of middlemen can be overcome by vertical integration. Tour operators for example can overcome the difficulty of selective brochure racking in this way.

Figure 5.5.   Some possible motivations for vertical integration.

Forward integration – purchasing retail outlets – is popular with AIT tour operators due to the volumes of business achieved for them by the retail sector. This, at the same time, provides both synergies and economies of scale.

Whilst linkages between tour operators and other organizations in the chain of travel distribution have clear advantages for the parties to the integration, the outcomes for consumers and destinations are not always as positive. Indeed, many independent travel agents claim that directional selling is used in the industry. This involves tour operators in favouring promotional efforts through travel agencies which belong to the same group.

For a variety of reasons the accommodation element is often not included in these large integrated structures although both Thomson and Airtours have a handful of hotels in their portfolios. Burns and Holden (1995) describe Air-tours first move into hotel ownership with the purchase of the Majorcan hotel Bouganville Park Hotel. They further quote the prediction made by Airtours chairman, David Crossland, in *The Times* (29 June 1993) that more pur-chases of hotels would be made: 'mainly for hotels the company already featured in its brochures that had borrowed heavily and then suffered a downturn in custom'.

A major reason against the purchase of accommodation units is that this does not allow sufficient flexibility to react to changes in market demand. A typical vertically integrated structure would therefore only consist of a tour operator, a travel agency chain and a charter airline. Agreements with scheduled carriers are also evident in the market. Vertical expansion has occurred at both Thomson and Airtours through ownership of airlines, seat-only divisions and direct sell operations.

Tour operators are currently the most integrated of all industry players as they integrate both forwards and backwards. Airtours bought several travel agents and has developed Going Places into a 728 branch group. This helped the company to achieve vertical integration. Airtours has also integrated horizontally notably through acquisitions such as Aspro, a budget AIT brand. Not all of Airtours' attempted bids were successful however as their renowned bid for First Choice, then called Owners Abroad, failed to win acceptance.

Integration ensures that the majority of the money paid for a package holiday finds its way to the same large, integrated company. Indeed this process extends beyond the travel trade and transport sector with banks for example also wanting to own tour operators as a way of increasing their involvement in the foreign exchange and related aspects of the travel business. The issues surrounding vertical integration have attracted much attention over recent years particularly as they have greatly influenced the structure of the AIT market in the UK.

INVESTIGATIONS

It is the belief of many that high levels of power shared amongst a few operators might be against the public interest. The Monopolies and Mergers Commission (MMC) investigated the industry in the mid-1990s. In 1996 the Director of Fair Trading referred to the MMC despite having concluded in 1994 that such a move was not required. The MMC report which was published at the end of 1997 concluded that vertical integration between the large multiple travel agents, the major tour operators and charter airlines did not adversely affect consumer choice. Some major mergers and acquisitions, such as those of Unijet and Hayes & Jarvis by First Choice, in the industry then followed in 1998.

There has, as noted above, been a series of official investigations into vertical integration between holiday suppliers and retailers. This process commenced in 1995 yet it was not until 1997 that the government were able to provide feedback on this.

The latest government report at the time of writing has largely been in the favour of the industry as it is but does make clear certain stipulations for the major operators particularly in relation to clarifying their ownership of travel agency branches. A high concentration of ever-larger tour operators which are increasingly global with cross-holding agreements is therefore becoming more common.

DIVERSIFICATION

The discussion of vertical integration above hints at ways in which tour operators have diversified in recent years. This section examines further tour operator diversification incorporating some consideration of internationalization. We commence with a look at the diverse product offering from Thomson in Figure 5.6.

The following aspects of Thomson's business are indicative of the company's diverse product.

The core brand

The Summer Sun programme (600 page brochure); Winter Sun, Villas & Apartments, Small & Friendly, A La Carte, Freestyle (youth), Young at Heart (over 50s), Cruise, Cities and single-destination holidays (e.g. Thomson Turkey)

Separate major brands

Other major brands operating out of the UK are Skytours (economy), Holiday Club International and Portland Holidays (direct sell market leader)

Hotels

Thomson owns 21 hotels in Mediterranean resorts (Sun Hotels)

Cottage holidays

Thomson acquired several cottage-letting groups in the early 1990s resulting in the UK's largest cottage holiday group, Country Cottages. Cottage holidays have also been offered in France

Seat-only

Air Fares is the name of the seat-only operation on Britannia flights

Cruises

Thomson is now a major cruise operator in the Mediterranean

Thomson International Group

Acquisition of Budget Travel (Ireland) was followed by that of Fritids Resor (the second largest tour operator out of Scandanavia)

Figure 5.6. Thomson's diverse product. *Source*: based on Mintel (1998).

In common with Thomson, Airtours has shown an increase in international development to the extent that less than 50 per cent of turnover now derives from UK outbound businesses. Since 1990, Airtours has acquired the following international brands:

• Sunquest and Alba Tours (Canada) and SunTrips (California)
• Scandanavian Leisure Group (Sweden, Norway and Denmark)
• Spies (Denmark and Finland)
• Sun International (Belgium).

(Mintel, 1998)

Recent international acquisitions by Thomson and Airtours have resulted in them having a dominant share of the market out of Scandinavia at the end of the 1990s. First Choice similarly has an overseas operation with Signature Vacations in Canada and JWT in the Republic of Ireland. In the travel agency market Thomas Cook operates through a network of other associated companies with a total of 5000 outlets in 120 countries around the world. A further example of diversification is provided by Airtours Timeshare division. Another aspect that Airtours shares with Thomson is the fact that it operates a separate division for specialist holidays incorporating cruises, city breaks, skiing, lakes and mountains and youth holidays.

Diversification is not always successful. Mintel (1998) cites the example of the diversification of Club 18–30 into Florida in 1997 which failed due to age restrictions on both drinking and car hire.

FRANCHISING

Whilst the use of franchising has not to date been evident in the tour operations sector the concept has been applied to the travel agency sector, with varying degrees of success, over the years. We will now look at the strategic use of franchising within the travel agency sector considering some of the current issues surrounding this.

Franchisee motivations in general, such as increased market share and benefits from the franchisor's marketing budget, have been well covered in the more general literature on franchising and can be applied also to the travel agency sector. Specific motivations can however be added to these and some of these are outlined below:

- increased negotiatory power with principals;
- low initial investments (working from home, no stock to purchase etc.);
- override commissions; and
- heavily discounted personal travel.

A popular example of a franchised travel agency chain is the Canadian company, Uniglobe with over 1000 franchisees worldwide. Bonanza Travel and Advantage Travel Centres also became involved in franchising more recently.

The adoption of franchising by the retail travel sector has relied upon the creation of a number of 'enabling factors' as past failures in this sector, discussed below, testify. We will now examine these enabling factors.

Entry Barriers

The travel agency sector traditionally had low entry barriers but these have increased along with requirements for more sophisticated technology. Price competition has also influenced entry barriers.

Appointments

IATA appointments could not be guaranteed for franchisees.

Legal factors

The splitting of commission used not to be allowed and this is effectively what the payment of royalties amounts to.

Illustrating the levels of vertical integration within the travel trade sector was Airtours' 15 per cent stake in a new franchise company within the Advantage Travel Centres link-up. This particular arrangement had a number of interesting aspects to its operation. Advantage Travel previously operated solely as a consortium of independent travel agents. There was a 66 per cent membership vote, in a secret ballot, in favour of the establishment of a franchise-operating subsidiary. All 950 branches then received formal franchise offers with those members choosing to sign up before Christmas 1998 paying only £1 joining fee as opposed to the £3000 fee from the beginning of 1999. Monthly royalty payments were set at £90. Almost half of the Advantage membership had signed up to the deal by the end of February but this was followed by a series of difficulties. Strong initial resistance to the link with Airtours and a split in the membership ranks at Advantage took place. There was a climbdown by Airtours on certain key points (Noakes, 1998). Airtours then faced the challenge of having to satisfy franchisees' expectations whilst retaining the support of non-franchise members of Advantage Travel. The relationship to franchising that has occurred through the Airtours/Advantage link-up has been a significant development in terms of travel trade integration and could be indicative of future forms of collaboration as operators seek to increase distribution in the domestic and international marketplaces. This particular development was not, however, successful.

As mentioned above, early attempts at franchising by travel agents, including the British chain Exchange Travel failed. These agents often wanted to compete with the expanding multiples but found their efforts beset with problems instead. Exchange, for example, had difficulty achieving the required turnover to pay the 1 per cent management service fee due to low profit levels according to Holloway (1995).

Holloway has further examined more general difficulties in relation to early attempts at travel agency franchising and these are outlined in Figure 5.7.

- Travel agents offered neither price nor product advantages. A strong name and unique product are required if a franchise is to be successful
- Franchising did not guarantee the approval of principals and IATA appointments for example could not be assumed to follow a franchise agreement
- Inappropriate staff appointments led to inconsistent standards and quality problems
- There were legal problems caused by the fact that commissions could not be split between an agent and another organization which the payment of royalties amounted to
- In common with some non-travel related franchise agreements, problems arose as a result of exaggerated claims in relation to potential profits, a lack of marketing back-up and broken promises in relation to exclusivity.

Figure 5.7. Reasons for failed attempts at travel agency franchising. *Source*: based on Holloway (1994).

It was only once travel agents were granted freedom to discount and to split commission that franchising became a viable option and this has gained in popularity with the ability to negotiate higher commission levels and so improve profit margins (Holloway, 1995). The same author discussing franchising has said:

> Arguably a franchise, if it is to be successful, must offer a unique product of some kind which is not available through other distributive outlets; this a travel franchise signally fails to deliver.

DISINTERMEDIATION

A major issue faced by many in the travel business is the prospect of disintermediation or the effective removal of the middleman – the travel intermediary – from the chain of travel distribution. A recurring theme in the trade press is the warning that travel agents need to act now in order to avoid becoming obsolete in future. Whilst it is certain that the extent to which travel companies use direct methods to reach consumers is increasing and will continue to increase in the short term at least, less certain is what the future holds for the retail travel sector itself. Figure 5.8 summarizes the main arguments to emerge from the continuing debate as to whether the travel agency sector has a role in the future of travel marketing.

Argument	Reason
Yes	• Some consumers enjoy face to face contact when booking a holiday
	• Holidays are expensive and some customers therefore believe they deserve personal attention
	• Not all consumers have access to home booking technology
	• Some tourism products are highly complex and require detailed knowledge on the part of the person making the booking
No	• Advances in technology have made home booking easier
	• The number of tourism organizations offering a variety of different methods of booking has greatly increased
	• Some tourism products are extremely simple and require little knowledge on the part of the person making the booking
	• Travel agency payments have been reduced by a number of principals

Figure 5.8.   Has the travel agency sector a future in travel distribution?

There are despite the amount of discussion surrounding the possibility of disintermediation many reasons why the travel agency sector could succeed in the changed environment. Responding appropriately to the threats they currently face will be crucial however. Some possible means of survival have been put forward by the trade press and others. These are summarised in Figure 5.9 below.

• Development of a niche position in the market place for example through product specialization as evidenced by travel agencies dealing solely with ski business or cruises and those dealing only with the top end of the market.
• Development of a focus on customer care for example through creation of a pleasant environment, the provision of refreshments, highly trained travel counsellors and such like.
• Development of a specialism in respect of travel technology offering access to the Internet, virtual reality and CD-Roms and such like as well as highly trained personnel.

Figure 5.9.   Possible means of survival for travel agents

SUMMARY

This chapter has considered a number of trends and issues including those which were evident in the past and which have helped to shape the travel trade as it is today. More recent trends and developments were also discussed. Integration was a central focus of this chapter.

DISCUSSION QUESTIONS

1. Account for factors leading to the economic situation in the tour operations sector today.
2. Critically evaluate the involvement of the travel trade in vertical integration.
3. Examine the applicability of franchising to the travel agency sector.

REFERENCES

Burns, P. and Holden, A. (1995) *Tourism – a new perspective*, Prentice Hall.

The Department of Trade and Industry (1995) *Looking into The Package Travel Regulations; a guide for organisers and retailers*, January.

Holloway, J.C. (1995) *The Business of Tourism*, Pitman.

Key Note Market Research (1998) *Travel Agents and Overseas Tour Operators*.

Laws, E. (1997) *Managing Packaged Tourism – relationships, responsibilities and service quality in the inclusive holiday industry*, International Thomson Press.

Mintel (1998) *Inclusive Tours, Leisure Intelligence*, March.

Mintel (2000) *Travel Agents, Retail Intelligence*, January.

Noakes, G. (1998) Advantage and Airtours tie-up attracts 350, *Travel Trade Gazette*, 10th February, p. 7.

Pender, L. (2000) Travel trade and transport, in C. Lashley and A. Morrison (eds), *Franchising Hospitality Services*, Butterworth Heinemann.

Poon, A. (1993) *Tourism, Technology and Competitive Strategies*, CAB International.

Renshaw, M.B. (1997) The Travel Agent, Business Education Publishers Ltd.

PART 2

Transport for Tourism

The development of transport, both public and private, has had a major impact on tourism growth and direction. This is especially true of mass market tourism.

Good internal and international transport infrastructure are important to successful travel and tourism development and so this text now moves on to look in more detail at the transport sectors of the industry. These sectors comprise train companies, coach operators, ferry operators and airlines. Cruises are considered together with ferry operators although arguably these could have been examined in Chapters 1 and 2 as they offer inclusive packages.

CHAPTER 6

Rail Transport

INTRODUCTION

This chapter first of all provides some necessary background to the association between rail travel and travel and tourism, as well as the background to the operation of rail services in the UK. Rail services in relation to travel and tourism are then discussed in detail. International and packaged rail transport are then discussed in turn. The chapter concludes with some consideration of likely relevant future developments in the rail sector.

BACKGROUND

Rail travel has long been associated with travel and tourism. Indeed, the advent of the railway had a profound effect on the growth of travel generally. Holloway (1994) describes the first package tours on excursion trains as having been in operation by 1840. These enabled people to travel to the seaside and helped to make seaside resorts popular destinations for pleasure travellers. Another development for which the railways have been noted was that of providing hotel accommodation to meet the needs of the early rail market. The railway terminus hotels could therefore be seen to be early examples of vertical integration within the industry. Indeed, Holloway describes the railway companies as playing a significant role in the hotel industry for the next hundred years. Similarly, Holloway's description of the railway companies' links with the cross-channel ferry operators in the mid-1800s provides an early example of horizontal integration. By 1962 these railway companies had gained the right to own and operate the steamships and they quickly expanded cross-channel services whilst control was in their hands. Rail travel has traditionally met the needs of both independent holiday-makers including the visiting friends and relatives (VFR) category as well as packaged travellers. Chapter 1 described Thomas Cook's first excursion as a rail journey from Leicester to a temperance meeting in Loughborough. For the cost of one shilling, 500 people travelled the distance of 12 miles and back.

Trains are the most important form of public transport in the UK according to Key Note (1999c), accounting in 1997 for almost half of all domestic tourism trips taken on public transport. The same source informs that the volume of passengers travelling by rail has greatly increased in recent years to reach an estimated 43 billion passenger kilometres in 1998. Trains account for 10 per cent of all domestic tourism trips and almost 50 per cent of domestic tourism trips on public transport. Rail travel has many advantages for tourists as discussed in this chapter. Rail travel is often considered to be environmentally friendly at least in comparison to travel by private car. Travel by train also has the advantage of city-centre-to-city-centre transport whilst avoiding problems of parking and traffic congestion. The introduction of high speed trains has had an effect on the air and road transport markets. Price and the duration of the journey both influence customer choice as to mode of transport. For journeys of around three to four hours it is widely recognized that a direct high-speed train is an attractive alternative. A number of major European city-pairs with large populations fall into this category. Train travel does have the disadvantage however of being slower than air travel for journeys beyond a certain threshold. In these circumstances it is often only those with the time and desire to take a train journey across a country or continent for example who are likely to choose rail over air travel. Rail travel does however often suit those passengers with a fear of flying.

There is insufficient room in a chapter of this nature to describe the structure and operation of the rail industry in different countries. Instead, discussion will concentrate on the example of the UK. Van de Velde (1999) examines the legal, regulatory and organizational frameworks for rail travel in a number of different countries for readers wanting a broader perspective.

Following the nationalization of the railways in 1947, rail services in the UK consisted of the following:

Intercity

These long-distance routes were easy to run commercially. Indeed they were therefore more attractive under privatization.

Regional

Passenger routes outside the main conurbations including 'branch' lines. These mainly existed for social or political reasons in the UK and many have now closed as they were unprofitable.

Urban

Passenger routes serving the major urban conurbations and providing links with their dormitory towns and commuter belt.

Private and tourist railways

These existed purely as tourist attractions or holidays in their own right. Examples include the popular privately owned locomotives, especially steam locomotives.

Luxury trains

Those, such as the Venice-Simplon Orient Express, operating at the top end of the market.

RAIL TRAVEL IN THE UK

Rail privatization

The publicly-owned national rail network under British Rail was divided into 25 passenger train operating franchises and sold to the private sector between 1994 and 1997.

The structure of the industry in the UK

The structure of the passenger train industry has greatly changed since acceptance of the White Paper on the privatization of the nationalized train network by Parliament in 1992.

Franchising

Rail franchises were put up for tender in 1995. Following this, UK government support through subsidies for the railway operating companies to 2004 will be about 50 per cent less than the level prior to privatization.

By 1997 there were 25 passenger train franchises and 13 franchise owners. In Northern Ireland, however, the Northern Ireland Railway is still state-owned and part of Translink which also has the Province's bus operators in its portfolio.

A number of separate companies therefore constitute the new rail industry providing one another with services under contractual arrangements. The main organizations are discussed below.

Railtrack PLC

Railtrack Group plc assumed ownership of the national rail infrastructure on 1 April 1994 and has been in the private sector since May 1996. This infrastructure

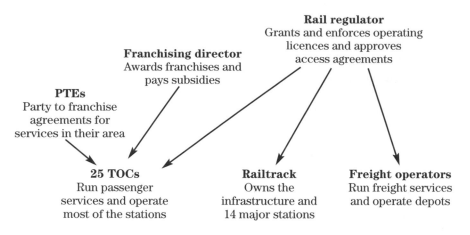

Figure 6.1. The structure of the national railways following privatization, 1999. *Source*: Annual Company Report and Accounts/Mintel Rail Travel, Leisure Intelligence, Sept. 1999

includes the track, stations, depots, signalling, electrical control equipment and route structures. The organization charges for access to the network. They are responsible for maintenance and renewal of network as well as signalling and managing the timetabling. Railtrack charges operators to use its track.

The train operating companies (TOCs)

These companies have responsibility for passenger rail services in the UK, operating under fixed-length (5 to 15 years) franchise agreements with the Office for Passenger Rail Franchising (OPRAF). The TOCs have introduced a wide range of different fare types. Further details regarding the process of franchising are provided below.

Office for Passenger Rail Franchising (OPRAF)

As mentioned above OPRAF has a role letting the 25 passenger rail franchises but its position has evolved to also include the monitoring and management of these franchises. Railway investment and service quality are seen to be important aspects of this role.

Rolling Stock Leasing Companies (ROSCOs)

Rolling stock is supplied to TOCs by these organizations who also oversee its maintenance and provide finance.

Strategic Rail Authority (SRA)

This body has only been in existence since 1999. It has overall responsibility for rail planning and was set up partly in response to criticism levelled at the rail industry.

Office of the Rail Regulator (ORR)

Protection of railway users' interests is the duty of the Regulator in addition to promoting the use and development of the network and ensuring competition in railway service provision. The Regulator grants licences under which he can impose conditions. Finally the ORR deals with competition issues and licenses Railtrack.

Rail companies are required to publish statistics on performance and operators can be fined, as has already happened, for not reaching targets.

Cooper *et al.* (1998) describe this privatized system as having had no noticeable impact on transport for tourism whilst highlighting fears that it leads to less integration of tourist product components as a result of localized network provision.

Regulation

The government's Integrated Transport White Paper 'A New Deal for Transport: Better for Everyone' has many implications for rail transport. The new strategic rail authority (SRA) discussed above has also been developed.

In common with the other travel trade and transport subsectors discussed in this book the passenger rail industry is highly concentrated. As mentioned above only a small number of companies or consortia have been successful in being awarded franchises and the effect of this has been compounded by consolidation amongst franchise holders. Stagecoach Holdings, for example, acquired a 49 per cent stake in the Virgin Rail Group in 1998 for around £158 million. (Key Note, 1999c).

THE INTERNATIONAL RAIL SCENE

Whilst travel by rail is traditionally regarded as a mainly domestic activity, there has been a growth in international rail travel in recent years. This is, for the UK market at least, in no small part due to the development of the Channel Tunnel as discussed below. Rail travel in general is suited to international journey travel times of around 3 hours. The advantages of city-centre-to-city-centre trains, capable of speeds up to 225 kph, are also significant in addition to which there are no parking problems or congested motorways for tourists travelling by train.

It often pays for overseas tourists coming to the UK to purchase rail tickets in their home country for the following reasons:

- Some products, available overseas, are not for sale in the UK.
- Tourists need not queue for tickets during their holiday time.
- Holiday budgeting is easier when tickets are purchased in advance.

BritRail Ltd markets and sells rail travel worldwide to international visitors. BritRail passes currently offer unlimited access to the entire rail network in England, Scotland and Wales. Fifteen thousand daily departures are available from 2400 stations throughout Britain.

Rail travel in Europe

Long distance high-speed rail services are those which compete most effectively with other transport modes for custom.

High speed rail services in Europe

Advances in high-speed train technology during the past two decades have contributed to a growth in the passenger traffic on long distance, inter-city routes. Examples of high-speed services include the Train á Grande Vitesse (TGV) in France, discussed below, the Alta Velocidad (AVE) in Spain and the German Inter-City Express (ICE) as well as the Pendolino tilting trains in Italy. These trains offer airline style service, improved punctuality and travelling speeds of 200–300 kilometres per hour. The growth of passenger traffic travelling by high-speed rail in Europe is illustrated in Table 6.1. A new high speed rail service was launched in Belgium in 1997 with plans to extend this to the Dutch and German borders creating a Brussels hub linking Cologne, Amsterdam and London according to *The Sunday Times* (1997).

Table 6.1. Growth in passenger traffic travelling by high-speed rail in Europe, 1989–98
Source: Reproduced by Russell (2000) from International Union of Railways (UIC).

Year	Million passenger kilometres	Annual change (%)
1989	12.4	–
1990	16.3	31.4
1991	21.6	32.5
1992	26.5	22.7
1993	28.9	9.0
1994	32.1	11.1
1995	32.9	2.5
1996	37.4	13.7
1997	42.3	13.1
1998	48.5	14.7

Note: High-speed rail is defined as 200 kilometres per hour or above. Data are based on nine European railways including those of France, Germany, Italy and Spain

These high-speed rail services are capable of offering so-called 'seamless' rail services between different countries. There is however still much room for improvement to the international high-speed network. Indeed, seamless services on international routes can be hindered by the fact that railways tend to be organized on a national rather than an international basis. This can lead to differences both technically and administratively between the rail networks of different countries. Different track gauges on either side of an international border for example occurs as is the case with Spain and France. It is possible however to equip trains to run on both. Similarly, different electrical requirements can cause problems. According to Russell (2000), approval was given, in 1990 by the European Community, for TENS, a Trans European Network of high speed road and rail links. A further relevant development in terms of high-speed trains has been the introduction of tilting train technology which enables faster speeds on existing tracks without new high-speed lines.

The world's first high-speed passenger train was the Shinkansen, or 'bullet train' which entered into service in Japan in 1965. Europe has also developed significant provision of high-speed rail services so expanding the size of rail markets on some routes. The French example of the Train à Grande Vitesse (TGV) is provided in Figure 6.2.

The first TGV line between Paris and Lyon became operational in stages between 1981 and 1983. This was an attempt, on the part of the French government, to reduce the country's dependency on oil following the 1973 oil crisis. Three further TGV lines have been developed with specially developed tracks. These are

TGV Atlantic:	Paris – Brittany/Bordeaux
TGV Nord:	Paris – Lille
TGV Rhône-Alpes:	Lyon – Valence

In addition, the following line is under construction

TGV Mediterranee:	Valence – Nimes/Marseilles

Planned for the future is

TGV Est:	Paris – Strasbourg

France has the most extensive high-speed rail network in Europe

---

Figure 6.2. TGV. Source: based on Russell (2000).

Inter-railing

Inter-rail passes entitle the holder to unlimited rail travel on the national rail network of the countries or zones purchased. These passes are available to any person who is normally resident in Europe or who has lived in Europe for six months prior to the trip. They are also available in two forms, those for travellers aged less than 26 years old and those for travellers of 26 years and above.

NIGHT TRAINS

European railways are developing overnight sleeper trains between countries in the hope of attracting new markets such as the business market. There is however less need for sleeper services for domestic travel in countries such as the UK due to shortened journey times. Indeed, most of the UK services have ceased operating.

THE CHANNEL TUNNEL

A significant development in terms of European rail travel has been the Channel Tunnel which has been in operation since 1994, providing alternative modes of travel between the UK and the Continent. The Channel Tunnel has provided a link for both the road and rail networks of the UK and continental Europe. Whilst this development has not been without its difficulties, including a fire in November 1996, the Channel Tunnel has forced rationalization in the Cross-Channel Ferry industry. Eurotunnel owns and operates the physical infrastructure whilst Eurostar offers rail connections via the tunnel and 'Le Shuttle' provides a vehicle-carrying rail service operation. These two services are now considered in turn.

Le Shuttle

Le Shuttle meets the needs of road vehicles, linking the M20 motorway in Kent with the A16 and A26 autoroutes in France. This rail service operation carries vehicles between Cheriton (near Folkestone) and Sandgatte (near Calais) in a journey time of 35 minutes. Vickerman (1995) describes the three separate types of Le Shuttle service as the following:

Freight shuttle

This service carries lorries in semi-open wagons whilst their drivers are accommodated in a separate club coach. Further consideration of this service is beyond the requirements of this chapter.

Double-decker tourist shuttles

This service is provided for cars and other vehicles up to 1.85 m in height. By April 1995, 270,000 cars and more than 500,000 passengers had travelled on this shuttle service. The drive-on/drive-off trains are designed to carry passengers in their own cars.

Single-decker tourist shuttles

This service accommodates coaches, caravans and other vehicles over 1.85 m in height.

Eurostar

Services on Eurostar started in 1994 with a limited inter-capital service between Paris/Brussels and London competing with airlines for business traffic. The planned high-speed Channel Tunnel rail link between Kings Cross St Pancras in London and the tunnel's UK entrance has been delayed but construction work finally began in late 1998 with the first stage due to open by 2003. Further planned services to regions throughout the UK would, it is claimed, offer tourism marketing opportunities to the regions.

London and Continental Railways (LCR) operate the Eurostar service. The company failed, at the start of 1998 to provide a suitable proposal for the construction of the high-speed rail to the Channel Tunnel. Instead, a new consortium comprising National Express (40 per cent), French Railways (35 per cent), Belgian Railways (15 per cent) and British Airways (10 per cent), is to finance the high-speed service and the construction of the link according to Key Note Ltd (1999c).

Eurostar's electrically powered trains, with pneumatic suspension, travel at speeds up to 186 miles per hour. Each train has eighteen air-conditioned coaches split into First and Standard class accommodation. The trains have two bar/buffet coaches and a trolley service. There are also separate compartments for luggage and public telephones. Passport and Customs controls take place on the trains speeding up the check-in process. The trains depart from Waterloo, an international rail terminal that can handle up to 6000 passengers an hour and which has a special international departures concourse. Many Eurostar trains also call at the new Ashford International Terminal in Kent. Eurostar journeys between London and Brussels take only 2 hours and 40 minutes whilst those between London and Paris take 3 hours. Eurostar, in common with scheduled air travel offers more than one class of travel. Indeed, first class travel is split into Business First and Premium First. Interestingly, Virgin Group, the operators of Virgin Atlantic, purchased the Eurostar franchise. Virgin Atlantic is BA's main UK-based long haul competitor. Eurostar through train services are clearly competing with air travel on the routes served.

According to Russell (2000), more than 25 million people had travelled by Eurostar by the fifth anniversary of its operation in November 1999. The same source attributed the London–Paris route with particular success, informing that it won 60 per cent of all passenger traffic between the two cities. This has had an effect on the number of flights operating this route in recent years. Indeed, the *Travel Trade Gazette* reports that CAA statistics reinforce the fact that Eurostar rail services have had a significant impact on the air market from London to Paris. In more general terms, Le Shuttle and Eurostar services have gained more than 10 per cent of the market since the opening of the Channel Tunnel at the end of 1994. Offering city-centre-to-city-centre transport, they are competitive alternatives to air travel. Day trips to Paris are available on Eurostar as are direct services to Disneyland Paris's own station which, with Disney characters waiting to greet passengers on arrival, appeals to the family market.

The Channel Tunnel has had some success to date despite the delays and financial and operational problems that beset the project in the early days. It is only once regional services are developed however that the benefits of this development will be apparent to those in the UK living at distance to the south east of England. Nevertheless, the Channel Tunnel has become highly significant in terms of the integration of road and rail networks in Europe with the rail service in particular offering 'seamless' journeys. Vickerman (1995) describes in more detail the problems encountered in establishing the Channel Tunnel services and how these were overcome.

RELATIONSHIPS WITH AIRLINES

Cooperation between airlines and rail companies is something that is likely to develop in future due to customers' preferences for rail travel for journeys between specific city-pairs. Current examples of such cooperation include American Airlines and the French railway, SNCF (Société Nationale des Chemins de Fer Français). The two companies signed an agreement to allow air passengers to buy TGV tickets to onward destinations in France when booking their flight. This results in a cheaper overall ticket price than the sum of the two fares would be. TGV services connect Paris Charles de Gaulle (CDG) airport with Brussels and more than 50 French cities with around 850,000 passengers transferring between air and rail at CDG (Russell, 2000).

AIRPORT SERVICES

Of clear importance to tourists is the provision of public transport between main cities and the airports that service them. Both London's main airports, Heathrow and Gatwick offer such services. The British Airport Authority (BAA) operates a non-stop rail service from central London to Heathrow airport. Services run every 15 minutes from 0502 to 2347 hours (from Heathrow). This Heathrow–Paddington Express service carries over five million passengers a year. Luggage and check-in facilities for some flights are now available at Paddington station up to two hours prior to the departure time or one hour before departure for passengers with hand luggage only. Boarding cards and seat numbers can be issued and so passengers can proceed immediately to the departure gate at Heathrow. Similar services operate to Gatwick and Stansted airports and a new rail station has been developed at Luton. Outside London and the South East, there are established rail connections at a number of UK airports including Manchester and Birmingham. For independent travellers, these improved rail links make it easier to book transfer arrangements independently and remove some of the difficulties of accessing major airports.

PACKAGED RAIL TRAVEL

That the first inclusive tours used travel by rail has been mentioned elsewhere in this book. Despite that air inclusive tours have now become the norm, packages by rail still have a share of the market. The use of high-speed trains and Eurostar is having an impact on short-haul winter holidays for example. Indeed, Key Note (1999b) describes Eurostar services as the main growth area for overseas short break packages in winter as more overseas operators offered Eurostar within their short-break programmes. Eurostar already works with existing tour operators. In the UK one company – Superbreak – is significant in this market and details of their operation are provided in Figure 6.3.

Superbreak Mini Holidays Ltd. are short break specialists offering a large selection of UK destinations and flexible itineraries that can be geared to personal requirements. Prime overseas markets include Northern Europe, Southern Europe and North America.

Part of the Holiday Break company Superbreak and Golden Rail are sister companies to other specialist holiday companies including Eurocamp and Keycamp. Superbreak Mini Holidays are short break specialists offering a large selection of UK based holidays. Flexible itineraries can be geared to personal requirements.

Based in York the company has a turnover of £40 m per year, carries in excess of 500,000 customers and prints over 6 million brochures, whilst Eurocamp Plc has a turnover in excess of £140 m per annum.

Travel by train has always been associated with the company although they also offer non-rail based packages. Rail inclusive options are a popular customer choice and rail fares are quoted throughout the Superbreak brochure. Both viewdata and the company's Reservations Advisers also provide rail inclusive prices.

Figure 6.3. Superbreak. *Source*: Superbreak Mini-Holidays Ltd (2000).

LUXURY TRAINS

Throughout the world there are a number of luxury trains offering exceptionally high quality travel. The most notable example of a luxury train is the Venice–Simplon Orient Express. Other examples include The Royal Scotsman and the The Blue Train. Operation of The Royal Scotsman is discussed in Figure 6.4. Some Spanish services including Barcelona to Madrid offer special airline-like trains which even have a 'hold' for luggage.

The Royal Scotsman is a luxury hotel train and coach tour operated by The Great Scottish and Western Railway Company Limited (GS&WR), using train haulage supplied by English Welsh and Scottish Railway Ltd. Launched in 1984, The Royal Scotsman is acknowledged as one of the most exclusive trains in the world. The train promotes itself as offering 'a revival of the romantic age of railway travel, combining Edwardian splendour with modern luxury'.

Accommodating just 36 passengers, the train is always stationary at night so as to ensure a good night's sleep. Two and four-night programmes are offered covering areas of Scotland including the West Highlands, Perthshire and the North East. Visits to private homes, historic castles and places of cultural interest are also offered. A team of guides and a liveried motorcoach form an integral part of the travel experience. At the time of writing the cost, per person in a twin or single cabin, was £1390 for a two-night tour. This tour rate includes a State cabin with private ensuite shower and toilet facilities, table d'hôte meals daily including wine and all alcoholic and other beverages, all applicable taxes and all visits arranged by GS&WR.

Private and corporate charters are available on The Royal Scotsman. As an alternative to the standard tours, customized tours can be arranged to customer requirements by incorporating activities such as golf or shooting. Where a party size is greater than 36, back-to-back tours can be offered by splitting a group and combining a tour with a stay at a Scottish hotel.

Figure 6.4.   The Royal Scotsman. *Source*: The Royal Scotsman and ZFL Public Relations (2000).

RAIL PRODUCT DEVELOPMENTS

The rail product is increasingly becoming more like that of the airlines. It must be recognized however that developments, such as those listed below, tend at present to be confined to a particular train company or service or to a handful of these at the most:

- seat-back videos
- music channels
- sockets for lap-top computers
- children's play areas and baby-change facilities
- 'silent' cars
- loyalty schemes
- child escorts.

RAIL DISTRIBUTION

There has been a shift in distribution strategies used by train operating companies in recent years. Europe's railways have for example started to distribute via the global distribution systems (GDS) used by travel agents. In the past it was difficult to achieve middleman support for rail products for a number of reasons including that margins were low and the booking process was not easy. Attempts to resolve this situation have included the payment, to travel agencies, of improved levels of commission and the development, by Eurostar, of Elgar. Elgar is a system that interfaces with the major GDS in the UK.

Europe has a significant number of rail ticket issuing agents. Worldchoice, for example, has Railchoice which is also a Continental Rail Agents Consortium member. There have also been examples of rail companies appointing air consolidators to sell tickets on their behalf. This, Eurostar did with Globepost.

In addition to the above, there has been an increase in the number of international journeys by rail and an increase in business travellers' use of rail travel. These moves have had an effect on the use of both leisure and business travel agents for the booking of rail travel. Whilst the use of e-commerce by the rail sector has been developing slowly, a number of train operating companies have full web-based reservations facilities.

CHESTER-LE-TRACK

Chester-le-Track is a north-east based company which was set up to provide access to the rail network on the Internet. It's owner purchased Chester-le-Street railway station, a small railway station in Chester-le-Street in County Durham, England, to enable him to sell rail tickets. The web site has live hypertext links to enable browsers to connect to other relevant transport sites. A copy of the home page is provided in Figure 6.5. Browsers are able to buy rail and coach tickets as well as London Transport Travelcards via the Chester-le-Track site.

Figure 6.5. The Chester-le-Track homepage. *Source*: http://www.chester-le-track.co.uk/

TRADE ORGANIZATIONS

The International Union of Railways (UIC) is a worldwide industry association of more than 130 railway companies. According to Russell (2000), the organization's main functions are to share best practice between its members, to establish common technical and operational standards and to promote the business of railways in general.

THE FUTURE OF RAIL TRAVEL

UK

Prospects for the future of rail travel in the UK are, subject to certain factors, likely to be good. Reasons for this are listed below:

- Railtrack has announced an investment programme aimed at reducing delays and expanding the network.
- Worsening road congestion if accompanied by improved rail service levels, could lead to changed passenger perceptions.
- investments are being made in new rolling stock which should improve service quality.

Concerning the last point, it deserves mention that investment decisions are long-term – much longer than a typical franchise – and this can cause obvious problems.

Europe

It is highly likely that even faster trains will be introduced to Europe before too long.

Magnetic levitation, or Maglev, trains are undergoing trials in Japan but are not planned for the European market in the short-term. These effectively float above an electro-magnetic field at speeds of up to 450 kilometres an hour. More development in terms of integration between airline and rail ticketing and marketing are also likely in future. Rail partners in the global airline alliances are a further possibility. Intermodal developments, particularly in Europe, offering seamless travel between airports and city centres may be significant. Finally, improvements in rail travel, together with air traffic congestion problems in Europe, could further reduce the appeal of air travel. On the other hand, for certain journeys, the possibility of customers booking cheap flights on low cost carriers acts as a threat to rail travel. The development of low cost carriers is discussed in Chapters 9 and 11.

SUMMARY

Having outlined some of the necessary background to the structure of the rail network in the UK this chapter then discussed this form of transport in relation to travel and tourism. International and packaged transport forms were then covered in turn. The chapter concluded by speculating as to the likely future of rail transport in the context of travel and tourism.

DISCUSSION QUESTIONS

1. Examine the structure of the rail industry in the UK.
2. Compare and contrast the product offered by two different organizations involved with packaged travel by rail.

3. Discuss the effect on both the provision of rail transport and on competitive transport forms of the development of the Channel Tunnel.

REFERENCES

Cooper, C., Fletcher, J., Gilbert, D.,Wanhill, S. (1998) in R. Shepherd (ed.) *Tourism: principles and practice*, Pitman.

English Tourist Board (1994) *Rail Privatisation and its Impact on Local Authority's Transport Role*, Insights Guide.

EIU Travel and Tourism Analyst (1995) *The Channel Tunnel – a progress report*, No. 3.

Holloway, J.C. (1994) *The Business of Tourism* (4th edn), Pitman Publishing.

Key Note Ltd. (1999a) *UK Travel and Tourism*.

Key Note Ltd. (1999b) *Winter Holidays*.

Key Note Ltd. (1999c) *Rail Travel*.

Mintel (1999) *Rail Travel, Leisure Intelligence*, September.

Markson, N. (1995) *Channel Vision, English Tourist Board Insights*, Tourism Intelligence Paper, A-88, January.

Russell, P. (2000) Rail travel in Europe, travel and tourism analyst, *Travel and Tourism Intelligence*, No. 2.

The Sunday Times (1997) Brussels Comes Closer, 14 December, p. 6.

Travel Trade Gazette, Eurostar Derails Paris Air Traffic, 14 May, p. 37.

Van de Velde, D.M. (1999) *Changing Trains*, Ashgate Publishing Ltd.

Vickerman, R. (1995) The Channel Tunnel – a progress report, EIU Travel and Tourism Analyst, No. 3.

Westbrooke, J. (1996) Fast track into Europe, *Financial Times*, 7 October.

www.chester-le-track.co.uk

CHAPTER 7

Ferries and Cruising

INTRODUCTION

Despite the popularity of air inclusive tours, both ferries and cruising perform important roles in travel and tourism. Whilst this chapter introduces other forms of water based travel and holidays, the main focus is on ferries and cruising as reflected in the title. The chapter outlines the importance of water-based travel and transport before going on to examine these individual forms in more detail. Ferries and the fast growing cruise sector are covered in turn. There is also a brief discussion of both sailing and canal boat holidays.

BACKGROUND

The shipping industry, including ferries and cruising companies, has a longer history than many transport forms. Indeed, Holloway (1994) describes some of the companies that are active in this area today, including P&O and Cunard, as having been in existence since the Victorian era. Like air and rail transport providers these companies do not deal exclusively with the transport of passengers but also with cargo. It is only with the transportation of tourists that this chapter is concerned. It has already been mentioned elsewhere in this book that, in most developed countries, private cars account for more leisure journeys than does any other form of transport. Developments to enable international car travel have therefore been formed. Specifically car ferries and tunnel developments have been important. These also have the benefit of accommodating rail and foot passengers.

Prior to the introduction of air travel, the international movement of tourists was greatly accommodated by the shipping companies who enjoyed healthy profits. Holloway (1994) describes the early days of the steamship as summarized in Figure 7.1. Britain can be seen to have pioneered deep-sea services and dominated world shipping in the latter part of the nineteenth century. Holloway further describes the global growth of shipping as leading to shipping conferences which would develop cartel-like agreements on fares as well as conditions applicable to the carriage of traffic ensuring year-round profitability in a highly seasonal market. This has much in common with practice in the airline industry prior to deregulation.

1821	The first regular commercial cross-channel steamship service was introduced in 1821 on the Dover–Calais route. The importance of their links with these cross-channel ferry companies was quickly recognized by the railway companies of the day
1838	The Peninsular and Oriental Steam Navigation Company (later P&O) is credited with establishing the first regular long-distance steamship service with operations to India and the Far East
1840	The Cunard Steamship company, with a lucrative mail contract, began regular services to the American continent in1840
1862	By now the railway companies had gained the right to own and operate the steamships themselves. These railway companies rapidly expanded the cross-channel services in a short period
1869	The opening of the Suez Canal stimulated demand for P&O's services to India and beyond as Britain's Empire looked eastwards

Figure 7.1. The early days of the steamship. *Source*: based on Holloway (1994).

THE CONTEMPORARY FERRY MARKET

Ferries, of differing types, offer short-distance transportation both for local communities, on short domestic routes, and for tourists. The latter utilize short and longer domestic and international routes. A key distinction that can be drawn is that between local ferries and sea-going ferries. Both play a significant role in travel and tourism. Local ferries can help tourists to access areas that otherwise would be difficult to reach. Sea-going ferries often operate on key tourist routes between countries. Particularly relevant to this chapter are ferry services linking countries separated by water and meeting the needs of international car, coach and foot passengers. These services may be provided by regular ships, hovercraft, seacat or high-speed sea service (HSS). Modern vessels have greatly increased manoeuvrability and turn-arounds in ports and reduced requirements for dock facilities.

Some countries, such as Greece, have extensive provision of ferry services connecting islands, particularly the more remote islands without airports, to the mainland and to one another. Independent tourists, arriving in Athens by air, often proceed to the ferry ports to travel onward to their holiday destination or destinations.

The UK has reasonably well developed international ferry services and Key Note (1999) describes these ferry operations in and around the UK as falling into the following three main geographical route categories:

- UK to continental
- UK to Eire
- domestic.

These routes were serviced by twelve companies operating internationally in 1998 as well as several domestic operators. Stena is the only operator to service all three of the above sectors. International ferries in the UK are operated by companies from a variety of countries including Britain, Ireland, Scandinavia, France and Belgium. The leading companies, by volume, are P&O European Ferries, Stena Line, Brittany Ferries and Seafrance. Caledonian MacBrayne is the largest ferry operator on the West coast of Scotland, connecting the islands to the mainland and running inter-island ferries. Around half of all ferry traffic out of the UK – 20 million passengers per year in each direction – are travelling on the crucial Dover–Calais route. Other significant routes are Harwich–Hook of Holland, Ramsgate–Dunkerque/Ostend, and routes to Ireland from Holyhead, Stranraer and Liverpool to name but a few.

The European ferry market is a healthy one, possibly stemming from the popularity of holidays by car and coach. The development of new ferry routes has no doubt helped to grow the market. Among the busiest routes are those across the narrowest points of the channel from Dover to Calais. Large roll-on, roll-off vessels, capable of carrying several hundred cars and several thousand passengers operate on these routes. Bateson and Hoffman (1999) discussing Sealink Ferries, one of the operators on these routes, examines the company's pricing structure. This is based on raising fares during peak periods such as school holidays and lowering them in mid-week and midwinter. This is a common strategy across most ferry companies and indeed most transport forms.

HOLIDAY INITIATIVES

A number of significant holiday initiatives have evolved around transportation by ferry. Companies such as Brittany Ferries operate holiday programmes to France and Spain for the UK market. The company offers a choice of 1500 gites in France alone. Channel crossings range from four to nine hours, operating between Portsmouth, Poole and Plymouth to St Malo, Roscoff, Caen and Cherbourg. For destinations in southern France as well as the Spanish destinations, it is possible to sail to Santander in Spain.

The established ferry market between the UK and France/Spain was greatly challenged by the opening of the Channel Tunnel

THE CHANNEL TUNNEL

Development of the Channel Tunnel has been significant in terms of European transportation. Arguably this is not merely a form of sea transportation, incorporating as it does elements of travel by both car and train. The infrastructure itself nonetheless offers consumers a route across the English channel that otherwise would not be available to them. Linking Britain and France, this transport system has three main elements shown below:

- Eurotunnel: owns and operates the physical infrastructure.
- Le Shuttle: rail service moving passengers, cars and freight on road trucks.
- Eurostar: direct services by rail.

The provision of rail services by Le Shuttle and Eurostar are discussed in more detail in Chapter 6 whilst the remainder of this chapter's coverage of the channel tunnel is concerned with the impact on ferry services and their responses to this.

Statistics relating to the cross-Channel routes confirm that the Tunnel services have expanded the overall market for travel between the UK and Continental Europe. Mintel (2000) describes Eurostar's passenger numbers as having risen by 4.5 per cent in 1999 to reach 6.6 million. For independent travellers in particular, who mostly 'turn up and go', this offers an easy means to undertake Eurostar journeys without the use of a tour operator or travel agent.

Impact on ferry services

Despite the opening of the Channel Tunnel, ferry services still account for over half of the sea holidays out of the UK. Competition from Eurostar and Le Shuttle has however had a considerable effect on cross channel ferry operations not least of all in forcing some rationalization in the UK industry. In common with air transportation on competitive routes, the ferry companies have lost passengers to the tunnel. By some measures the Channel Tunnel now accounts for between 40 and 55 per cent of the market. Prior to development of the Channel Tunnel, the only real competitor to the cross-channel ferries were the airlines or other water-borne services such as hovercraft and jetfoils. The former were then an expensive option whilst the latter encountered problems during poor weather. The Channel Tunnel, by contrast, was a strong competitor, offering uninterrupted services which are both frequent and considerably faster than the ferry services.

The response from the ferry companies

The ferry operators responded to this challenge at the time in a variety of ways as outlined in Figure 7.2. Principally this involved the ferry companies in investing heavily in their fleets and increasing the frequency of services on short sea routes – those considered to be most at risk. Promotional activities, some of which were in collaboration with British Tourist Authority (BTA) or other tourist boards, were undertaken and there was much emphasis on the creation of incoming tour programmes. The merger of the short-sea crossing routes operated by Stena and P&O European Ferries into a new company, P&O Stena, in 1998 is an example of this. P&O Stena Line is now the largest UK ferry operator and the merging of the two companies was only allowed after a lengthy inquiry by the authorities. There had been long-standing restrictions on ferry companies working together but the Office of Fair Trading (OFT) finally agreed to 'pooling' of cross channel services given the impact of the Channel Tunnel on traffic. Individual applications are still looked at by the competition authorities however. Finally, there were fears of a price war following the opening of the Channel Tunnel. Whilst this did not occur immediately, later moves by Le Shuttle to slash their prices were met by price cuts from the ferry companies also.

- Rationalization in the sector
- Heavy investment in their fleets (several hundred million pounds)
- Increased frequencies (especially on short routes)
- Intensive marketing activities including competitive pricing and involvement with promotions
- Increased collaboration with the travel industry (e.g. tour operators, hotels)

Figure 7.2.   The ferry companies' responses to competition from the Channel Tunnel.

The shipping lines have also introduced fast ferries to compete with Eurostar and Le Shuttle. Some ferry journeys have been reduced by half as a result of this. Mintel (2000) describes Stena Line's fast ferry service from Harwich to The Hook of Holland as having cut sailing time from seven hours to three hours and 40 minutes. A further development has been the addition of leisure services (particularly to longer crossings) as illustrated below, making the journey part of the overall holiday experience. Many of the leisure developments also have potential to stimulate on-board spending. Whilst facilities vary from vessel to vessel, the table below provides an indication of those onboard Stena Line ferries to Ireland, Holland and Scandinavia from the UK. Improved catering, retailing and entertainment all went some way towards making some ferry journeys resemble mini-cruises. Indeed, this was an explicit objective on the part of some ferry companies. In addition to the development of the Channel Tunnel, the ferry companies at the end of the 1990s were acutely aware of the threat posed by the loss of duty-free sales. This was discussed in the lead up to the Single European Market and came into effect in 1999. By the end of the 1990s, facilities onboard ferries were often extensive.

General	Bars	Lounges
Information desk	Globetrotter	Club lounge
Shopping	Spikes	Globetrotter lounge
Viewing gallery	Stingers	Panorama lounge
Bureau de Change		
Entertainment	**Restaurants**	
Casino	Ben & Jerry's	
Children's areas	Cupa Cabana	
Children's cinema	Globetrotter	
Onboard entertainment	Hot Sticks	
Video lounges	Maximes	
Video wall	MacDonald's	
Video warp	New York Pizza	
	Rudi's Diner	

Figure 7.3. Indicative onboard Stena Line ferry facilities. *Source*: based on Stena Line, Fast Ferry and Ferry Guide, Edition 2 (2000).

A number of new modes of transport are available on some ferry routes and are often faster on these short routes. In some cases these transport forms can cover different types of terrain. These include the Hydrofoil/Jetfoil, the Seacat and the

Hovercraft. Horner (1996) describes hovercraft as travelling on a cushion of air so that they ride above rather than on the waves. They are therefore more reliant on good weather than traditional ferries but given this they are faster. These have however recently been withdrawn from some routes. The same author describes Seacat as a catamaran service and HSS as drawing heavily on aircraft design to offer increased speed and comfort. Whilst not new, paddle steamers are a further form of transport used by tourists.

PACKAGED TRAVEL

The main suppliers of water-borne packaged travel are the cruise lines who offer more of a leisure product than a mode of transportation. The passenger shipping industry has, since the virtual demise in the 1950s of the ocean liners that operated across the Atlantic and to the Empire become more concerned with the provision of leisure cruises. Passenger ships were the forerunners to the present-day cruise ships and have more or less been replaced by them. Small numbers of tourists are still transported by cargo ship. These call at cargo docks rather than passenger terminals.

THE CRUISE INDUSTRY

Cruising is a dynamic sector of the tour operations industry that has experienced phenomenal growth in recent years. Indeed, it is one of the fastest growing sectors of the travel business with bookings currently growing at least 15 per cent year on year. The industry has shown record numbers of orders for new vessels in recent years. There are currently around 50 new cruise ships either on order, under construction or on the drawing board. The majority of these new ships are large vessels capable of carrying 2000 passengers or more. Indeed, ships which can carry in excess of 3000 passengers are now being built. At the same time other companies are preparing to launch smaller and medium sized vessels. Despite all of this activity further growth potential is still evident. According to Buchanan (2000), the number of Britons taking cruises in 1999 was greater than the number that skied.

Industry structure

A high degree of concentration is evident in the cruise industry. Consolidation in the form of mergers and alliances have led to the creation of a small number of 'mega-carriers.' Indeed, the industry has experienced a number of high profile takeovers. In common with other travel trade and transport areas, a number of dominant groups have emerged in the cruise industry and look set to continue to do so in the short term at least. There are four of these dominant groups – Carnival Corporation, Royal Caribbean International/Celebrity Cruises, P&O Princess Cruises and Star Cruises/Norwegian Cruise Line – as detailed in Figure 7.4. According to Wild (2000), Carnival, the current leader, also has the greatest share of new orders with fifteen ships capable of carrying 33,000 passengers and costing $6.3 billion on order. Together the big four are taking 87 per cent of the new capacity due to come on stream and bearing 83 per cent of the cost.

Carnival Corporation	**Royal Caribbean International/ Celebrity Cruises**
Carnival Cruise Lines	Royal Caribbean International
Holland America Line	Celebrity Cruises
Windstar Cruises	
Cunard Line	
Seabourn Cruise Line	
Airtours Sun Cruises (26 per cent stake)	
Total capacity of existing fleet: 71,344 (including Airtours Sun Cruises 4196)	Total capacity of existing fleet: 32,992
Total capacity on order: 33,192	Total capacity on order: 56,656
P&O Princess Cruises	**Star Cruises/Norwegian Cruise Line**
Princess Cruises	Star Cruises
P&O Cruises	NCL
Swan Hellenic	Orient Lines
Aida Cruises	Norwegian Capricorn Line
Festival Cruises	(dissolved October, 2000)
Total capacity of existing fleet: 11,338	Total capacity of existing fleet: 24,236
Total capacity on order: 26,404	Total capacity on order: 15,004

Figure 7.4. The 'big four' cruise lines. *Source*: adapted from *Travel Trade Gazette*, 22 May 2000.

Specialist cruise lines

In addition to the main cruise companies outlined above there are smaller, more specialist operators such as Disney Cruise Line which offers family holidays. Gusets can combine a stay at Walt Disney World Resort in Florida with a visit to Disney's exclusive Caribbean island: Castaway Cay. The Disney fleet includes two vessels – Disney Magic and Disney Wonder – which visit destinations in Florida and the Bahamas. Further specialist cruise companies are Fred Olsen Cruise Line and Louis Cruise Lines. The former is a Norwegian operated shipping company which has been in existence for 150 years and is still owned by the Olsen family. The latter operates two, three and seven day mini-cruises from Cyprus. Clipper Cruise Lines is a further niche player offering unusual cruises and Windstar Sail Cruises of Miami are a well-known sail cruise company.

Globalization

Once again, in common with the other travel trade and transport sectors, the cruise industry is becoming more global in outlook. This should help them to attract the demand necessary given the increased capacity that the sector has on order. Wild (2000) describes both Carnival and Royal Caribbean as having a largely North American focus, with some more international aspects to their operation, Star and P&O are both far more global in operational terms. P&O for example has built a pan-European niche as well as which it has cruise activities based in the USA and Australia. P&O/Princess Cruises was due to demerge from the rest of the P&O Group at the time of writing.

Having introduced the nature of the industry it is important also to consider the cruise product itself.

Flexible offerings

Poon (1993) has described cruise lines as the leaders in flexible production in the tourism industry for the reasons outlined in Figure 7.5. She also attributes cruise ships with 'mass customizing' the market by using their enormous economies of scale to produce 'flexible' holidays at relatively low prices for large numbers of clients.

> - Varied ports of call
> - Varied activities at each port of call/onboard
> - Varied attractions at each port of call/onboard
> - Global sourcing of materials
> - Global sourcing of labour
> - Segmentation opportunities (e.g. romantic cruises, adventure cruises, sophisticated cruises)

Figure 7.5. Accounting for the 'flexibility' of cruise lines. *Source*: adapted from Poon (1993).

The cruise industry has already been described above as a dynamic one. To many, familiar with the traditional image of cruises as travel products aimed at an elderly, upmarket clientele, this description may seem unlikely. The traditional image of cruising is provided in Figure 7.6. Many within the industry have worked hard at trying to change this image of cruising not only through new product developments but also through the use of public relations campaigns. Cruise lines have had a common interest in working both separately and together to break down traditional consumer perceptions and expand the market.

- Expensive
- Up-market clientele
- Emphasis on high service levels
- Provision of security and comfort (whilst visiting destinations often that had a lack of developed tourist infrastructure)
- Itineraries that included visits to several destinations (in comfort as opposed to most mobile holiday forms)
- Destinations in the Mediterranean and Caribbean popular

Figure 7.6. The traditional image of cruising.

New product developments

The industry has however successfully managed to attract a far broader customer base in recent years by varying its product offering. Some of the ways in which this has been done are outlined in Figure 7.7. An important development in the 1960s was that of Fly Cruises which transport passengers by aircraft to the departure point for the cruise. This helped to overcome problems caused by poor weather and rougher seas closer to home so helping to fuel the growth of the cruise market. These fly cruises also mean that companies can consolidate passenger numbers from different locations. This helps to maximize load numbers. At the opposite end of the scale to these fly cruises are domestic cruises operated in the waters around Britain. Destinations for cruises are discussed further below. Large amounts of money are being invested in new ships with some companies preferring this method of growth to mergers and acquisitions. These new ships can offer greatly improved facilities. Royal Caribbean International's mega-ship, Voyages of the Seas, even has a rock-climbing wall, an ice rink, an in-line skating track and a mini-golf facility. One of the main strengths of the cruise industry can now be described as the wide variety of cruise formats it offers.

Floating resorts

The giant ships now available and carrying huge numbers of passengers are often described as 'resorts at sea' offering passengers a range of facilities and entertainment options. These ships are however restricted in terms of the destinations they can visit due to their size

Mini cruises

Short cruises enable those with less time or on a restricted budget to experience cruising

Themed cruises

Some cruises are organized around a 'theme'. Interests covered include architecture, gardening and wine. Cultural cruises with expert lecturers are also available

Sailing ships

Cruises can be taken on board sailing ships. These are smaller than average cruise ships and the entertainment tends to be more basic. Like smaller luxury ships, these vessels can access small coves and out-of-the-way harbours

Family cruises

Some cruise ships have been designed with the family market in mind, incorporating children's swimming pools, play and social areas. Large ships with giant waterslides, computer centres, climbing and adventure areas and virtual reality games rooms meet the needs of this market

Cruise and stay

The ability to combine a cruise with a stay at a resort has increased the flexibility of cruising. In Alaska, for example, land stays enable cruise passengers to explore the Canadian Rockies and/or the Alaskan interior

World cruises

World cruises, which last around three months, have much in common with the traditional lengthy cruises which were only really available to those with the necessary time and money

Figure 7.7. Product offerings in the cruise sector. *Source*: based on Passenger Shipping Association Cruise Information Service (2000).

Destinations

The spatial distribution of cruising is also changing. The once popular destinations, whilst still attractive to many, have been joined by newer cruise destinations. Parts of the Far East including Singapore have increased in popularity as ports of call. Less traditional destinations such as South America are also growing in popularity. The development of mini-cruises has increased visitation to some locations closer to home. Private islands are also increasingly popular. Operators in the Caribbean in particular offer small coves or peninsulas that are not easily accessible other than by sea. These are sometimes leased from government or may even be shared between competitors. Laws (1997) attributes Norwegian Cruise Line (NCL) with pioneering this concept when it landed cruise ship passengers by tender on Great Stirrup Cay in the Bahamas for the first time in 1977. In 1986 NCL purchased the island and invested $1 million to upgrade facilities. A final trend is that of the larger ships towards becoming floating resorts which are like destinations themselves.

Cruise passengers

Cruise passengers can no longer be simply categorized as elderly and rich. Many of the product developments, described above, have helped cruise operators to attract a more varied clientele. Indeed, the development of mini-cruises has meant that the average price of cruises has fallen quite considerably. There has also been a shift in the age of the average cruise passenger from nearly 60 in 1993 to 54 in 1997. Age varies however from ship to ship and between destinations. The majority of cruise passengers worldwide are American and it is therefore noteworthy that the American market has long been broader than that in Europe. The family market has been a target for cruise lines in recent years. Despite often being a seasonal market, some operators have had success with this segment.

Tour operators and the cruise market

Tour operators have long been involved in the cruise market in the USA but have traditionally had far less involvement in the European cruise industry. Holloway (1994) describes attempts by European tour operators to enter the market in the 1970s by chartering or part-chartering cruise ships. These moves met with problems. Efforts to reduce prices led to dissatisfaction with standards of service and operation. More recent tour operator ventures into the cruise market have met with more success and cruising is now an important business for many of Europe's mass market tour operators.

In May 2000, First Choice announced a tie-up with the cruise company Royal Caribbean, allowing the operator to step up competition with its vertically integrated rivals. Banjeree (2000) describes the deal as giving First Choice extra funds for expansion while the cruise line secures vital retail distribution. A squeeze on sales had been spurred by directional selling. At the same time this creates a joint-venture cruise company targeting the European market. Royal Caribbean effectively gains 20 per cent of First Choice as well as a seat on the board and an option to raise its stake to 29.9 per cent.

Several major tour operators have introduced cruise holidays, often combined with the option of a land based holiday. The buying power of these companies, together with their links with airlines, means they can offer competitively priced holidays. Airtours launched its cruise division, Sun Cruises, in 1995. The Airtours cruise operation is discussed more fully in Figure 7.8.

Airtours portfolio of cruise products contains the following three brands:

Sun Cruises

Sun Cruises, Airtours own fly/cruise brand, operates exclusively for the Airtours Group and includes options to select accommodation from the major tour operator brochures. Sun Cruises carried 167,000 customers on a variety of Mediterranean and Caribbean cruises in 1999. One of the Sun Cruises vessels, MS *Sunbird*, was based in Palma, Majorca throughout summer 1999 and then moved to Barbados for winter

Costa Cruises

Costa Cruises specializes in /Mediterranean cruising and has a fleet of six ships. Costa Cruises carried 362,000 passengers in 1999

Direct Cruises

Direct Cruises offers cruises from the UK. These cruises operate from three UK ports – Glasgow, Dublin and Liverpool. Direct Cruises, which entered the UK market in 1998, was developed exclusively for Direct Holidays, one of Airtours UK tour operators. Direct Cruises currently charters a 962 birth cruise ship, SS *Apollon*, from a third party cruise operator and had 15,000 customers in 1999.

Figure 7.8. Airtours cruise operation. *Source*: Airtours (2000).

Distribution

Cruise lines have traditionally relied rather heavily on travel agents for distribution and this has been a lucrative source of commission earnings for agents. Specialist cruising agents have been developed including Cruise World, Mundy Cruising and The Cruise Line. The Passenger Shipping Association, introduced below, provides full lists of local agents. The tour operator-owned vessels can clearly benefit from the full distribution power of their parent companies. The use of technological distribution is also developing within the sector. According to Huxley (2000), Thomson opened a new call centre in 2000 and some of the 1000 staff employed work in a dedicated section to deal specifically with cruise enquiries and bookings.

Density

It is not only the facilities onboard cruise ships that vary but also the size. The density or passenger space ratio (PSR) is one means, described by Horner (1996) to measure this. A ship's gross registered tonnage (GRT) indicates its size and this can be found in manuals such as the *ABC Cruise and Ferry Guide* as can the maximum number of passengers for a ship. Dividing the GRT of the vessel by the number of passengers gives the density of the ship.

Trade associations

As with other forms of transport, there are associations with a cruise line membership. In the USA, the American Cruise Lines International Association (CLIA) is important whilst in the UK the Passenger Shipping Association is significant. The role of the Passenger Shipping Association (PSA) is outlined in Figure 7.9.

Formed in the 1950s, the Passenger Shipping Association (PSA) promotes passenger travel by sea. A cruise information service provides news and information for both holidaymakers and travel agents interested in cruising. Factsheets are available covering both geographical areas and types of cruise. A selection are listed below:

Caribbean
Mediterranean
Alaska
Far East
Baltic and Scandinavia
Luxury cruising
Family cruising
Singles cruising
Themed cruising
Wedding, honeymoon and anniversary
Working ships
Conference and incentive

Figure 7.9. The Passenger Shipping Association (PSA). *Source*: Passenger Shipping Association (2000).

The negative impacts of cruising

In common with the tour operations sector more generally, cruising has attracted criticism for the effects that it can have on destinations and eco-systems. Some of the criticisms levelled at cruising are outlined in Figure 7.10.

- Main ports can become very crowded when ships arrive
- The infrastructure of the port and/or resort visited can come under a great deal of pressure as large tourist numbers arrive for what is often a short spell
- Eco-systems can be disturbed by the numbers of visitors/frequency of calls
- There is a possibility of oil seepage
- Dredge disturbs reefs and other organisms
- The short time often spent at ports reduces the economic opportunities for local businesses

Figure 7.10. Criticisms levelled at cruising.

More detailed information covering cruising and cruise ships is available in the form of travel guides published by Berlitz and Fodor amongst others. Travel agents obtain details of both car ferries and cruise ships in the ABC Cruise and Ferry Guide.

BOATING HOLIDAYS

Coastal and inland waterways offer popular holiday options. Demand has grown for sailing holidays. Popular holiday options include canal boat trips or flotilla packages. Whilst France is a popular destination for canal boat holidays for UK holidaymakers, both the Greek Islands and the Caribbean are attractive for flotilla holidays. The latter involves individually hired yachts sailing together in flotilla formation. Learn-to-sail package holidays have also captured some market share. Sailing is also one of many water-based sports activities offered by many of the all-inclusive holiday resorts such as Sandals.

SUMMARY

This chapter concentrated on two forms of transport that are water-borne. These two principal forms of transport – ferries and cruising – offer important travel alternatives. The ferry market was considered first together with competition to this sector from the Channel Tunnel. Discussion of the fast growing cruise market then followed and the chapter concluded with a brief look at boating holidays.

DISCUSSION QUESTIONS

1. Examine developments that have contributed to the growth of cruising in recent years.
2. Account for the intensity of competition in the cross-channel market.

REFERENCES

Airtours PLC (1999) *Annual Report and Accounts*.

Banerjee, T. (2000) First Choice gains £200m for expansion, *Travel Trade Gazette*, 22 May.

Bateson, J.E.G. and Hoffman, K.D. (1999) *Managing Services Marketing; Texts and Readings*, The Dryden Press.

Berlitz (2000) *Complete Guide to Cruising and Cruise Ships*, Berlitz Publishing Ltd.

Buchanan, G. (2000) Supercruise; six stars all the way to South America, *Sunday Times*, 11 June, p. 6.1.

EIU Special Report (n.d.) *The World Cruise Ship Industry in the 1990s*, No. 2104.

EIU Travel and Tourism Analyst (1995) *The Cruise Ship Industry to the 21st Century*, No. 2.

Fodor's Worldwide Cruises and Ports of Call.

Holloway, J.C. (1994) *The Business of Tourism* (4th edn), Pitman Publishing.

Horner, P. (1996) *Travel Agency Practice*, Addison-Wesley Longman.

Huxley, L. (2000) Thomson Cruises eyes USA tie-ins, *Travel Trade Gazette*, 19 June.

Key Note Ltd. (1999) *UK Travel and Tourism*.

Laws. E. (1997) *Managing Packaged Tourism – relationships, responsibilities and service quality in the inclusive holiday industry*, ITP.

Markson, N. (1995) Channel vision, English Tourist Board, *Insights*, A-88, January.

Peisley, T. (1992) *The World Cruise Ship Industry to the 1990s*.

The Passenger Shipping Association (2000) *Cruise Information Service, Choose to Cruise*.

The Passenger Shipping Association (2000) *Cruise Information Service, Cruise 2000; Choose to Cruise – the Cruise Lines*.

Poon, A. (1993) *Tourism, Technology and Competitive Strategies*, CAB International.

Travel Trade Gazette (2000) TTG's Guide to the Big Four Cruise Lines, 22 May, pp. 32–3.

Vickerman, R. (1995) The Channel Tunnel – a progress report, *EIU Travel & Tourism Analyst* No. 3, The Economist Intelligence Unit Limited.

Wild, P. (2000) Takeovers grip cruise industry, *Travel Trade Gazette*, 22 May, p. 34.

CHAPTER 8

Bus and Coach Travel

INTRODUCTION

This chapter covers both inclusive tours by coach and the express coaches used by independent travellers. The traditional image of coach based holidays as being a product produced for and purchased by the elderly describes perfectly one part of the market. What this image fails to cover is the remainder of the market composed of city breaks, budget winter sports holidays and package holidays for those unable to fly or drive. Buses are also often used by tourists for local travel within or between destinations. A clear distinction between bus and coach transport is difficult to make. *Travel and Tourism Analyst* (1994, No. 4) describes the coach market as one for leisure trips as opposed to urban or inter-urban transport systems. Limited coverage of the bus sector is provided here in comparison to the discussion of coach travel. This chapter outlines the industry structure discussing recent change to this. The role of the coach tour wholesaler, incoming coach tour operators and several trade associations are considered.

BACKGROUND AND MARKET OVERVIEW

Travel by bus and coach can be seen to fall within the overall category of road transport and Holloway (1994) examines developments in road transport since the seventeenth century, describing the introduction of the stage-coach as greatly aiding mobility for small groups of travellers. These stage coaches relied upon teams of horses which were changed at regular points along the route. Improved roads helped lead to faster journey times and comfort levels for passengers.

According to Key Note (1999), buses and coaches account for 8 per cent of all UK domestic tourism trips and almost 40 per cent of all public transport tourism in the country. Whilst scheduled express coaches and local bus services account for most public transport trips by road, organized coach trips, as discussed below, account for more in terms of spending. Coach holidays offer an inexpensive alternative to air inclusive tours and so can be attractive. Indeed, coach travel offers 'direct-to-accommodation' transport and luggage delivery. Direct services to small towns and villages are also provided. Travel by coach is however less suited to longer journeys than it is to short and medium distance journeys. There is a point at which the generally cheaper price of coach travel becomes less relevant for many travellers due to the loss of comfort and speed advantages offered by other modes of transport.

Whilst representing only a minority player in the total holiday market, coach tours have grown in both the domestic and international markets in recent years. This growth looks set to continue in the next few years. Barton (2000b) quotes research from the Confederation of Passenger Transport (CPT) which states that the UK coaching market was worth £1487 million and supported at least 79,000 jobs in 1998. The sector, which involves some 4.2 million coach tours of one or more nights, is clearly important to tourist destinations, attractions and other businesses throughout the UK.

Mintel (1999) informs that the majority of coach holidays purchased in the UK are domestic yet coach holidays still account for 8 per cent of all holidays abroad. Coach companies are also involved in the transportation of incoming tourists. In the UK for example, National Express offers travel passes for travel in the UK which are only available at selected overseas agents. Their *Tourist Trail* passes are however available in the UK.

Coach holidays are purchased by independent holidaymakers as well as package tourists. Independent coach holidays are however preferred by the younger part of the overall market for coach travel. Hired coaches are also used to supply the package holiday market with transfers to and from terminals. Demand for domestic sightseeing trips is also met by coach companies. Cooper *et al.* (1998) describe local towns within destinations as making use of the mini or microbus giving the example of Kenyan safari holidays which use the adapted microbus in particular for sightseeing and game watching. A further market for coach travel which tends to attract a broader spectrum of society than coach trips generally is airport shuttles. Price can be seen to be a major factor in purchase decisions made by passengers selecting to travel by coach. The coach transport sector is seen to be environmentally friendly. The Department of the Environment, Transport and the Regions (DETR) suggests that average car occupancy is 1.5 as against 30 for a bus. In common with rail transport, opportunities for increased market share of bus and coach travel could result from any government policy of support for 'sustainable' transport alternatives.

INDUSTRY STRUCTURE

The bus industry has developed differently in different European countries. This can, in part, be attributed to their backgrounds including the legal framework and tradition of public or private ownership. Dostal (1999) describes several thousand private companies existing in just three European countries. There are several hundred public enterprises in Germany. Mintel (1999) describes the coaching sector as a fragmented one with a localized structure and for which it is impossible to give exact figures regarding numbers of operators. Approximately 1250 coach operators are listed in the *Travel Trade Gazette Annual Directory* with around half of these believed to offer holiday packages.

In common with the tour operations sector in general, the coach holiday operations market is dominated by just a few companies. The main players are Shearings, Wallace Arnold and Cosmos. In 1996–7 both Wallace Arnold and Shearings achieved independence through management buyouts.

Legislation has had a significant influence on development of the UK bus and coach industry. The bus and coach industry has been completely altered as a result of legislative changes between 1980 and 1994. The deregulation of express coach services occurred in 1980 followed by deregulation of local bus services outside London in 1986 following acts passed in 1980 and 1985 respectively. Prior to 1986, bus operations were heavily regulated under a system which followed these territorial monopolies by giving network subsidies. Small private companies did exist but tended to serve niche markets which the larger companies found unremunerative. Most UK local bus services were owned and operated by territorial monopolies which were either state-owned or municipally owned. Key Note Ltd (1998) describes the 1980 Transport Act as deregulating express services in the UK, removing fare controls and replacing vehicle licensing with operator licensing in 1981. Further deregulation was facilitated by the passing of the Transport Act of 1985. This act abolished road service licensing for local services outside London whilst also stopping public transport support for local services other than where unprofitable services are required to meet a social need. Privatization of the National Bus Company and the Scottish Bus Group, which had both been set up as nationalized companies in 1969, was provided for. Municipal operators were transferred into separate public transport companies. Most changes took effect from 1986 although privatization of the National Bus Company and the Scottish Bus Group were completed in 1988 and 1991 respectively.

Deregulation allowed any suitable operator to run any specified service without subsidy. Public involvement in local bus and coach services was removed by privatization of state-owned companies and by putting at 'arms length' those companies owned by municipalities/local authorities. Initial competition saw the emergence of new private operators but subsequent buy-outs and take-overs have left today's scheduled bus and coach industry structure dominated by several large private operators with numerous small operators and some municipal companies.

There are, according to Key Note (1999), now five main bus operators in the UK. These five have, since deregulation and privatization, been involved in the consolidation and rationalization of the industry. They are Arriva, Stagecoach, First Group, National Express and the Go-Ahead Group. The percentage share of the bus market held by these five companies in 1998 is shown in Table 8.1 together with approximate fleet sizes. The top five bus groups clearly dominate the industry with 67 per cent of the market whilst National Express alone dominates the scheduled coach market with a share of around 75 per cent. National Express offer services under franchise agreement. The holiday excursion and contract hire market by contrast remains highly fragmented.

Table 8.1. Top five companies' share of UK bus market. *Source*: adapted from Key Note Ltd (1998).

	Share (%)	Fleet size (approx)
First Group PLC	23	8050
Stagecoach Holdings PLC*	18	8500
Arriva PLC	15	7000
National Express Group PLC	7	2963
The Go-Ahead Group PLC	4	2400
Total top five	67	28,913

Note: * This figure has increased substantially following acquisition.

According to Key Note Ltd (1998) the UK industry has matured rapidly and 95 per cent of the bus and coach sector is now in the private sector. Key Note Ltd (1998) informs that in 1985 private operators carried only 3 per cent of local bus passengers whereas by 1997 they carried 93 per cent. Some public operations were bought out as management/employee buyouts and were later taken over by a main operator. Others were sold directly to private bus companies. The change to privatized companies was dramatic.

Growth of these dominant groups emerged out of a period of takeovers and acquisitions of public transport companies and the component parts of both the National Bus Company and Scottish Bus Group. This has all occurred following deregulation and privatization. Dostal (1999) argues that since deregulation some new entrant companies have found it difficult to compete against the incumbent operator, National Express, and that independent competition remains limited both domestically and internationally.

Under deregulation buses have diversified in a variety of ways. Organic growth has been a main goal of many companies. First they have diversified into other transport areas notably trains, metro systems and airport transport systems. Possibly the most significant move has been that into rail operations. All five of the dominant groups have interests in at least one rail franchise. National Express Group with five franchises has more than any other group. Most would now classify themselves as land-based passenger transport operators and continue to strive to become more integrated passenger transport providers. Indeed, some scope remains for integration into other passenger transport forms. Bus operators have also diversified geographically with companies such as Stagecoach becoming obvious international players. According to Dostal (1999), the ongoing liberalization of bus and coach transport in Europe opens up new opportunities for bus and coach companies who have so far been limited to their national or often more regional or local markets. Incumbents are however at the same time trying to protect their traditional markets. Mergers and acquisitions offer means by which international bus or multi-modal transport groups can enter other countries. Stagecoach acquired Coach USA in 1999.

Great advances have been made in the industry in recent years and the following in particular deserve mention:

- information provision;
- bus shelters; and
- integration.

The latter of these, integration, includes interchanges between different transport forms and ticketing integration whereby ticketing initiatives extend to other operators and competing transport forms.

SCHEDULED LONG-DISTANCE SERVICES

The UK has an established network of coach operators offering medium and long distance routes. In some other European countries however these operate as niche services. International journeys offer more scope for development, according to Dostal (1999), as the organization of railways is nationally focused. One interesting development internationally has been the growth of 'shuttle services' between Britain and the Continent. In North America there has been a long tradition of cross-country travel offered by companies such as Greyhound Lines.

EXPRESS COACH COMPANIES

An example of an express coach company is provided in Figure 8.1.

National Express PLC is the leading express coach company in the UK as well as being a good example of an integrated transport operator having interests in both the bus and rail sectors as well as in airports. National Express has also diversified internationally and adds a European dimension to its services through Eurolines.

The coach division includes the following three sectors:

- UK express coaches
- Airport coach services
- European coaches

Coach services served 1200 UK and 500 European destinations in 1997 with 15.6 million journeys.

National Express dominates the coach sector with around three-quarters of the scheduled coach market.

Figure 8.1. National Express PLC. *Source*: based on Key Note (1999).

VERTICAL INTEGRATION

Horizontal integration within the coach industry was shown in the example of National Express provided above. Vertical integration also takes place in the industry. Within the domestic market, two market leaders, Wallace Arnold and

Shearings, have both developed hotel chains. This can have the advantage of helping to guarantee control of standards and facilities on certain types of holidays.

FINANCIAL SECURITY AND CUSTOMER PROTECTION

Major coach operators are members of ABTA for reasons of financial security. The Confederation of Passenger Transport's (CPT) Bonded Coach Holiday Scheme is a source of financial security. The Coach Tourism Council (CTC), discussed below, includes many of the largest companies amongst its membership and the Coach Marque standard provides a guarantee of standards.

COLLABORATION WITH PRINCIPALS

The coach tour is associated with the operation of packaged travel including day trips and tours. They do not always run these themselves and may deal with others who share the risk. In some cases coach operators deal directly with principals themselves. Coach companies offering tours of one or more nights' duration have long had arrangements with hotels and other accommodation providers. Whilst this aspect of the tour is often taken care of by coach tour wholesalers, as discussed below, some coach companies will deal direct with accommodation providers. Hotel chains such as Swallow in the UK have departments dealing with this type of group business.

Larger chains often have popular coaching brands as does Accor with Ibis and Novotel. Once again Accor has a coaching division which is concerned exclusively with this market segment. Coach tour companies have long had involvement with schools providing school trips both domestically and internationally. The private hire market serves the needs of this particular segment as well as others such as clubs and hotel groups. Operators sometimes organize additional elements of a trip on behalf of the charterer. In this respect their role can resemble that of a tour operator.

More recently coach companies and wholesalers have, due to an extension of their product range, had to deal with other principals in the travel industry. Whilst the majority of UK based coach holiday companies operate in the domestic market and the rest of Europe, long haul holidays are also available, often using air travel to and from the holiday destination as shown by the example of Shearings in Figure 8.2. These fly/coach holidays have, in general, opened up opportunities for UK coach operators to include long-haul destinations such as China and Hong Kong in their programmes.

Shearings offers special deals on long haul departures from regional airports in the UK with free parking at certain ones. They similarly offer discounts on National Express scheduled services to airports. Shearings works with partners in destination countries advertising leading operators such as American Tours International in the USA and Scenic Tours in Australia. The Worldwide escorted tour programmes also cover Canada, New Zealand and South Africa. The air-coach option is offered to European destinations with flights to the relevant countries and coach link-ups rather than coach travel from the UK.

Figure 8.2.   Shearings long-haul holidays.

A further main development in the coach market has been the introduction of the coach-cruise where the cruise passenger is transported to the cruise ship departure point by coach. Greatdays group travel guide for example includes a range of cruises for coach operators. The same brochure also reflects the increasing popularity of air packages among coach operators, offering a broad range of destinations from two-night city breaks in Paris to seven-day safaris in South Africa. New coach/TGV packages to destinations including France and Switzerland are also being offered by some operators. The most established transport form used in combination with coaching however is the ferry and even this area is becoming increasingly competitive as regards attracting coach business. P&O Stena Line's latest move in the ultra-competitive Dover–Calais route was, according to Barton (2000a), the introduction of a huge, (28,838 tonne), state-of-the-art Superferry. This is the largest cross-channel ferry on the route with capacity for up to 2000 passengers and 600 cars. The same company has a loyalty scheme offering coach operators the chance to earn gift rewards for frequent day excursion bookings on its Dover–Calais service.

The coach holiday market has, of course, benefited greatly from the development of the Channel Tunnel as discussed in Chapter 6. International coach travel to and from the UK for example has increased since the opening of the Channel Tunnel.

NEW MARKETS FOR COACH HOLIDAYS AND TRAVEL

In addition to the introduction of new forms of collaboration with other transport providers, new markets are being targeted by coach operators. *Coach and Bus Week* (Barton, 2000a) provides the example of National Express which was, at the time of writing, targeting the youth market with offers that package coach travel and accommodation together with discounted entrance to night-clubs in the night-life centres of London and Leeds.

Product development is a further area in which significant moves have been made by the sector in recent years. Inclusive themed tours in particular are also becoming popular with coach groups. For 2000 a number of coach operators offered inclusive tours to the millennium dome in Greenwich. At the time of writing, National Express offers the following three and five day themed short breaks:

- Sandringham and Althorp;
- BBC Gardeners' World Live;
- Gardens of the English Riviera; and
- TV Yorkshire and Emmerdale.

COACH TOUR WHOLESALERS

Coach tour wholesalers buy hotel accommodation which they then sell on to small coach companies. There are a proliferation of small, often family-run, coach companies. These intermediaries earn a profit by purchasing rooms at discount, by buying in bulk, and adding a mark-up to this. At the same time the small coach operators, without the bargaining power to negotiate the rates that the wholesaler can achieve, obtain less costly accommodation for their clients. This has the added advantage of having already been inspected by the wholesaler. Coach tour wholesalers are also involved in booking ferry transport for coach companies as well as which they purchase museum passes and such-like on their behalf. Whilst the role of coach tour wholesalers was traditionally domestic in nature this is, in common with many sectors of the travel industry, increasingly international in scope.

There are only a handful of these intermediaries in the UK including Greatdays and Independent Coach Travel. The example of Greatdays is discussed more fully below. Independent Coach Travel is a specialist Irish wholesaler providing wholesale tours, ranging from basic bed and breakfast to inclusive themed programmes, for coach operators to book. In common with other coach tour wholesalers, the company produces brochures for coach operators. These include suggested itineraries, locator maps, price panels and hotel descriptions and are distributed to the travel trade. Another company, Leisure Breaks, which was formed in 1991 to provide London theatre breaks to the coach and group market, now offers a full range of short breaks and tours throughout Europe.

A family business since 1985, Greatdays is now one of the largest wholesale tour operators in Britain employing a team of 50 between their offices in Altrincham, London and Dallas, USA. For the first four years the company concentrated on selling British hotel accommodation to British tour operators. Since then, the company has been developing its inbound department, selling Greatdays UK products to the European and worldwide incoming markets. The associated company, Greatdays Holidays Ltd, offers a full range of air travel tours from weekend and short breaks to specialist mid- and long-haul destinations. A profile of the group is provided below.

Group profile

Greatdays Holiday Services Ltd
Surface travel arrangements, coach hire, ferry crossings, hotels, guide services and theatre and concert bookings. Groups from 15–500 + persons in hotels from 2–5 star in Great Britain, Ireland, Central Europe and Scandinavia

Greatdays Holidays Ltd
'Flight-only' or 'air package' deals for groups. Student, tourist class and luxury accommodation, transfers and tours for groups from 10 to 500 persons

Greatdays conference and incentive travel
A specialist division offering transport, quality hotel accommodation, meeting and conference facilities, incentive ideas and event management for the corporate markets

Academy of Knightsbridge
This is a further specialist division offering language courses to overseas students in the UK

Greatdays Incoming Services, London Greatdays Panita Travel
A full ground handling service in and around London including 'meet and greet' service, airport transfers, hotel reservations, multi-lingual guides, sightseeing tours, river cruises, concert and theatre bookings, apartments, sporting events, limousine and coach hire

Greatdays European Travelhouse, Greatdays Panita Travel
Deal with fully inclusive tours (FIT) reservations and ground arrangements for individual foreign visitors to Great Britain and Central Europe

Greatdays London Visitor Welcome Centre
In a prime location just 200 metres from Harrods and opposite the Victoria and Albert Museum, the welcome centre offers hotel accommodation, excursions and tours, theatre and show tickets and a range of essential services for groups staying in London.

The company, which has a multi-lingual staff, produces a biannual group travel guide with suggestions for groups. They also conduct an on-going programme inspecting hotels and resorts across Britain and Europe. They encourage, and can arrange, pre-tour visits to hotels and venues for clients. There is also a department offering tour support and free leaflet design and printing. The company has membership of the following: BAWTA (British Association of Wholesale Tour Agents; BITOA (British Incoming Tour Operators' Association); CTC (Coach Tourism Council); GTOA (Group Travel Organizers' Association); ASTA (American Society of Travel Agents); RDA (German travel association for the bus and coach industry), RSC (official reservations agency for the Royal Shakespeare Company); LTB (London Tourist Board); MVC (Manchester Visitor and Convention Bureau); ETOA (European Tour Operators' Association).

Around 90 per cent of Greatdays business is group travel and around 70 per cent of this comes from coach operators. The company works with more than 300 coach operators throughout Britain and deal with semi-professional organizers from organizations with more than 1000 staff that have regular holiday programmes. The average group has 35 people. Greatdays, which has a turnover of £9 million, works with all major hotel chains. Jarvis Hotels, for example, is a main UK supplier.

Figure 8.3. Greatdays Travel Group. *Source*: Greatdays (2000) and Group Leisure (2000).

INCOMING COACH TOUR OPERATORS

According to CPTs report, *The Role of the Coach in the Economy* (2000), 1.6 million overseas visitors arrived in Britain by coach, staying a total of 13.1 million nights and spending £396 million. In addition to this incoming coach tourism, many overseas visitors arriving by modes other than coach then go on to take coach tours and trips within the UK.

MASS MARKET TOUR OPERATORS AND COACHING

In the past, mass market tour operators have often shown little interest in the coaching holiday sector of the market. This may change in future as the travel industry becomes yet more concentrated than it is at present and as competition intensifies still further. One example of a mass market player moving into this sector is provided by Airtours' purchase, in the first half of 2000, of Leger Holidays, one of the largest coach tour specialists. This move enables Leger to benefit from Airtours Travelworld and Going Places travel agencies which together account for around 800 outlets. At the same time this provides a successful and profitable specialist coach tour operator for Airtours portfolio.

DISTRIBUTION

Direct sell is a popular option amongst coach operators who will often utilize direct mail and direct response advertising. In addition to these direct methods, brochures are sometimes distributed to travel agents and bookings taken through them. Lack of CRS adoption within the sector has however hindered relations with travel agents for some operators and as the purchase of coach travel often involves fairly simple transactions, the need to use travel agents is often not great. Some larger operators now take brochure requests through the Internet. Bus and coach operators sometimes run their own sales outlets or indeed in some cases tickets may be purchased via competitors. Self-ticketing machines have been located at many of the larger coach stations.

TRADE ASSOCIATIONS

The Coach Tourism Council (CTC) was established by Gerry Topioi of Groupways as an association of coach operators and suppliers with the aim of promoting coach tourism through good, positive public relations (PR). With a membership of over 300 today, the objectives of CTC remain unchanged. Indeed, the association's constitution is: 'To enhance the image of travel and tourism by coach to consumers, travel journalists, travel trade press, travel agents and any other person or body connected with the industry.' CTC also conducts an ongoing programme of research.

The British Association of Wholesale Tour Agents (BAWTA) also has many coach operator members. BAWTA Ltd is a non-profit making organization, founded in 1987, whose objectives are:

- To promote the quality, public image and growth of coach tourism.
- To represent and promote the interests of British wholesale tour agents and operators.

The association has both a code of conduct for members' dealings with clients and a repatriation scheme.

Coach and bus shows are held regularly and it is claimed that 'Coach and Bus 99' featured the biggest array to date of group tourism stands. These included attractions, wholesalers, tourist boards, hotels, and cross-channel operators amongst others. This hints at the importance of coaching trips to travel and tourism and the importance of travel and tourism to coaching companies. There is an increasing partnership approach being adopted between coach operators and coach tourism outlets. Poynter (1993) examines factors to consider when selecting a tour bus. The same author provides a practical introduction to business management plans for one day tours as well as tour bus negotiation skills.

COACH HOLIDAYS AND TOURISM – GETTING THE BALANCE RIGHT

Popular tourist destinations have, in the past, often viewed coach tours negatively partly because they bring high visitor numbers to areas. This can cause congestion in addition to which large numbers of tourists require the infrastructure to support them. Often these coach tours are stopping at attractive towns and villages or tourist sites for only short periods of time. They therefore can be low spend visitors as accommodation and food are provided elsewhere on the trip.

Despite the above coach tours can make a crucial contribution to local economies, they are less seasonal than most tourism alternatives and there are ecological arguments in favour of coaching. The latter include the way in which transporting groups by coach has a less detrimental effect on the environment than would numerous individual or small groups travelling by car.

THE FUTURE FOR COACH HOLIDAYS

The consolidated groups of integrated travel companies have been showing interest in niche markets and market expansion for coach specialists could result in moves by the major groupings into this market. Further consolidation is in itself likely within the sector.

SUMMARY

This chapter considered the role of express coaches used by independent tourists as well as inclusive tours by coach. The industry structure was described together with an explanation of deregulation and privatization in the sector. The focus was on the importance of this form of transport to tourism. The role and function of coach tour wholesalers was therefore covered in detail.

DISCUSSION QUESTIONS

1. Outline the structure of the coaching sector in the UK.
2. Explain the role of coach tour wholesalers.
3. Discuss recent developments in coach holidays.

REFERENCES

Anon (2000) Greatdays ahead, *Group Leisure*, February.

Barton, M. (1999a) Fifty new packages in latest WA brochures, *Coach and Bus Week*, week ending 23 September 2000.

Barton, M. (1999b) Superferry, *Coach and Bus Week*, week ending 23 September 2000.

Barton, M., (2000a) Airtours buys Leger Holidays for £23.1 m, *Coach and Bus Week*, week ending 6 March 2000.

Barton, M., (2000b) UK Coaching market worth £1,487 million, *Coach and Bus Week*, week ending 10 February 2000.

Cooper, C., Fletcher, J., Gilbert, D. and Wanhill, S. (1998) in R. Shepherd (ed.) *Tourism: principles and practice*, 2nd edn.

Dostal, A.W.T. (1999) Bus & coach operators in Europe, *Travel and Tourism Analyst*, No. 5, Travel and Tourism Intelligence.

Holloway, J.C. (1994) *The Business of Tourism* (4th edn), Pitman Publishing.

http://www.bawta.co.uk

Key Note Ltd. (1998) *Bus and Coach Operators*.

Key Note Ltd. (1999) *UK Travel and Tourism*.

Mintel (1999) Coach Holidays, *Leisure Intelligence*, January.

Poynter, J.M. (1993) Tour Design, Marketing and Management, Prentice Hall.

CHAPTER 9

The Airline Industry

AN OVERVIEW OF THE AIRLINE INDUSTRY

That this book's coverage of the airline industry is spread over three chapters is indicative of both the importance of air transportation to the travel business and the complexity of the industry. The first of these three chapters introduces the airline industry and many of the factors that influence its operation including the freedoms of the sky, bilateral agreements and deregulation. Those organizations involved in the remaining regulation of the industry are then discussed. The chapter concludes with a comparison of scheduled and charter airlines. Chapters 10 and 11 go on to examine issues and trends within the industry. Air transportation in the 1990s has been described by Vellas and Becherel (1995) as being characterized by the following three conditions which these chapters hopefully portray:

- exceptional growth;
- increasingly competitive markets; and
- extreme vulnerability to international economic and political crises.

BACKGROUND

The majority of international passenger movements both to and from the UK involve air transportation. This form of transport has developed greatly since the Second World War when a surplus of aircraft became available for civil use. The cost of air transport has a direct influence on the cost of tourism products and indeed on the choice of destination. International tourism has thus been extended with the distribution of tourists greatly influenced by flight provision. The air transport sector is a key part of not only the tourism industry but also the world economy.

The first recorded powered, piloted flight took place in 1903 when The Wright Flyer – the Wright brothers plane – flew a short distance at Kittyhawk fields. Although it was not then known, air transportation was to become extremely important to the development of international tourism, particularly influencing travel patterns.

A significant aspect of the development of the airline industry has been a steady reduction in the cost of travel, making this a more competitive form of transport for tourists. This was, in part, a result of improved technology. As aircraft became larger and faster they could carry more passengers so spreading costs. Technical developments also meant that airlines upgraded their fleets making available second-hand aircraft in good condition and at low cost to other airlines including charter carriers.

There are, according to Hanlon (1999), approximately 1200 scheduled airlines in the world with some 300 operating on international routes. There are a variety of different sizes of airline from those carrying less than 10,000 passengers a year to major carriers serving in excess of 80 million passengers per year. Despite the scale of the industry, Key Note (1997) believes that there remains much opportunity for further development particularly in areas of the world where international leisure travel markets have yet to be created.

Hanlon (1999) informs that the air transport industry now caters for 1.5 billion passengers a year, employs approximately 1.7 million people and generates some $300 billion in revenue. He further describes the industry as having consistently grown at a very fast rate over the past 50 years. Indeed, the only time during this period that world air traffic has fallen was in 1991 when a 3 per cent drop resulted from economic recession, the Gulf War and threats of international terrorism directed at commercial aviation. In Europe alone world passenger traffic in terms of passenger-kilometres performed by scheduled airlines of International Civil Aviation Organization (ICAO) contracting states, grew from 428.2 billion to 549.3 billion between 1985 and 1995. Hanlon describes ICAO, the source of these figures, as forecasting that by 2005 world passenger traffic will have reached 970 billion. Variations in growth can be observed between different regions. The industry is not, despite this growth, characterized by high levels of profitability and some years have witnessed both excess capacity and heavy losses. A further source, Mintel (2000), describes the demand for flying as growing inexorably as exemplified by a growth in the number of passengers handled at UK airports between 1993 and 1998 of 29 million per year. They believe that this growth rate will increase in future.

Prior to looking at issues and trends affecting the airline industry it is necessary to understand the context within which international aviation takes place. This chapter therefore now considers the freedoms of the sky and bilateral agreements.

THE FREEDOMS

Much of the framework, or legal guidelines, within which the modern day airline industry operates was set at the Chicago Conference in 1944. Whilst the aim of the conference was to develop a multilateral air service agreement what actually resulted was a system to facilitate the operation of bilateral agreements between countries. This system was built around the concept of the *five freedoms of the air*. These freedoms are as listed in Figure 9.1.

---

1. The right of an airline company of one state to fly over the territory of another state
2. The right of an airline company of one state to land on the territory of another state
3. The right of an airline company to carry passengers, mail and goods from its own state to another state
4. The right of an airline company of one state to embark passengers, mail and goods in another state and carry them to its own state
5. The right to operate between two states other than the airline company's own country

Additional freedoms to develop since the Chicago Convention are listed below

6. The right to carry passengers, mail or freight between two countries on an airline which is of neither country but is operating via the airline's own country
7. The right to carry passengers, mail or freight 'directly' between two countries on an airline associated with neither of the two countries

---

Figure 9.1.   The five freedoms of the air.

In the absence of political or military problems the mutual exchange of the first two freedoms is the norm whilst governments bargain hard for the remaining freedoms as discussed below. Holloway (1995) provides some interesting practical examples.

BILATERAL AGREEMENTS

It is on the basis of the above freedoms that bilateral agreements such as the well-known *Bermuda Agreement* between the UK and the USA introduce fifth freedom rights. Whilst the traditional view would support equitable exchanges, a number of factors including the size of the bargaining countries influence the outcomes. The freedoms have influenced the extent of regulation in the industry. Indeed, services have often been provided by a series of bilateral monopolies consisting of the two national airlines at either end of the route only occasionally supported by the fifth freedom operations of other airlines. Competition has therefore been severely curtailed within the international airline operating environment. The freedoms of the sky are still important to international air transportation today with fifth freedom rights commonly in use.

An important concept in international aviation is that of cabotage. Essentially this describes the right of an airline of one country to embark passengers, mail and freight in another country and then to carry them on to another point in the same country. Vellas and Becherel (1995) describe this as introducing competition between domestic and international carriers and as one of the most debated aspects of the liberalization of air transport.

An additional layer of complexity in the airline industry is created by the allocation of slots (take-off and landing times). These are negotiated, on a historical basis, at IATA's bi-annual slots conference. This system is currently the subject of much debate but essentially it could be argued that in the past there tended to be little variation to slot allocation year on year. Airlines usually keep any slots they have been operating, with priority given to year round business and regular services. This aspect of the industry is likely to become even more complex in future as a result of the predicted growth of air traffic worldwide.

FLYING THE FLAG

State owned airlines have traditionally been significant players in the international air transportation industry. These carriers of course were popular with governments due to the power and prestige that their operation afforded the country. They therefore met objectives that had little to do with efficiency and profitability. Indeed, there remain today many subsidized state carriers that are often lacking in competitive edge yet in many parts of the world opportunities are reserved for them. (Key Note Ltd., 1997). Factors that led to the existence of so many so-called *flag carriers* include the nature of bilateral agreements. Governments have, as a result of these agreements, much control over the operation of routes starting or finishing in their country. According to Hanlon (1999) these flag carriers dominated the industry for most of the post-war period and even where they did not, as in the USA, government control was exercised over where airlines could fly and what they could charge.

Despite the above, privatization of airlines has been a major trend to affect the industry and the extent of this together with reasons for it are examined in Chapter 10.

DEREGULATION AND LIBERALIZATION

The airline industry has, for a variety of reasons, traditionally been a highly regulated industry. It is unsurprising given the nature of air travel that safety in particular has long been regulated. Aspects such as the mechanical condition of equipment and the qualifications of pilots are clearly important. Economic control was however also traditionally associated with air travel. This included route entry, timetables and air fares. More recently the industry has, in common with other industries, been subject to consumer protection controls as well as environmental controls.

Deregulation in North America

A major change in respect of regulation which resulted in the effective removal of much of this control, has occurred in many parts of the world through the process of deregulation of the airline industry. This first occurred in the USA in 1978 with the passing of the Airline Deregulation Act which led to an open-skies policy although pressure for change to the highly politicized nature of civil aviation in the USA had emerged before this. The British government was advocating a more liberal policy around the same time but other countries in Europe did not share this enthusiasm. The Airline Deregulation Act in the USA significantly affected both the structure and the operation of the airline business in the domestic market by reducing state control and allowing market forces to operate. It was in the economic areas of route entry, timetables and air fares that deregulation removed control. Deregulation transformed the structure of the domestic airline industry. This act was passed despite strong arguments against it as well as strong arguments in its favour, both of which are summarized in Figure 9.2.

For	Against
Possible lower prices	Possible reduction of air safety levels
Possibly more consumer choice	Possible reduction to the number of scheduled carriers as operators go out of business
Possible consumer benefits of increased competition (e.g. improved service)	Consumer benefits could be short term

Figure 9.2. Arguments for and against deregulation.

The US example of deregulation is fairly extreme. The Civil Aeronautics Board (CAB) was phased out following the act and finally disbanded in 1984. By subjecting the domestic market to free competition it was expected that smaller airlines, with lower overheads and better productivity, would be able to undercut the inefficient larger carriers. Whilst this happened in the shorter term, with fares falling and new carriers emerging, the longer term results of deregulation were not however as expected. The dramatically changed structure of the industry was to experience a reversal of much that had taken place. Few of the new low cost carriers survived in the longer-term leading to the return of higher fares and a reduction in consumer choice. Consolidation once again became a feature of the US airline industry from the mid-1980s on. Competition was fierce and many airlines were pushed into either bankruptcy or merger. With the collapse of many of the new entrants, the industry even became slightly more oligopolistic than prior to deregulation. Some possible reasons for airline failures are provided in Figure 9.3. The outcomes of deregulation are discussed further in the following two chapters.

---

1. Some airlines expanded too quickly
2. Labour and fuel costs were high for large companies and these were passed on to consumers pre-deregulation. Post-deregulation this was not competitive as the cheaper companies existed with non-unionized employees and more efficient planes etc.
3. Established carriers, shaken by the early effects of deregulation recovered, cut costs and learned to exhibit their advantages through aggressive pricing and the like

---

Figure 9.3. Possible reasons for airline failures in the US post-deregulation.

There has, since deregulation, been much discussion of the concept of 'Open Skies' and the spread of deregulation to routes to and possibly also within Europe. Discussions to date have been inconclusive and it remains to be seen what form such an Open Skies policy will take.

Liberalization in Europe

The privatization of British Airways (BA) in 1997, as discussed in Chapter 10, was accompanied by a reduction in state control over airline operations which essentially created an environment more conducive to liberalization. Indeed, BA was one of the airlines to argue in favour of liberalization whilst other airlines – mainly those receiving state funding – argued against it. The British government had, for some time, favoured an open skies policy but European liberalization evolved far more slowly than had deregulation in the USA. Overall the process was one of a more managed approach than that in the USA.

The US experience of deregulation had influence on the European stand-point and ultimately a far more moderate system, known as liberalization, resulted in Europe. The timing of implementation partly reflects the fact that a compromise had to be reached in Europe where some countries were desirous of a long transition period. The process of liberalization occurred through three packages of measures which commenced in 1993 and were completed when cabotage rights took effect in April, 1997. There are also significant differences between the airline environments of North America and Europe which affected the processes of deregulation and liberalization. The public sector role of airlines in Europe is a key difference. Even today state aid is given to a number of airlines despite opposition to this. There are also clear geographic differences. These key differences are summarized in Figure 9.4. In common with the US situation there were both those in favour of deregulation and those against it. Indeed, Key Note (1997) suggests that whether airlines viewed this as an opportunity or a threat depended very much on the airline itself. Those airlines in a healthy financial and operational position were more likely to welcome competition on equal terms.

USA	Europe
'One country'	Numerous countries with different cultures, languages etc (pre-European *harmonization*)
No state-aid	State-aid given to some airlines
No experience of deregulation	US experience of deregulation

Figure 9.4. Differences between European and US airline environments prior to deregulation.

A principal step towards European liberalization was to move the many countries towards a single market or a single aviation policy with all countries treated as one for the purposes of air travel. Liberalization effectively means that European airlines have freedom in setting tariffs, albeit in the context of regulations to avoid the fare-wars that occurred in the USA. A standardized European operating environment has also been created for all EU carriers enabling them to operate from any EU country given certain conditions. Finally, cabotage rights enable EU carriers to operate flights commencing in other EU countries as discussed above.

The third package of measures was forwarded to the Council of Ministers by the EC Commission in 1991. This was the final stage necessary for the creation of a single international EC airline market. This third package of liberalization measures was accepted despite that it was surrounded by controversy, not least of all because of the continuing issue of state aid. The original proposals had however been diluted somewhat. In April 1997, cabotage rights came into effect and any European carrier can now treat any other European country as its home base for the purposes of air travel. The fact that international aviation experienced a number of difficulties in the early 1990s added to the problems experienced in progressing European liberalization. Substantial losses by airlines increased pressure for continued protection and regulation.

Deregulation has had enormous impact on airline strategies. Vellas and Becherel (1995, p. 140) attribute the transformation of the industry to three main factors:

1. Deregulation of the domestic market in the United States has been the catalyst for a general lowering of domestic and international prices.
2. The strategies of airline companies towards tourism radically changed after the competition introduced by the charter companies in the 1980s. Companies like Wardair and Capitol, although they failed, have transformed the industry.
3. General discounts on scheduled airlines have been introduced. Tour operators can now sell seats at very competitive prices to cover tourism demand, thus generating a new clientele for the airlines (this amounts to selling charter seats on scheduled airlines at an advantageous price).

As mentioned above the process of liberalization in Europe was a lengthy one and Figure 9.5 outlines the key stages leading to liberalization.

1974	The European Court of Justice ruled that the Treaty of Rome's competition rules applied to air transport
1975	The Commission recommended the establishment of a European market in aviation
1979	The Commission's Memorandum 1 called for a liberalization of the bilateral restrictions and a review of state subsidies. This led to the Inter-regional Directive which introduced free access on inter-regional routes by certain size of aircraft on certain lengths of route. This did not greatly influence air transport services in Europe as a whole
1984	The Nouvelles Frontieres ruling
1987	The first package of measures
1990	The second package of measures
1993	The third package of measures
1997	Full cabotage from April

Figure 9.5. EC developments preceding the third package of measures. *Source*: based on Morrell (1998).

NETWORK DESIGN

Network design is a central factor in airline costs and revenues.

Hub and spoke networks, characterized by routes radiating from a hub, became popular in the period following deregulation in the USA and more recently in Europe. This form of network design, as shown in Figure 9.6, combines passengers from various destinations (spokes) on flights from the hub along a trunk route to another hub. Passengers may then travel on to a variety of destinations (spokes).

For example, it can save time for a passenger from Glasgow to travel to Hong Kong via the hub at Amsterdam than to fly via London. Interline opportunities are often the reason for a choice of airline. Use of a hub is particularly suited to longer-haul travel where the time spent changing aircraft at the hub is relatively short in comparison to the overall journey time. Critical to the success of hubbing nonetheless is to time arrivals for onward travel to departing flights. Maximization of connection options is a priority with this form of network design. Figure 9.6 illustrates hub and spoke design diagramatically.

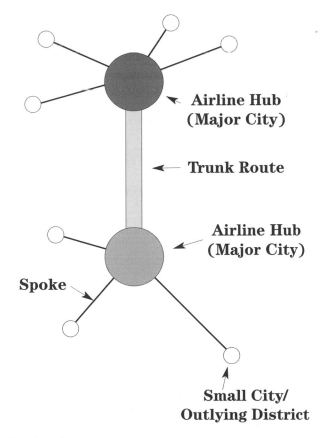

Figure 9.6. A hub and spoke system

Hubs and the networks built around them can become important strategic resources to airlines and indeed even sources of competitive advantage. More detailed accounts of hub and spoke networks are provided, together with discussion of alternatives including linear and grid networks, by Holloway (1997) and Hanlon (1999).

INTERNATIONAL ORGANIZATIONS

Despite the processes of deregulation and liberalization, international and domestic organizations are still involved in the regulation of the airline industry and some of those which are relevant today and which perform complementary roles are now discussed.

International Air Transport Association

The International Air Transport Association (IATA), which represents the world's scheduled airlines, was formed in 1919 and recreated in 1945. This is a non-governmental trade organization made up of member airlines. IATA is concerned with technical aspects of the operation of airlines as well as which it provides financial and legal services for members. IATA effectively controlled international air fares for many years and indeed was accused of being a legalized cartel, setting fares by agreement between different airlines and their governments. Some observers believed this led to high air fares and stifled competition whilst non-IATA airlines could compete more freely on both price and service aspects. Following deregulation the tariff setting and trade agreement functions have however been greatly reduced.

IATA also performs a facilitation role whereby it seeks to 'ensure that people, freight and mail can move on the vast global network as easily as if they were on a single airline within a single country' (Key Note, 1997).

IATA therefore provides a clearing house for the settlement of debts between airlines so enabling tickets of one airline to be freely used on the services of a fellow airline member of IATA. (Key Note, 1997).

International Civil Aviation Organization

The International Civil Aviation Organization (ICAO) is a United Nations organization. ICAO is mainly concerned with the technical side of operations including improving technical standards and conducting accident investigations. Securing international cooperation between government Agencies such as airport and air traffic control authorities is one of ICAO's key roles.

European Civil Aviation Conference
The European Civil Aviation Conference (ECAC) operates under the umbrella of ICAO in respect of its European membership which once again is drawn from governments as opposed to airlines.

Association of European Airlines
The Association of European Airlines (AEA) is a further body with a European membership which this time is composed of the major scheduled carriers. Whilst the role of the association is similar to that of IATA, the focus is on European airlines.

European Regional Airlines Association
The interests of Europe's regional airlines differ in many respects from those of larger European flag carriers and the European Regional Airlines Association exists to look after their interests.

Figure 9.7. International organizations.

UK ORGANIZATIONS

Having introduced the main international organizations concerned with air transportation it is helpful to consider the principal organization at the domestic level which, in the UK, is the Civil Aviation Authority (CAA). The CAA was introduced in Chapter 1 in relation to Air Travel Organizers' Licences (ATOLs). These are a legal requirement for travel organizers selling most air holidays and some air seats to the public. Discussion of the CAA is followed by an introduction to the roles of other organizations that have a role in respect of air transport in the UK context.

The Civil Aviation Authority
The Civil Aviation Authority is the independent, statutory body responsible for the economic and safety regulation of the UK industry. The National Air Traffic Services Ltd (NATS) is still, at the time of writing, part of CAA although the Government plans to sell 51 per cent of this. Navigation services are seen to be outside the scope of this book.

The Economic Regulation Group (ERG) regulates airlines and airports whilst also acting as an expert adviser to the Government on a number of economic matters regarding airlines and airports. The Group is also involved in the collection, analysis and publication of statistical information on airlines and airports. The promotion of air transport users' interests through encouragement of a diverse and competitive industry is the key function of ERG. The consumer representation arm of the CAA is the Air Transport Users' Council (AUC)

National Air Traffic Services (NATS)
NATS Ltd is a wholly-owned subsidiary of the CAA which plans, provides and operates air traffic services in the UK and North Atlantic airspace and at busy airports. In 1999 the Government proposed a Public Private Partnership (PPP) for NATS. It plans to sell 51 per cent of NATS and to retain 49 per cent. Under the Transport Bill which is before Parliament at the time of writing, CAA would become regulator of NATS.

Department of the Environment, Transport and the Regions (DETR)
In addition to the above the Department of the Environment, Transport and the Regions (DETR) in the UK is responsible for the following:

• Government policy for civil aviation including formulation of legislation
• International civil aviation, including the negotiation of international air service agreements and the issue of permits to overseas airlines
• Aircraft noise policy
• National airports policy
• Coordination of aviation security
• Investigation of aircraft accidents

The Air Accidents Investigation Branch (AAIB) is the part of the department responsible for the investigation of civil aircraft accidents and serious incidents within the UK.

Ministry of Defence (MOD)
The MOD is responsible for military aviation in the UK.

Figure 9.8. Airline related organizations in the UK. *Source*: based on www.caa.co.uk

There are further organizations, including the Department of Trade and Industry (DTI) and the Health and Safety Executive (HSE), involved in particular aspects related to civil aviation but the principal ones are those outlined above.

Having introduced much of the context of international aviation, this chapter now compares the operation of the two currently available forms of passenger transport by air – scheduled and charter flights.

SCHEDULED AND CHARTER OPERATIONS

There are both similarities and differences between scheduled and charter flights. The traditionally recognized characteristics of each are presented in Figure 9.9.

Charter	Scheduled
Smaller seat pitch	Larger seat pitch
Lower service levels	Higher service levels
Less catering	More catering
Less entertainment	More entertainment
Less comfortable	More comfortable
Less convenient times	More convenient times
Less convenient airports	More convenient airports
Lower ratio of staff to passengers	Higher ratio of staff to passengers
Cheaper	More expensive
Less frequent service	More frequent service
Predominantly aimed at package holiday-makers via tour operators	Predominantly aimed at business travellers and independent leisure travellers
More medium-sized aircraft	More varied aircraft sizes
Pre-booking often necessary	Pre-booking not always necessary
Smaller operators with lower overheads	Larger operators with higher overheads
Consolidation of flights takes place	Fixed departure airports and times

Figure 9.9.   A comparison of scheduled and charter airlines.

Scheduled airlines are widely considered to offer superior standards to charter carriers. Certain airports have become associated with one or other of these flight types. In London for example, Heathrow has traditionally been seen as the airport for scheduled air travel whereas Gatwick is associated with the charter carriers. Consolidation can occur in the charter sector, causing changes to flight details such as departure airport or time. This system is used to manage low bookings economically and may involve putting two different flights together.

In addition to the above only a small number of long-haul destinations can support the level of regular business needed for charter operations. Indeed, most charter operations exist within Europe, servicing in particular routes to popular tourist destinations in Southern Europe. The charter market is made up of tour operators making block bookings of seats or whole aircraft for a particular period such as a season of regular journeys (rotations). These airlines depend on high utilization of their aircraft and have high break-even points, sometimes as high as 80–90 per cent. At around 60 per cent, the break-even point for scheduled carriers is far lower. Flight only sales using charter seats are made to individuals but generally it is the market for scheduled air travel that is more likely to be composed of individuals reached via travel agents or directly.

Features	Typified by	Effect
Direct distribution	LCCs tend not to maintain offices in cities they serve. The direct purchase of tickets is by telephone and payment is by credit card.	Cuts out the middle man avoiding payment of commission to travel agents. CRS fees are also avoided.
Ticketless travel	LCCs often choose not to issue tickets but instead purchases are made by phone using a credit card and a reference number is issued and the passenger then shows some proof of identity at the airport.	Cuts out commission as above and improves productivity by freeing up check-in staff and also by removing the cost of the ticket itself.
Interline Agreements	There is a lack of ticket or baggage interline agreements with other airlines.	This helps maintain a simple booking system and so keeps reservation costs down.
Removal of the 'added value'	FFP are not usually offered by LCCs.	Removes the cost of running a loyalty programme.
Simplified pricing structure	Demand regulated fares or flexible return tickets.	Attracts business for the carrier.
Reduced service and entertainment levels	In-flight service on most flights curtailed or even eliminated. Beverage service, where provided, may be charged for. On flights where duty-free sales are applicable these are promoted as a means of revenue generation. In-flight entertainments are similarly often excluded or paid for.	Reduction in costs and labour. Faster airport turnarounds. These are often no greater than 30 minutes.
Free seating arrangements	Free seating arrangements using reusable boarding cards.	Boarding times are reduced and turnaround times improved. Utilization times can therefore be as high as 11.5 hours per day.
One-class travel	LCCs tend not to offer different classes of travel.	Sophisticated yield management systems are not required.
High-load factors	Seats are usually sold on a first-come-first-served basis with the cheapest seats sold first as opposed to the traditional approach of trying to sell as many high revenue tickets as possible.	Break-even load factors will be exceeded.
Fewer booking restrictions	LCCs generally offer fewer booking restrictions (sometimes achieved by selling one-way tickets). Generally the tickets are non-refundable and non-returnable.	Business travellers are attracted by the fact that there is no imposition of a Saturday night stay for cheap fares. Load factors of 100 per cent can be achieved.
Aircraft safety and comfort	The seat pitch on LCCs tends to be less	Increased passenger numbers per flight.
Lease v. buy	LCCs tend to lease rather than buy aircraft.	Wet leasing is a flexible option which enables airlines to increase or decrease schedules in response to demand. The rate for a wet lease includes all costs for the aircraft, flight, crew, maintenance and insurance.
Departure points	Most LCCs utilize airports other than the main established departure points. Routes are used which create parallels to trunk routes. Luton and Stansted are used instead of Heathrow, for example.	Access costs (landing charges) are reduced as are passenger handling charges. There is less congestion and turnaround timers are improved.
Reduced labour	The ratio of staff to passengers can be reduced on LCCs.	A reduction in labour costs.

LCC = Low Cost Carrier   FFP = Frequent Flyer Programme   CRS = Computer Reservations System

Figure 9.10.   Indicative features of low cost carriers.

Some more up-market tours utilize transport by scheduled carrier in order to offer continuity of service levels, more choice of destination and departure times and suchlike. These are also a better option for tour operators dealing with smaller numbers of passengers. Scheduled airlines are increasingly entering the leisure travel market as their cost structures become more akin to those of charter carriers. Similarly some charter carriers, especially those now operating on long-haul routes are adopting strategies traditionally associated with scheduled carriers. First Choice's Air 2000 for example claims to be the first charter airline to offer a choice of classes of travel on long-haul flights.

The regulatory differences between scheduled and charter air transport within the EU was abolished with completion of the single market. Prior to this a number of rules of charterworthiness, including those outlined in Figure 9.11, had to be observed by charter airlines.

- Could not sell direct to the public
- Restricted in the products they could sell e.g.
  - round-trip journeys
  - minimum stay requirements
- Restrictions on seat-only products

Figure 9.11. Some effects of the rules of charterworthiness for charter airlines prior to the single market.

Low cost carriers have had significant impact by lessening the distinction between scheduled and charter airlines. These are scheduled carriers displaying many of the features of a charter airline as shown in Figure 9.10.

Dennis (1999) compares the cost differentials between no-frills and mainstream scheduled carriers. His estimates, which are based on British Midland, an airline which is similar to low cost carriers in that it operates 737 aircraft, are shown in Figure 9.12.

	British Midland	Low Cost + 20% seats and flights
Flight and Cabin Crew Salaries	6.3	3.6
Flight and Cabin Crew Expenses	1.9	0.0
Fuel and Oil	6.1	7.3
Aircraft Rental/Depreciation	15.5	15.5
Training and Development	0.8	0.8
Maintenance	8.7	10.4
Airport Charges	14.7	4.9

Handling and Ground Charges	14.4	11.5
Passenger Services	6.5	0.0
Insurance	0.6	0.8
Sales and Reservations	5.5	12.0
Advertising	3.5	5.3
Commission	7.6	0.0
Cargo Specific	1.1	0.0
General and Administrative	1.9	1.0
Total	100.0	79.0
Per pax (index)	100.0	55.0
Cost per pax	£83.30	£45.80

Notes: British Midland data from CAA Statistics 1996
Load factors are assumed equal between the carriers

Figure 9.12. Estimated cost comparison: British Midland v. low cost carrier. *Source*: Dennis (1999).

It is not only the introduction, to Europe, of low cost carriers that poses a threat to the continuation of this key method of differentiating between types of airline. As mainstream scheduled carriers display more flexibility and become more efficient they are increasingly able to compete for business with charter carriers. Low cost carriers are discussed further in Chapter 11.

DISTRIBUTION

Scheduled carriers rely heavily on travel agents, including business travel agents, for distribution. Tour operators are sometimes also involved in this. Airline consolidators are also used. Charter airlines rely heavily on tour operators and leisure travel agents as well as seat-only operators for distribution. Indeed, seat only companies have become a main distribution channel for the airlines. Chapters 1 to 3 cover these distribution channels. The bucket shops that used to be associated with the distribution of air seats are no longer involved. Direct selling has however grown phenomenally in recent years and looks set to continue to do so.

In comparison with most industries, the airline industry has had high distribution costs. This is especially interesting given that there is no physical product to move. Costs include those listed opposite:

- in-house reservations staff;
- reservations fees for GDS;

- travel agents' commissions; and
- production/processing of paper tickets.

Airlines are constantly seeking to reduce these distribution costs. The low cost carriers have shown some success in this regard. Activities adopted by the airline industry in order to try to reduce airline distribution costs include the following:

- more direct sales (via the Internet for example);
- the introduction of ticketless travel; and
- reductions to travel agency commissions.

The last of these, reductions to travel agency commission levels, was portrayed as an emotive topic in the trade press at the turn of the century. As some of the major carriers reduced commission levels, others followed their lead prompting some travel agents in some cases to avoid booking those carriers where possible. Some low cost carriers avoid using travel agents as a method of distribution altogether.

Methods which take advantage of the new and emerging technologies such as the Internet and interactive TV are especially topical at the start of the third millennium. Chapter 4 discusses these developments in more detail whilst the use of CRS in airline distribution is considered below as this has been a main outcome of deregulation and is a feature of the greatly changed industry. Airline distribution is essentially being revolutionized and restructured by the Internet. Low cost airlines are equally breaking up the pattern of selling airline tickets. Finally there have been predictions that, as ticketless travel takes hold, the days of the paper ticket are numbered.

The remainder of this chapter examines charter airlines in more detail. This is intended to complement the discussion of tour operators and packaged tourism in Chapters 1 and 2.

THE CHARTER AIRLINE INDUSTRY

The origins of the charter airline industry lie in post-Second World War Europe. Servicemen, sent overseas during the war, developed a desire to return overseas. Added to this desire was a plentiful availability of aircraft developed for the war which was available to purchase at reasonable cost. Indeed, Laws (1997) describes the first AIT as having taken place when Vladimir Raitz flew seventeen people to Corsica in a war surplus Dakota accommodating them in old army tents. Package holidays are discussed more fully in Chapter 2.

The continued development of aircraft technology led to larger and faster planes and so to increased passenger numbers and reduced air fares. As newer and better versions became available, redundant aircraft became available cheaply in the second-hand market. The charter airlines developed, maximizing passenger seat numbers, reducing travel costs and increasing the market for overseas holidays. All of this had the effect of creating a highly competitive market.

Worldwide only 10 per cent of passenger air travel is provided by charter flights although this figure increases in areas with a well-developed package holiday industry such as Europe.

Laws (1997) provides a useful figure describing the different types of charter flight arrangement as shown in Figure 9.13.

Type of charter	Key features
Whole charter	A contract to hire the entire capacity of an aircraft
Part (or split) charter	A contract in which several tour operators share one flight individually contracted to the airline
Ad hoc charter	An arrangement for a single rotation
Series charter	A contract for a regular sequence of flights
Time charter	A contract for the exclusive use of an aircraft throughout a season

Figure 9.13. Different types of charter arrangement. *Source*: Laws (1997) based on Medlik (1993) and Wheatcroft (1994).

Charter airlines are used to deploying aircraft for seasonal demand perhaps through fleet relocation to areas with more business in, say, winter. Most of the summer capacity on Britannia Airways is accounted for by Thomson tour operations whereas in winter some of the capacity is chartered by ski operators according to Key Note (1999). Using flight series charters enables tour operators to reduce costs and fill their aircraft by transporting clients who are going to different resorts or accommodation but in a similar location in the same aircraft. This back-to-back system takes one group of holidaymakers to a resort and returns with another group who have finished their holiday. Empty legs occur at both the beginning and end of season when the first return flight and the last outbound flight are empty.

The largest charter airlines (by the number of seats available) are provided in Figure 9.14 together with their tour operator owner.

Major charter airlines in the UK include Britannia Airways, Airtours International Airways, Monarch Airlines, Air 2000, Caledonian Airways, Leisure International and Flying Colours. These charter airlines are also capitalizing on the seat-only market for air travel.

Britannia Airways, part of the Thomson Travel Group, is the UK's leading charter airline and provides an interesting illustration of a charter airline striving to maintain high levels of fleet utilization. This Britannia achieves by balancing subcontracting

Largest Charter Airlines (by seats available)	Tour Operator
Britannia	Thomson
Monarch	Cosmos
Airtours	Airtours
Air 2000	First Choice
Caledonian Airways*	Carlson

Note: * Caledonian Airways, together with Flying Colours, are now known as JMC Airlines part of Thomas Cook's new mainstream holiday brand, JMC

Figure 9.14. The largest charter airlines in the UK. *Source*: based on Mintel (1998).

and chartering. For example Britannia contracted three TransAer aircraft using Britannia's livery, uniform and in-flight service levels in summer 1998. An example of the opposite whereby spare capacity is chartered to others was given above. The accounts for Thomson Travel Group show that Britannia Airways contributes around 45 per cent of sales and the inclusive tours, 55 per cent. Britannia Airways has, with 29 aircraft, a 27 per cent share of seats sold on charter flights out of the UK. Over a quarter of flights sold are long haul and about 10 per cent of Britannia's seats are sold to third parties such as other tour operators (Mintel, 1998).

The charter airline sector is extremely concentrated with the top five charter airlines controlling 85 per cent of the outbound market in 1997 (Key Note, 1997). Significantly the sector also displays high barriers to entry.

Relationships to tour operators

As seen above, almost all major charter airlines are owned by leading AIT operators. A notable exception to this is identified by Key Note (1999) as Monarch. This vertical integration between tour operators and charter airlines is discussed in Chapter 5. The picture is not quite as simple as it may appear however as not all tour operators own a charter airline and so many have to contract for capacity to meet their demand for holidays. At the same time, integrated charter airlines may only utilize a proportion of their capacity for their parent tour operator's business. Laws (1997) informs that Air 2000 provides only 65–70 per cent of its seats to First Choice. In this case, tour operators themselves act as clients. Typically, the specialist operators will contract for their requirements early on as will the major operators who often launch their brochures, with full costings, ahead of the competition, aiming to offer convenient departure dates and times. Other tour operators may contract their capacity in response to actual demand. A tour operator requiring more certainty in their flight arrangements may have to weigh this against the charter rate they will pay.

Major tour operators are in general opposed to using one another's charter carriers partly as a consequence of the highly competitive nature of the industry. It may however be that a consolidator – a middleman involved in the sale of spare capacity on behalf of the airlines – undertakes to negotiate such a situation. The role of consolidators and air brokers is discussed in the context of the distribution of travel and tourism products in Chapter 3.

One of the longest-established UK charter carriers, Britannia Airways Ltd is the in-house charter airline of Thomson Group. The group provides a good example of vertical integration within the UK travel industry as it also owns the travel agency chain, Lunn Poly. Originally operating under the name Euravia Limited the airline was established in 1962. More recently, Britannia has modernized its fleet and has won the *Travel Trade Gazette* 'Top Charter Airline' award several times.

Figure 9.15. Britannia Airways Ltd. *Source*: adapted from Key Note (1997).

The second largest charter airline in the UK is now JMC Airlines, the in-house charter carrier of Thomas Cook's new mainstream holiday brand, JMC. The airline is discussed in further detail in Figure 9.16.

The former Caledonian and Flying Colours fleet were given a new brand identity in September 1999 giving it the same 'personality' as its sister company, JMC Holidays Ltd. This aimed to create a seamless link between the company's tour operating and airline divisions. It was confirmed, at the launch, that four Boeing 757s would be leased, representing an investment of £100 million over the next five years, replacing the decommissioned L1011s with a younger and more modern fleet. This provides greater flexibility, reliability and an increase in utilization all of which are important aspects of charter airline operations. Recognizing the important role of the air transport component of a package holiday to travellers' overall enjoyment, the airline aims to maintain their reputation as a punctual airline, improve in-flight service and offer pre-allocated seats to all JMC customers. The fleet itself underwent an extensive refurbishment programme throughout the winter converting aircraft to fly the new JMC livery. New uniforms for flight and cabin crew were also introduced and check-in desks at UK departure airports were dramatically branded to strengthen the bond between the two companies.

Figure 9.16. JMC Airlines. *Source*: Thomas Cook and JGPR (2000).

Having discussed the nature of contracting for charter airline capacity it is now worth mentioning the details of the charter contract itself. This document lays out the necessary information in relation to the parties to the agreement as well as the agreed terms of the contract such as the number of aircraft and relevant seating configurations, fees, fuel, catering and suchlike. This can help to clarify the legal position in the event of a problem and helps both parties to understand their position.

Charter airlines can be seen to have low priority in the allocation of slots at airports for the reasons outlined earlier in this chapter. A final important aspect of the operation of charter airlines is that of pricing. Figure 9.17 summarizes some factors of influence in respect of this.

Exchange rates

ABTA has traditionally used an agreed date for tour operator costings such as currency exchange rates, which forms the basis for charter pricing. Tour operators will also need to build into their pricing strategy the requirement to account for the following

Empty legs
The first homeward flight and last outbound flight of the season for example cannot be part of a charter rotation.

Reduced load factors
An allowance is usually made for the fact that any flight is likely to be less than full.

Flight-time reductions
Reductions are usually made for both mid-week and night flights.

Passenger taxes
Taxes levied by authorities are passed on to tour operators and are usually invoiced to passengers.

Figure 9.17.   Tour operators and the costs of charter flights.

SUMMARY

This chapter introduced the framework within which international aviation takes place. Having discussed the background to international aviation, the chapter then moved on to examine the freedoms of the sky, bilateral agreements, slot allocations and the processes of deregulation and liberalization. Network design was then introduced followed by consideration of the role and function of the many associations and regulatory bodies that are involved with the air transport sector. Finally, there was a discussion of the differences between scheduled and charter airlines including extended consideration of charter airlines. Each of these topics provide essential background to the concepts discussed in Chapters 10 and 11.

DISCUSSION QUESTIONS

1. Discuss the extent to which you agree with the view that the airline industry is characterized by layers of complexity.
2. Compare and contrast the processes of deregulation in the USA and liberalization in Europe.
3. Examine differences between scheduled and charter airlines. Is the differentiation between the two lessening and if so, why?

REFERENCES

Civil Aviation Authority (1998) *The Single European Aviation Market: the first five years*, CAP 685.
Davidson, R. (1994) *Business Travel*, Pitman Publishing.
Dennis, N. (1999) *Low Cost Carriers and Scheduled A Airline Operations*, Operations, Aviation and Tourism: Developing the Travel Inter-relationships, University of Westminster, 25–27 January, Unpublished Conference Proceedings.
Hanlon, P. (1999) *Global Airlines – competition in a transnational industry* (2nd edn), Butterworth Heinemann.
Holloway, J.C. (1995) *The Business of Tourism*, Pitman.
Holloway, S. (1997), *Straight and Level: practical airline economics*, Ashgate.
Inkpen, G. (1998) *Information Technology for Travel and Tourism* (2nd edn), Longman.
Key Note Ltd. (1997) *Airlines*.
Key Note Ltd. (1999) *UK Travel and Tourism*.
Laws, E. (1997) *Managing Packaged Tourism – relationships, responsibilities and service quality in the inclusive holiday industry*, International Thomson Business Press.
Medlik, S. (1993) *Dictionary of Transport, Travel and Hospitality*, Butterworth-Heinemann.
Pender, L.J. and Baum, T.G. (2000) Have the frills really left the European airline industry?, *International Journal of Tourism Research*, 2, 423–36.
Renshaw, M.B. (1997) *The Travel Agent*, Business Education Publishers Ltd.
Vellas, F. and Becherel, L. (1995) *International Tourism*, Macmillan Business.
Wheatcroft, S. (1994) *Aviation and Tourism Policies*, Routledge.
Wheatcroft, S. and Lipman, G. (1986) *Air Transport in a Competitive European Market*, EIU.

CHAPTER 10

The Scheduled Airline Industry: An Overview

INTRODUCTION

Having considered the background to air transportation including bilateral agreements, deregulation and liberalization, and the difference between scheduled and charter carriers, we now go on to look at scheduled air transport in more depth. This chapter considers the structure of the industry, the traditional national flag carriers, privatization, airline pricing and yield management and frequent flyer programmes.

BACKGROUND

The airline industry has long been viewed as an important one by countries and their governments. This stems in part from the external benefits that a national airline can offer. These potential benefits are summarized in Figure 10.1. The majority of international airlines used to be wholly, or at least to a large extent, owned by governments. This was not however true of the US carriers nor indeed a handful of others. Air transport can be seen below to be limited by the the concept of 'sovereignty of the sky.' Indeed, Wheatcroft and Lipman (1986) describe aviation as having close links with sovereignty, airspace and defence. This relates to the political complexity of international aviation. Government control and regulation of air transport was discussed in Chapter 9.

- Source of foreign exchange
- Trade/foreign investment opportunities (created by improved access for example)
- Symbol of prestige (i.e. flag carriers)
- Stimulation of tourism development
- Support of home aerospace industry
- Guaranteed availability of stand-by fleet of trained crew in the event of an emergency

Figure 10.1. Possible external benefits of national airlines. *Source*: based on Hanlon (1999).

THE STRUCTURE OF THE INDUSTRY

There are, according to Hanlon (1999), around 1200 scheduled airlines worldwide with approximately one-third of these operating on international routes. These airlines vary greatly in size and scope of operation. Table 10.1 shows the top 50 passenger airlines in 1997 ranked by sales. The US industry is the largest in the world by a considerable amount. This stems from the size of the domestic air transport market particularly in comparison to smaller countries such as the UK.

Table 10.1. The top 50 airlines in 1997 ranked by sales. *Source:* Hanlon (1999) compiled from International Air Transport Association and World Airline Directory, *Flight International* (18–24 March, 25–31 March and 1–7 April 1998).

		Sales (US$ millions)	Passengers (millions)	Employees (number)
1	American	18,570	81.00	111,500
2	United	17,378	84.20	91,779
3	British Airways°	14,184	40.96	60,575
4	Delta	13,590	101.15	63,441
5	Lufthansa	13,354	44.40	58,204
6	Northwest	10,226	54.70	50,000
7	Air France°	10,185	33.50	46,348
8	Japan Airlines°	9936	31.36	18,127
9	All Nippon°	8798	40.83	15,200
10	US Airways	8514	58.70	40,246
11	Swissair	7356	10.80	16,833
12	Continental	7213	40.00	40,000
13	KLM°	6688	14.73	26,811

14	Qantas[b]	6131	18.61	30,080
15	SAS	5097	20.80	20,500
16	Alitalia	5085	24.55	18,676
17	SIA[a]	4992	12.00	28,196
18	Air Canada	4024	14.00	21,215
19	Cathay Pacific	3958	10.02	15,747
20	Southwest	3817	50.40	23,974
21	Iberia	3562	16.07	20,000
22	TWA	3328	23.39	25,000
23	Varig	3151	10.65	18,203
24	Thai Airways International[c]	3120	14.38	24,186
25	Korean	3029	25.58	17,139
26	Japan Air System[a]	2651	19.13	6094
27	Ansett Australia[b]	2538	11.52	17,067
28	LTU International Airways[d]	2349	7.20	5159
29	CAIL	2221	8.60	14,233
30	Air New Zealand	2031	6.63	9340
31	Sabena	2012	6.87	9500
32	American West	1875	18.33	9615
33	Alaska Airlines	1863	12.25	6477
34	China Airlines	1740	7.40	8490
35	Malaysia Airlines[a]	1731	15.66	2354
36	Vasp	1667	4.57	7156
37	Austrian	1597	3.94	4149
38	Garuda	1571	6.69	13,727
39	China Southern	1541	15.24	7820
40	Finnair[a]	1445	6.86	10,780
41	Aeroflot RIA	1399	3.90	15,000
42	South African Airways[a]	1393	5.10	10,612
43	THY Turkish Airlines	1347	10.30	8958
44	EVA Air	1292	4.16	5800
45	El Al	1220	2.90	3407
46	Philippine Airlines[e]	1181	7.31	13,587
47	TAP Air Portugal	1155	4.40	8000
48	Aeromexico	1125	7.52	5516
49	Emirates	1114	3.68	4978
50	Virgin Atlantic[a]	1075	2.81	6400

Key: [a] Year to 31 March 1998   [d] Year to 31 October 1997
       [b] Year to 30 June 1997   [e] Year to 31 March 1997
       [c] Year to 30 September 1997

The scheduled air transport industry consists of both major airlines and smaller niche players. The major airlines are in many cases resolved to become key forces in future aviation markets. There also exist a variety of niche players targeting a more limited market with a more limited product.

NATIONAL FLAG CARRIERS

The development of the scheduled industry in some countries by state owned airlines often led to the following:

- airlines acting more or less as an arm of government;
- airlines having to meet objectives that take precedence over efficiency and profit;
- a requirement to 'fly the flag';
- a requirement to operate routes that were desired for social reasons; and
- a requirement to support local aircraft suppliers.

These national airlines, traditionally associated with particular countries, were considered to be of enormous strategic importance (see Figure 10.1) and so the industry experienced a great deal of government intervention. Nationalized airlines predominated in Europe in the early days of air travel. The existence of routes between city pairs dominated by the two national carriers of the the two countries at either end of the route has already been described in Chapter 9.

PRIVATIZATION

The situation, described above, whereby national airlines predominated, is now changing as airlines are increasingly moving into private ownership. The entire framework in which airlines operate is therefore changing. This is partly a result of many governments' policies of reduced public sector involvement. Vellas and Becherel (1995) describe the objective behind these privatization strategies as being to implement market concentration plans and diversification programmes as well as to open up to international competition. Deregulation has also played a part in that the development of merger and alliance activities are not always compatible with the public service role of airlines. Privatization strategies can help carriers to become more competitive. Most European airlines are now in private ownership or are progressing along the road to either total or at least partial privatization.

British Airways (BA), which was privatized in 1987, is an early example of total privatization and one that has been well documented (Morrell, 1997; Vellas and

Becherel, 1995). BA had to undergo substantial change prior to privatization and this resulted in a greatly streamlined airline. It took seven years for the process to be completed however as the company had financial problems that needed to be addressed prior to privatization. The entire UK airline industry has now been privatized. The UK's charter airlines always had been in private ownership.

Privatization can occur in a variety of different ways. Morrell (1997) describes the following processes of privatization, providing detailed examples of each method.

1. Sale of a minority government stake to the private sector as happened with Finnair
2. Sale of a majority in a number of stages as happened with Lufthansa
3. Sale of a majority in one stage as happened with Kenya Airways
4. The outright sale of a 100 per cent government shareholding as happened with British Airways.

Figure 10.2. Processes of privatization. *Source*: based on Morrell (1997).

Liberalization had highlighted attention on the effect that state aid could potentially have on competition. Prior to this, bilateral and other restrictions to cooperation often masked the effects of subsidies somewhat.

FLYING AT HALF MAST

Despite the privatization policies described above, the legacy of the national carriers is still apparent today in many countries. The public sector has often retained a substantial equity in a country's airline company. This can be as much as 50 per cent. Even where there has been a total privatization, normally 50 per cent of the equity has to come from citizens of the airline's home country. According to Vellas and Becherel (1995), it is the evaluation and also the economic and political objectives of the country which will determine if the privatization is to be complete or partial. The different privatization programmes are subject to different legal and political traditions. The subsidized state carriers can however lack competitive edge as well as which they can be slow to innovate. Carriers which previously benefited from more protectionist regulatory conditions feel threatened when this is removed.

It is not merely the privatization policies being implemented by airlines that are affecting a change to the identity of airlines but also the merger and alliance activities that have swept across the industry. These are discussed in the following chapter.

A further area of significant change in the industry is that of pricing.

PRICING OF AIR TRAVEL

The pricing of air travel, once a highly regulated business, now strikes many consumers as a complex and ever-changing area. Influences on price include those presented in Figure 10.3.

- The date of travel (peak/off-peak)
- The length of stay (will it exceed a certain length/include a Saturday night?)
- The class of travel (first/business/economy)
- The size of travelling group
- The age of the traveller (adult/child)
- The route (demand levels/supply/length of journey)
- The purchase point (method of distribution)

Figure 10.3. Influences on the price of air travel. *Source*: based on Hanlon (1999).

The complexity of this area is helped by the fact that airlines have numerous fare categories for some routes. Indeed, Holloway (1997) describes some airlines as applying 30 or more different fare categories on any one flight. He further describes individual airlines in the deregulated environment of the USA as being capable of thousands of price changes daily. This can obviously lead to substantial differences in the fares that people on the same flight are paying. In addition to these differences on the same flight, there are regional differences in the price of air travel. For example, there are differences between North American and European air fares. Even within Europe there are differences on routes between some city pairs as some will be more competitive than others. Hanlon (1999) makes reference to 'high-fare' and 'low-fare' cities. There are some factors that certain consumer groups are willing to pay more for and these include prestige and flexibility.

Classes of travel

It is usual for scheduled carriers, other than low cost carriers, to offer different classes of travel. Typically these are first or business class and economy. Class of travel used to be defined by regulatory authorities but this is now normally defined by the airline as indicated, to an extent, by the fare category.

Price discrimination

Hanlon (1999, p. 186) describes discriminatory pricing in the context of economic theory as being held to take place in the following circumstances:

when a producer charges different prices for different units of the same commodity, for reasons not associated with differences in the costs of supply. It occurs where price differentials do not directly correspond to differentials in cost.

Hanlon therefore concludes that both peak/off-peak pricing and differentials and discounts for quantity purchases do not represent discretionary pricing on the following basis:

1. Peak/off-peak price differences reflect additional capacity costs of catering for peak demand.
2. Quantity discounts reflect economies of bulk sales.

Price discrimination can occur in two different scenarios. First, where prices charged are uniform yet costs differ significantly and second where differential prices are charged yet costs are the same. Hanlon (1999) discusses the operation, competitiveness and desirability of discriminatory pricing in detail.

Airlines have researched the price that different market segments are willing to pay and found price elasticity to vary with wealthy business travellers unsurprisingly less price elastic than leisure travellers. Market segmentation by purpose of travel has therefore resulted in the industry. Space allocation and average load factors influence market segmentation by purpose of travel. Restrictions placed on certain fare categories are therefore often intended to prevent customers 'trading down' from more expensive fares as this could dilute the revenue the airline achieves. Computer reservation systems (CRS) are useful in helping with seat allocations to maximize profits. This idea of 'charging according to willingness to pay' has attracted criticism for obvious reasons as it can be seen to be unfair. Counter-arguments however include that certain services could not operate under a system of uniform pricing and that differential pricing has long been accepted on the basis of age across a variety of product types. Clearly this is an area in which universal agreement seems unlikely to emerge in the short term.

Another controversial aspect concerning the pricing of air travel and one which has attracted attention is the use of predatory pricing.

Predatory pricing

Holloway (1997, p. 402), defines predatory pricing in the following way:

tactical pricing, by a dominant carrier, at low levels which are either below cost or substantially lower than what the market will bear.

He further describes the intent of such actions as frequently being to drive competitors from the market and presumably to create opportunities for prices to be raised again thereafter and supernormal profits to be earned. Alternatively, this may have the objective of deterring market entry through demonstration that prospective profitability would be limited by less revenues than might otherwise be expected from these segments (technically this would amount to what is known as 'limit pricing').

Predatory pricing can force all of the carriers operating a route into a loss making situation. A dominant carrier, even by just offering a restricted number of low cost seats, could deter new entrants or the expansion of existing competitors.

The use of predatory pricing is however extremely difficult to prove. Whilst allegations of predatory pricing have been made in the industry, formal inquiries into this have been less common. One example of a case based on alleged predatory pricing occurred when easyJet made a complaint in 1996 that KLM was abusing its dominant position in the air transport market between Amsterdam and London. easyJet claimed KLM had reduced its lowest fares to less than that of easyJet when the latter entered the route. The complaint was withdrawn in 1997 on the grounds that KLM had stopped its alleged anti-competitive behaviour. This case had, however, gone further than any other predatory pricing case brought before the commission (CAA, 1998). It is not only predatory pricing that has been an issue as the highly public case brought by Virgin against British Airways highlighted. This case was concerned with allegations of specific non-price predatory behaviour. In general terms, Holloway (1997) provides the following examples of non-price predatory behaviour.

- Manipulation of CRS displays
- Domination of slots at congested airports
- 'Swamping' a route with additional frequencies (overscheduling)
- 'Sandwiching' or 'bracketing' a low-frequency competitor's departures
- Scheduling arrivals away from a competitor's connections
- Refusal to interline
- Imposing discriminatory conditions on access to ground services (e.g. passenger-handling or ramp maintenance support)

Figure 10.4. Indicative non-price predatory behaviour in the airline industry. *Source*: based on Holloway (1997).

Linked to the issue of pricing of air travel is that of yield management.

YIELD MANAGEMENT

According to Holloway (1997, p. 133), yield management essentially involves

> the controlled release of scheduled output from inventory. Its earliest manifestations were simple 'space control' and overbooking, but more sophisticated systems now use statistical techniques to forecast sales probabilities based on current booking profiles as a guide to the release of inventory on any given flight and the price at which it should be released.

Holloway further describes yield management as using discriminatory pricing for the following two reasons:

1. To accommodate the innate perishability of the airline product.
2. To exploit price elasticities of different market segments to generate more revenue from a given level of output.

There are however differences between yield management and price discrimination basically accounted for by the fact that yield management makes constant adjustments to the availability of seats at different prices.

Holloway believes CRS to be invaluable tools for this type of inventory control in addition to their communication and distribution functions. Some airlines apply 30 or more fare categories on any one flight to manage yield and without CRS this would be very difficult to manage. CRS offer real-time inventory management and pricing flexibility. This helps to maximize revenue from the various fare classes and booking categories on different flights. The complex fare structures that have developed following deregulation and liberalization as well as from hub and spoke networks require this. CRS are discussed more fully in Chapters 4 and 11. Holloway (1997) examines yield management in detail.

MARKETING INITIATIVES

The range of marketing initiatives employed by the airline industry are too numerous to detail in a text of this nature. There is however room to mention some of the initiatives to dominate the industry and those which have effected change in the industry operating environment. Specifically, frequent flyer programmes are seen to fall into this category.

Frequent flyer programmes

The creation of customer loyalty is for airlines, in common with many service organizations, a goal that requires constant attention. Customer loyalty programmes have therefore become an important marketing tool for airlines. Their use has however attracted a great deal of criticism as highlighted by the discussion below.

Frequent Flyer Programmes (FFPs) act as incentives to consumers to purchase air travel from a particular airline or a member airline of a particular group of carriers. They encourage loyalty in that travellers receive credits or mileage points for accumulation. Once a certain threshold has been reached these credits can be exchanged for rewards. Eligibility and rewards vary from programme to programme not only leading to complexity but also making comparability difficult. Typical rewards are outlined in Figure 10.5. The concept of FFPs initially was that passengers purchasing a ticket were entitled to extra free travel according to the number of miles flown. This is now only one of a variety of ways in which FFPs are operated. Points can be accumulated for credit card purchases, hotel stays, the purchase of petrol, telephone calls and the use of hire cars to name just a few.

> - Free flights/tickets
> - Free companion tickets
> - Upgrade to business/first class
> - Non-travel rewards

Figure 10.5. Typical frequent flyer programme rewards.

American Airlines launched the first FFP in 1981 taking advantage of the ability to offer free flights as a promotional tool to result from deregulation in 1978. The popularity of this venture encouraged similar programmes to be introduced in the USA particularly as some carriers felt threatened that the US airlines would have a competitive advantage as a result of running these programmes. Liberalization in Europe paved the way for European carriers, led by British Airways, to develop similar schemes in the 1990s. Prior to this, these schemes would not have been allowed to operate. BA's scheme, in common with some others, enables consumers of purchases other than air travel to earn awards. Most major airlines now have an FFP of their own or are members of a collaborative scheme. Access to a scheme can be seen to be an important aspect of an airline's marketing effort with approximately 80 schemes worldwide and a total membership of around 120 million. Some frequent travellers are members of a number of different schemes.

A number of issues surround the use, by airlines, of FFPs. Whilst introduced to offer additional benefits to travellers, the value of the programmes is reduced by the fact that so many programmes are in existence today. Some of the problems to result from their use influence the organizations implementing them whilst some have an effect on other airlines.

Loss of differential advantage
The existance and similarity of so many programmes has led to a dilution of the advantages of operating a scheme

Anti-competitive behaviour
FFPs can be used by airlines in an anti-competitive manner

Higher fares
FFPs could lead to higher fares being charged by dominant airlines than others to/from hubs

Increased switching costs
FFPs can act to increase the costs of switching from one airline to another

Entry barriers
FFPs can erect entry barriers in domestic markets by creating artificial linkages between different services so they deter entry. This they do by creating a need for airlines to establish from the outset a network of a certain size or link an FFP to those of other carriers

Unnecessary travel
Unnecessary travel is sometimes undertaken/more circuitous routes selected by employees in order to achieve more points. This can lead to a corporate backlash as described below.

Corporate backlash
A corporate backlash has been described as FFPs can be seen as a way of circumventing company travel policies. Some business managers believe points should be poured into a collective company pot instead of benefiting the individual. Some employees reject fare-saving opportunities in their quest for extra mileage points. Some companies have displayed hostility towards programmes which reward their employees especially as these can lead to distortion of company travel policy guidelines

Under-the-counter dealings
Under-the-counter dealings in free tickets including attempts to sell them on have occurred. In the USA frequent flyers have cheated by getting friends to fly under their names to boost their points

Negative effects on profits
FFPs can lead to increased costs for the airlines operating them especially where they employ indiscriminate use of rewards (not blacking out periods such as popular times for example)

Low redemption and future uptake
Unredeemed miles carry a heavy liability for airlines

Low cost carriers
The emergence of low cost carriers in Europe has attracted some business traffic that previously valued frequent flyer points as important.

Figure 10.6. Problems encountered with the use of FFPs. *Source*: based on Gilbert (1996), Bray (1996) and Hanlon (1999).

Some critics believe that these schemes act against the interests of the smaller carriers. These carriers have however often attempted to overcome the disadvantages posed by their smaller networks through partnership with other airlines' FFPs. An example of this is the linking of Braathens Safe's FFP with that of KLM. The use of FFPs has not, to date, given rise to any formal proposals for regulatory intervention. The regulatory authorities in Germany did however act against Lufthansa's 'Miles and More' scheme.

The popularity of FFPs is phenomenal with many travellers belonging to a number of schemes. Business travellers in particular are greatly influenced by the availability of FFPs and so it is difficult to imagine airlines being easily able to replace these with some other marketing initiative in the short-term at least.

It may be that the FFPs of the future are very different from those used in the industry today. Further exploitation of the databases that FFPs provide seems likely providing lists of potential consumers for late sales of cut price services. It may be that FFPs develop into a club-like format.

TECHNOLOGICAL DEVELOPMENTS

Technological developments have led to significant advances in the airline industry. These have been especially evident in terms of the aircraft themselves and their distribution systems. Developments in relation to the aircraft are mainly considered to be outside the scope of this text. It is worth mentioning however that technological improvements have led to change in terms of the economics of aircraft utilization.

Other than in aircraft design, it is in the area of airline distribution, reservations and ticketing that technological development has had most impact. The first significant development was the introduction of videotext to travel agents in the 1970s, enabling airlines to sell their seats without having to provide a telephone sales team as agents could now be 'hard-wired' to the airline. Computerized reservations systems (CRS) then appeared in the 1980s when American Airlines introduced a system designed to help control the carrier's inventory. This was something that airlines found problematic in the aftermath of deregulation with the proliferation of routes and fares that were on offer. Most reservations systems are now computerized and can carry out a number of functions including those listed in Figure 10.7.

> - Provide information on schedules, tariffs, space availability
> - Enable reservations to be made
> - Facilitate ticket and boarding pass insurance
>
> *Note*: This description excludes information-only systems.

Figure 10.7. CRS functions. *Source*: based on Holloway (1997).

There are many clear advantages of these systems for their airline owners and these are outlined in Figure 10.8.

Revenue generation	Fixed access fees for example for participating airlines, booking fees for carriers, enhancement fees (for ancillary services) etc
Incremental revenue	The so-called 'halo effect' whereby agents tend to book more passengers on an airline owning their CRS than would otherwise be expected.
Control/analysis of information	
Monitoring of agents' use of the CRS	

Figure 10.8. The advantages of CRS for their owners. *Source*: based on Holloway (1997).

The sales potential of CRS and their administrative applications were both quickly realized following their introduction. More recently it has been their ability to meet the requirements of travellers on a global basis that has been important as they have turned into global distribution systems (GDS). CRS have developed greatly in the last two decades and have now expanded into a major distribution channel used not only for the sale of air seats but also for travel related products such as hotels and car hire. A fight for domination has been described as CRS are driven by the possibility that only one system will ultimately dominate the global travel market. There are at present four major players in the market and further consolidation is likely.

By the mid-1980s, the US based CRS, notably American Airlines Sabre system, were moving into Europe and European carriers, concerned at the possibility of losing ticketing and distribution possibilities in their home market developed their own CRS which later split into the well-known systems, Galileo and Amadeus. In the Far East Abacus was developed. Taken together all of the CRS have had a market effect on the competitive structure of travel distribution.

Despite the advantages of these systems for their owners, as introduced above, criticisms have been levelled at CRS for a number of reasons including the fact that the fees charged often do not distinguish between the length of journey booked or the type of ticket. A number of the problems associated with the use of CRS are outlined in Figure 10.9. Various codes of conduct have been formed to address some of the concerns that have been put forward. Holloway (1997) provides summaries of both the US CRS rules and the CRS regulations in the EU together with coverage of other relevant CRS codes of conduct.

Display bias

CRS can be programmed to give host airlines' flights superior positioning

Halo effects

Even without superior positioning there is a tendency for travel agents to book on the CRS of the parent airlines as opposed to those of their competitors

Code-sharing

Code-sharing between major and niche carriers and linkages between their flight schedules can give smaller carriers advantageous displays. The larger carriers obtain increased market penetration at the same time.

Commission over-rides

Travel agents can receive additional commission for the sale of a particular carrier's seats as inventoried by their CRS.

Marketing intelligence

CRS enable trends to be monitored and the resultant information could be used to commercial advantage

---

Figure 10.9. Problems associated with CRS. *Source*: adapted from Travel and Tourism Analyst (1994).

More recently it is the Internet that has attracted attention for its potential to become a main aspect of airlines' distribution policies. This and further existing and emerging technologies suited to the distribution of airline seats are discussed more fully in Chapter 4.

SUMMARY

Following on from the introduction to air transport in Chapter 9, this chapter attempted to describe the structure of the scheduled air transport industry discussing factors such as the tradition of national airlines in some parts of the world and the process of privatization. Clearly deregulation and liberalization have led to a variety of developments within the air transport sector. Amongst those considered in this chapter was pricing. Discriminatory and predatory pricing both received attention. This was followed by an examination of two further significant developments – CRS and FFPs – both of which helped to shape air travellers' expectations by the end of the twentieth century.

DISCUSSION QUESTIONS

1. Examine reasons for variations in air fares.
2. Why might a number of airlines be described as 'flying at half mast?'
3. Critically evaluate the use, by airlines, of frequent flyer programmes.

REFERENCES

Bray, R. (1996) Frequent flyers' bonanza, *Financial Times*, 7 October.
CAA (1998) *The Single European Aviation Market: the first five years*, CAP 685, Westward Digital Ltd.
Davidson, R. (1994) *Business Travel*, Pitman Publishing.
Hanlon, P. (1999) *Global Airlines – competition in a transnational industry* (2nd edn), Butterworth Heinemann.
Holloway, S. (1997) *Straight and Level: practical airline economics*, Ashgate Publishing Ltd.
Key Note Ltd. (1997) *Airlines*.
Key Note Ltd. (1999) *UK Travel and Tourism*.
Morell, P. (1997) *Airline Finance*, Ashgate Publishing Ltd.
Travel and Tourism Analyst (1994) No. 4, Economist Intelligence Unit.
Vellas, F. and Becherel, L. (1995) *International Tourism*, Macmillan Business.
Wheatcroft, S. and Lipman, G. (1986) Air transport in a competitive European market: problems, prospects and strategies, *Travel and Tourism Report* No.3, EIU.
Wheatcroft, S. and Lipman, G. (1990) European liberalization and World air transport: towards a transnational industry, *Special Report* No. 2015, EIU.

CHAPTER 11

The Scheduled Airline Industry: Partnership and Globalization

INTRODUCTION

The hub and spoke network design introduced in Chapter 9 creates opportunities for code-sharing and relationships which require code-sharing as their basis such as franchising. Code-sharing is a commercial agreement between two airlines under which an airline operating a service allows another to offer it to the public using its own flight designator code even though it does not actually operate the service. This chapter discusses the relationships that stem from these arrangements in detail. Mergers, alliances, global groupings and franchising are all considered in turn. The emergence of competing groupings of airlines is a significant aspect of the industry and so is worthy of attention. Consolidation is now occurring within the many strategic alliances across the international industry.

BACKGROUND

Prior to discussion of mergers and alliances in the international airline industry it is worthwhile examining barriers to organic growth. A main reason for airlines choosing not to expand in this way is the problem of capacity constraints at major airports. This has prevented airlines from entering the European market to offer intra-European services. It has also prevented other airlines operating these routes from expanding their services. Airports including London's Heathrow and Gatwick, Madrid, Zurich, Frankfurt and Brussels are fully or nearly fully subscribed over most of the operating day according to the CAA (1998). Regulatory constraints also prevented airlines from operating routes they might otherwise choose to serve.

These are discussed in Chapter 9. Airlines have therefore looked towards partnership agreements as a method of expanding their marketable networks as well as to meet other needs which are discussed below. Bennett (1996, p. 214) exemplifies the variety of partnership that 'range from the formal to the informal and the tactical to the strategic'.

She goes on to argue that there is no universally agreed definition of a strategic alliance, adopting the following for the purposes of the paper:

> a relationship between two or more organisations which is based on a foundation of common goals and objectives and entered into to fulfil strategic ambitions which may or may not be mutual.

MERGERS AND ALLIANCES

The formation of mergers and alliances has been one of the defining characteristics of the air transport sector in the post-deregulation era. The industry has experienced a great deal of jockeying for position, some of which continues today. This activity has sometimes been misguided as airlines compete for partners for no better reason than the competition is doing so and they do not wish to be left behind. At other times this has been a carefully executed part of a well defined strategy.

Alliances

The business strategy of airline alliance formation is, according to French (1997), now a defining characteristic of the global air transport sector. The evidence of this fact can be found worldwide. Strategic alliance formation is as much in evidence in the airline sector as in any commercial sphere. When two or more airlines come together and pull their resources an airline alliance is formed. There are clear motivations for strategic airline alliance formation. These relationships can have the advantages shown in Figure 11.1.

- Increased market reach (including access to new markets via partner airlines and bypassing bilateral restrictions)*
- Cost control
- More efficient supply of capacity
- Traffic feed
- Economies of marketing

- Technical advantages
- Shared CRSs

Note: * as discussed in Chapter 9.

Figure 11.1. Advantages of airline alliances for airlines. *Source*: based on French (1997) and Hanlon (1999).

In addition to the above advantages of alliances, motivations for mergers came from the reasons shown in Figure 11.2.

Economies of scale and learning
- Access to benefits of another firm's assets
- Reduced risk by sharing it
- Defence of current markets
- Trend towards globalization
- The processes of deregulation and liberalization*
- The slow pace of liberalization of international air services†
- Survival

Notes: *As discussed in Chapter 9.
        †This has curbed airlines' abilities to grow and compete globally.

Figure 11.2. Additional motivations for airline alliances. *Source*: based on French (1997), Bennett (1996) and Hanlon (1999).

The objectives of partnership therefore include the creation of competitive advantages for the partners through complementary service provision, the achievement of economies of scale and the retention of independence. This is important especially as financially stretched airlines are not always suited to organic growth or acquisitions. Technological factors which include economies of aircraft maintenance can enable one airline to focus on one area of maintenance or one type of aircraft.

In terms of traffic feed, interline hubbing is important via cooperation between domestic and international services. This is particularly true where restrictions prevent carriers serving domestic routes or where bilaterals offer no traffic rights on relevant international routes. CRS development is also important as few airlines have the resources to develop a system alone. The processes of deregulation and liberalization clearly provided much of the impetus for collaboration of different sorts. The information revolution has done likewise. Airlines seeking to extend their global reach are attracted by this strategy. Given the regulatory constraints affecting the industry these alliances are likely to be long-term as opposed to a transitory feature of the industry.

Within the passenger airline industry strategic alliances cover diverse areas and indeed can incorporate any of the following:

- joint sales and marketing;
- joint purchasing;
- joint insurance;
- joint flights;
- improved flight connections;
- code-sharing;
- links between FFPs;
- shared airport facilities (check-in, lounge etc.);
- wet leasing; and
- block seat arrangements.

There are therefore numerous types of alliance 'relationship' and some of these require further explanation.

Code-sharing

Code-sharing occurs when one airline allows another to use its designator code, enabling the same service to be offered by more than one airline. Code-sharing is the most common characteristic of airline partnerships which grew substantially in the latter part of the 1990s.

Block seat arrangements

Blocked space agreements are an extension of the code-sharing concept whereby an airline leases a block of seats on the services of another airline on a route it does not operate itself.

Wet-leasing

Wet-leasing occurs when an aircraft is leased yet the crew, fuel and maintenance are all provided by the aircraft's owner.

The airline industry has a long history of cooperation albeit in a different format from the past. Pooling agreements were in evidence in the industry even prior to liberalization. Airlines are now more likely to look for partners with complementary networks e.g. trunk routes with feeder routes or those with geographically complementary routes. Deregulation and liberalization, which were covered in Chapter 9 led to a hectic period of takeovers and alliances, not all of which were successful. Vellas and Becherel provide the example of the failed Alcazar alliance, set up by medium-sized European carriers to rival BA and Lufthansa as well as the big US carriers. The merger was unsuccessful though as the partners could not agree on an American partner to operate the vital North Atlantic trade. Financially strong airlines and those receiving sufficient government backing have relentlessly pursued the relationships they desire. Vellas and Becherel (1995) provide the example of Iberia buying into several South American companies including Viasa of Venezuela and Aerolinas Argentinas of Argentina with the objective of establishing a dominant position on the European to Latin American routes.

The development of alliances on the current scale would have been impossible without the development of CRS (discussed in Chapter 10). These alliances are subject (in theory at least) to government approval. The US Departments of Transport and Justice are jointly responsible for policing air transport. Anti-trust legislation bars any form of market or price fixing. The many examples of consolidation in the USA in the 1980s were approved. More recently the proposed agreement between British Airways and American Airlines has met with difficulties. The EU similarly has the power to investigate monopolistic behaviour on the part of airlines as exercised once again in relation to the proposed AA–BA alliance. Further examples of airline partnerships are KLM with Alitalia and BA with Finnair.

Airlines can be, and often are, involved in several alliances at any one time although these are likely to have differing objectives.

Some alliances lead to outright merger and so these could ultimately lead to further concentration in the industry. Prospects for different airlines vary in this new air transport world.

Mergers

Mergers involve one airline in taking an equity stake in another airline. Richard Branson for example sold a share of his airline Virgin Atlantic Airways in 1999. Having reached a central position in airline strategy, airline alliances are likely to continue to be important in future. Should it become easily possible to purchase a majority holding or full ownership of any airline without restriction then current alliance patterns are likely to change however. At present the trend towards alliance formation seems far from abating.

There was an expected upsurge in merger activity in Europe following deregulation (CAA, 1998) yet this did not happen due to the effects of the recession and consequent need for carriers to consolidate their own positions before contemplating strategic expansion. More recently the focus has been on the establishment of and deepening of alliances in long-haul markets such as the North Atlantic.

In the UK, BA was formed through the merger, in the early 1970s, of the following two state carriers: British European Airways (BEA) and British Overseas Airways Corporation (BOAC).

Complementarity was evident as BEA served domestic and European routes whilst BOAC served Middle Eastern and long-haul intercontinental routes. Merger of the two gave BA the most comprehensive route network in the world.

The USA saw the highest levels of merger and alliance activity following deregulation and the consequent restructuring of the industry, albeit belatedly. This did cause some concerns regarding increases in market power. The mid-1980s in particular can be characterized by the wave of activity. By 1984 only fifteen carriers accounted for 90 per cent of the total domestic air travel market and by 1989 this percentage was held by just eight carriers. Important mergers included those of Northwest with Republic and TWA with Ozark. These two mergers both showed complementarity of networks prior to the mergers taking place. Northwest focused on long- and medium-haul whilst Republic focused on short- and medium-haul. Both used the same airport and many of the routes served were duopolies. The Department of Transport approved the merger none the less as they did with other mergers. TWA and Ozark used the same St Louis hub and shortly after merger they increased fares on what had been a competitive route.

GLOBALIZATION

International cross-border activity had often been constrained by governments for example by allowing only a certain maximum percentage of foreign ownership of carriers. Ownership of any EU airline is now open to nationals of any member state. Relaxation of restrictions can be seen generally now with some airlines taking a large share of a foreign carrier. BA for example took a 25 per cent share in Qantas.

Foreign investments have been made in the industry for some time and full mergers have sometimes resulted from this. This can lead to the formation of multinational airlines but usually this is limited to airlines from neighbouring countries and regional consortia formation. Most of the early impetus given to mergers and alliances by deregulation resulted in nationally based relationships. The constraints imposed by inter-governmental air service agreements and restrictions placed on ownership often prevented international agreements from occurring. The highest levels of activity took place in the USA where deregulation led to considerable restructuring of the industry. Global restructuring has more recently been taking place in the airline industry however as some carriers fight for their survival in the liberalized environments in many parts of the world.

Wheatcroft and Lipman (1989 p. 79) answer the question of what globalization means in an industry in which many of the major international airlines already service numerous destinations in every continent in the following way:

> in simple terms, the 'global airline' seeks to supply its services in any world market where it sees an opportunity for profitable expansion . . . the objective of globalisation is to improve competitive opportunities, to maximise new business openings, to enhance growth and to increase profitability.

In this respect, the global ambitions that can be observed in the airline industry are no different from those in other industries. Previously, airlines operated on an international basis but were not part of a global industry. Bidding for partners became intense as consortia formation began.

- The relaxation of government controls (e.g. market access)
- The relaxation of industry controls on pricing
- The shift towards privatization
- The development of CRS

Figure 11.3. Key developments facilitating the trend towards globalization. *Source*: based on Wheatcroft and Lipman (1989).

Most major airlines have global ambitions aiming to become a 'mega-carrier' of the future, operating services on a worldwide basis and participating in major geographical markets. Airlines which fail to meet these criteria are known as 'niche' carriers and are also hoping to have a place in the global industry of the future, possibly acting as 'feeder' airlines to the global carriers. The largest European carriers have been developing distinctive alliance groupings at the global level. The strengthening of their operations at their main hubs has been a particular focus in recent years.

The motivations behind the global ambitions show great similarity to those for mergers and alliances more generally. These are as follows:

- technical factors;
- cost savings;
- traffic feed;
- access to new markets;
- defence of current markets;
- economies of marketing; and
- development of CRS.

The major airlines have made no secret of their global ambitions. Indeed, the early 1990s witnessed a drive towards a 'global superleague' of carriers. Partnership agreements enabled airlines to merge their flights and distribution as well as their frequent flyer programmes and other marketing-based activities. In some cases these have also enabled them to offer so-called 'seamless services'. European carriers are heavily involved in this intensive global competition.

British Airways, as an airline actively pursuing its desire to be a global carrier, provides an excellent illustration of an airline that utilizes a variety of forms of collaboration to ensure strength in the major airline markets. Some of these are outlined in Figure 11.4.

In June 1996 BA announced plans of an alliance with American Airlines to commence in April 1997.

BA has consolidated its position within continental Europe and the UK via investment and franchise operations (see p. 208). The airline was involved in the launch of Deutsche BA with a 49 per cent stake in 1992 and took a 49.7 per cent stake in the French regional airline, TAT in the same year. BA also bought the scheduled services of the bankrupt Dan Air and in 1993 took a 25 per cent shareholding in Qantas. Overall BA's global alliances cover approximately 500 scheduled destinations in around 100 countries, involving more than 7000 departures per day.

Figure 11.4. British Airways exemplifies the business of mergers and alliances. *Source*: based on Mintel (1996) and Bennett (1997).

The fact remains however that to date most merger activity has been within national borders. Cross border attempts to break free of inter-governmental air service agreements and to extend marketable networks by involvement with complementary service providers can however be seen. Such moves are increasingly at opposite ends of long-haul routes. Motivations do vary for airlines from different countries though. Acquisition is now of interest to privatized companies as opposed to the previous situation of national airlines seeking to reduce their operating costs.

Having looked at mergers and alliances in the industry, it is now important to consider alliance patterns and the possible outcomes of these. Alliance patterns can, as discussed previously, take a number of forms and could be limited to marketing agreements for example. Previously though alliances were only between two airlines whereas the emergence of several major groupings or so-called galaxies of airlines has become noticeable as exemplified by Star and Oneworld. None of this activity is out of line with developments such as Joint Ventures and Licensing Agreements in other industries.

GLOBAL GROUPINGS

The emergence of global groupings and the rise of the so-called mega-carrier are topical aspects of the industry. Vellas and Becherel (1995) describe the rise of the airline 'mega-consortia'. Writing about airline partnerships, they use the illustration of European, Asian and American companies' attempts to consolidate their networks by entering into commercial agreements. Whilst the original alliances were mainly between two airlines, the emergence of several major groupings, or galaxies, of airlines is becoming more popular. Notable examples are discussed below.

At the time of writing membership of the two main global airline groupings is as follows:

Oneworld includes American Airlines, British Airways, Qantas, Cathay Pacific, Canadian Airlines, Finnair and Iberia.

The Star Alliance includes Lufthansa, SAS, United Airlines, Air Canada, Air New Zealand, Varig, Ansett Australia and Thai International. The 'star alliance' is a highly significant alliance development in the EU. The agreement meant that the partners had to terminate certain other partnerships.

Several authors including Wheatcroft and Lipman (1989) believe that the airline industry of the future will be dominated by just a few giant companies. Indeed, Wheatcroft and Lipman (1989) further believe that the 'global airline' concept of recent years is the major strategic issue of the international airline industry.

The takeover of BCal by BA, described earlier and which was followed by other national acquisitions, is viewed by Wheatcroft and Lipman (1989) as historically important. Control of feeder airlines by majors is an increasing phenomenon in the industry. In future, transnational developments are likely to continue to change the structure of the industry.

An efficient network strategy and schedule coordination are required if the full potential of an international airline alliance is to be realized. Dennis (2000) considers these two aspects comparing the effectiveness of the major alliance groupings in Europe and proposes strategies to optimize the coverage and connectivity of combined networks.

The emergence of dominant groupings as described is likely to have a knock-on effect in creating a reduction to the total number of carriers. Competition in the industry will inevitably continue to change. Concerns regarding monopolistic practices clearly exist especially where routes between particular hubs are dominated inhibiting route entry even more. This already occurs due to government restrictions and airport capacity constraints.

It is extremely difficult to keep abreast of the latest position regarding airline alliances as it is an ever-changing situation. For those readers wishing to track airline alliances, *Airline Business* magazine does however publish an annual survey of cross-border alliances. The number of airlines involved in alliances continues to grow and airlines are becoming better at identifying 'strategic fit'. Competition between alliance groupings is likely to increase in future. Consumer issues are also becoming more important as the BA-AA case testifies.

SEAMLESS SERVICES

 Airlines try to make journeys as smooth as possible even where passengers may have to change aircraft. By transferring luggage to the connecting flight and providing a similar service it is hoped that the journey will appear to be 'seamless.' The concept of offering a 'seamless service' is often based on provision of a common aircraft livery. Problems arise of course where carriers have to utilize different aircraft types for different journey sectors as levels of comfort can vary greatly as between jets and turbo-props. Hanlon (1999) discusses seamless service provision in further detail.

FRANCHISING

Franchises are basically licensing agreements. They display a level of standardization and draw greatly upon the experience of the franchisor. The concept of business format franchising (BFF) whereby the franchisor provides a brand name and proven formula for running a type of business, together with some assistance with this, has been tried and tested across a variety of types of service. Airline franchising involves smaller airlines in the adoption of the brand image, uniforms and livery of the majors whilst often acting as a feeder carrier for the franchisor. The concept of airline franchising shares much with the more general concept of franchising. These aspects are covered fully by sources including Lashley and Morrison (2000).

Advantages and disadvantages for both franchisors and franchisees that are generally associated with airline franchising are summarized in Table 11.1.

Table 11.1. Advantages and disadvantages of franchisors and franchisees generally associated with airline franchising. *Source*: based on Pender (1999).

Franchisors

Advantages

Access to domestic routes in countries where this might not otherwise be possible
- domestic volumes can greatly exceed international volumes
- domestic routes can provide feed for international flights

Franchising can overcome problems due to the shortage of slots at busy airports
Exposure on marginal routes which major airlines otherwise could not afford to operate in many cases
Network expansion is possible without heavy capital expenditure
Financial gains can be achieved
- franchise fees or royalties
- fees for ground handling and other services

Disadvantages

Difficulties can be experienced in controlling franchisees
Costs of controlling franchisees can be great
The reputation of the franchisor's brand is at stake

Franchisees

Advantages

Franchisees benefit from endorsement of the major's brand
Franchisor back-up is usually provided such as sales and marketing activities including access to distribution channels e.g. CRS and FFP access
Franchisees retain some commercial freedom

Disadvantages

Franchisees remain beholden to any franchisor problems
High maintenance standards must be maintained
Costs need to be kept low yet high degrees of sophistication paid for

Franchising appeals to major airlines with high cost structures operating under increasing price pressures. In the USA airlines have been expanding their marketable networks through franchising since domestic deregulation in 1978. A notable example of this is Air Florida's use of commuter flights provided by Air Miami. European airlines, including British Airways and Lufthansa, have only more recently become involved in franchising, partly in an attempt to achieve their global ambitions as outlined above. This form of partnership, involving less financial outlay, has advantages over equity investments for many airlines. Both franchisor and franchisee airlines can benefit from increased passenger numbers as a result of franchising. This can also be a means by which franchisors can expand internationally in an industry characterized by layers of complexity caused by problems of route and airport access. BA has a number of foreign franchisees in addition to those based in the UK. Franchising internationally has had particular benefits for BA in the Levant region due to restrictions on profitable operations to Beirut, Amman and Damascus resulting from the political situation in the Middle East. British Mediterranean now operates these routes under a franchise agreement for BA.

At the time of writing BA had signed a total of nine franchise agreements and had a fleet of 115 aircraft carrying more than six million passengers. The franchise partners accounted for a net revenue of £542 million providing 392,000 connecting passengers and adding nine countries to the network (British Airways, 1999). BA franchisees include the following:

- City-flyer Express;
- Brymon;
- Maersk;
- Loganair;
- British Regional Airlines (Manx);
- GB Airways;
- British Mediterranean;
- Sun-Air; and
- Comair.

Following BA's development of franchising, several other European national carriers have begun to form agreements of this type including Air France with Brit Air and Jersey European Airways (JEA) among others and Lufthansa with Augsburg Airways and others.

Airline franchising is not without its problems however and BA admits to experiencing problems controlling franchisees whilst being mindful of the fact that the reputation of their brand is at stake. Franchisee training and audit are attempts to control the process of franchising. Franchisees are also advised not to become too reliant on franchisors as this could render them vulnerable. Furthermore, business problems encountered by a franchisor can have a knock-on effect for franchisees. Franchisee independence can easily be compromised as a result of franchising. Airline franchisees are not exclusively start-up companies and not all operate exclusively as franchisees. Pender (1999) provides more detailed coverage of airline franchising.

DOMESTIC SERVICES AND FOREIGN CARRIERS

Since April 1997 it has been possible for non-UK airlines within the European Union (EU) to operate domestic services within the UK yet almost all domestic services are served by UK airlines. According to Key Note (1999) foreign carriers accounted for only 34 per cent of airline traffic at UK airports, representing 31 per cent of scheduled traffic but only 3 per cent of non-scheduled or charter airline traffic. British Airways dominates the market for scheduled passengers carried by UK airlines. British Midland and Virgin Atlantic Airways are further examples of UK-registered scheduled airlines.

VERTICAL INTEGRATION

Some vertical integration has taken place alongside all of the horizontal integration between scheduled carriers with examples from both the hotel and car hire sectors. These relationships have not always worked out however and airlines have often severed relations with hotels. Linkages with airport terminals have in some cases been more successful. Telecommunications linkages may develop further in future. Delta's relationship with AT&T who handle their internal computing requirements is one example of just such a relationship.

LOW-COST CARRIERS

The concept, and introduction to Europe, of low-cost carriers were outlined in Chapter 9. These can be seen to be one of the most significant outcomes of liberalization and have generally substantially stimulated new air traffic without serious detriment to incumbents' operations. They have however impacted on incumbents' business. British Airways introduced Go, a low-cost carrier of its own, in 1998 and this was subsequently followed by KLM's introduction of Buzz. According to the CAA (1998), these carriers, in aggregate, now account for around a third of overall non-national carrier output on some of the more dense international intra-European routes.

The emergence of European low-cost carriers post-liberalization is not out of line with the US experience. A variety of start-up airlines offering low fares operated in the early days of the deregulated environment. These carriers experienced problems in the resultant highly competitive market however. Some allowed standards to slip and this had an effect on consumer confidence. By the end of the 1990s low-cost carriers were responsible for only around a quarter of all internal passengers in the USA. Much of this low-cost traffic was accommodated by the major success story of US low-cost travel, Southwest Airline. Some of the pioneers of low-cost travel in Europe have admitted bringing the Southwest model to Europe. Other no-frills airlines in the USA to survive the initial shake-out in the early to mid-1980s include ValuJet (now AirTran) and Tower Air.

Surviving European examples of low cost carriers at the time of writing, include the following:

- Ryanair;
- easyJet;
- Virgin Express; and
- Air One.

Other 'no-frills' operators have had less success in the market place and neither Euroscot Express nor Debonair is still operating. Indeed, it cannot be assumed that low-cost carriers will continue to operate successfully in Europe. Comparison with the US experience as we have seen shows that although a number of low-cost carriers entered the US market following deregulation, the majority of these failed to survive in the longer-term. The USA airline environment is of course very different from that in Europe and in fact additional threats to the future success of low-cost carriers in Europe can be identified. These are outlined in Figure 11.5.

Any continuation of the policy of state-aid to some European carriers
Further development of high speed rail in Europe
Possible improved flexibility of charter airline operations
Possible responses of incumbents
Possible intra-airline rivalry displayed by low-cost carriers
Possible cessation of favourable airport charges at secondary airports

Figure 11.5. Threats to the survival of low-cost carriers in Europe. *Source*: based on Pender and Baum (2000).

Much of the discussion in this and the previous chapter has been concerned with the outcome of the processes of deregulation and liberalization. Morrell (1998) provides a detailed account of progress to date in relation to the achievement of liberalization and greater competition in the European air transport industry.

SUMMARY

Following on from the discussion in earlier chapters of the processes of deregulation and liberalization, this chapter considered some of the main outcomes of these. Attention was paid to the formation of airline mergers and alliances in particular leading to consideration of the increasingly global nature of air transportation. The emergence of global mega-carriers was discussed. The chapter then moved on to discuss further outcomes of deregulation namely the development of franchising and the emergence of low cost carriers.

DISCUSSION QUESTIONS

1. Account for the extent to which mergers and alliances have become a feature of the airline industry.
2. Why might franchising in the European airline sector be viewed as a short-term defensive strategy by major airlines?

REFERENCES

Bennett, M.M. (1996) Strategic alliances in the world airline industry, *Progress in Tourism and Hospitality Research*, Vol. 3.

British Airways (1999) http://www.british.airways.com

CAA (1998) *The Single European Market: the first five years*, CAP 685, Westward Digital Ltd.

Davies, R.E.G. and Quastler, I.E. (1995) *Commuter Airlines of the United States*, Smithsonian Institution Press.

Dennis, N. (2000) Scheduling issues and network strategies for international airline alliances, *Journal of Air Transport Management*, 6.

French, T. (1997) Global trends in airline alliances, *Travel and Tourism Analyst*, No. 4.

Gilbert, D.C. (1996) Relationship marketing and airline loyalty schemes, *Tourism Management*, 17(8).

Hanlon, P. (1999) *Global Airlines: competition in a transnational industry* (2nd edn), Butterworth Heinemann.

Holloway, S. (1997) *Straight and Level, Practical Airline Economics*, Ashgate.

Key Note Ltd. (1997) *Airlines*.

Key Note Ltd. (1999) *UK Travel and Tourism.*

Lashley, C. and Morrison, A. (2000) *Franchising Hospitality Services*, Butterworth Heinemann.

Mintel (1996) *Airlines.*

Morrell, P. (1998) Air transport liberalization in Europe: the progress so far, *Journal of Air Transportation World Wide*, 3(1).

Pender, L. (1999) European aviation: the emergence of franchised airline operations, *Tourism Management*, 20(5), October.

Pender, L. and Baum, T.G. (2000) Have the frills really left the European airline industry?, *International Journal of Tourism Research*, 2(6).

Pender, L. (2000) Travel trade and transport, in C. Lashley and A. Morrison, *Franchising Hospitality Services*, Butterworth Heinemann, Oxford.

Sull, D. (1999) Case study: easyJet's $500 million gamble, *European Management Journal*, 17(1), February.

The Economist (1999) Avoiding peanuts, 13 November, p. 104.

Vellas, F. and Becherel, L. (1995) *International Tourism*, Macmillan Business.

Wheatcroft, S. and Lipman, G. (1986) Air transport in a competitive European market: problems, prospects and strategies, *Travel and Tourism Report* No. 3, EIU.

Wheatcroft, S. and Lipman, G. (1990) European Liberalization and World Air Transport: towards a transnational industry, *Special Report* No. 2015, EIU.

Further Reading

Beaver, A. (1993) *Mind Your Own Travel Business: A Manual of Retail Travel Practice,* (3 Volumes), Allan Beaver Publishers, 3 ed.

Bray, R. and Raitz, V. (2000) *Flight to the Sun: The Story of the Holiday Revolution,* Continuum.

Brendon, P. (1990) *Thomas Cook, 150 years of Popular Tourism,* Secker & Warburg.

Bywater, M. (1992) The European Tour Operator Industry, EIU Special Report 2141

Davidson, R. (1994) Business Travel, Pitman Publishing.

Davies, R.E.G. and Quastler, I.E. (1995) *Commuter Airlines of the United States,* Smithsonian Institution Press.

Dobson, A. P. (1995) *Flying in the face of competition,* Ashgate.

Doganis, R. (1985) *Flying Off Course. The Economics of International Airlines,* Allen & Unwin.

Downes, J. (1993) Legal liabilities in the European travel trade: the EC Package Travel Directive, *Travel and Tourism Analyst,* No. 1, pp. 81–97.

Downes, J. and Paton, T. (1993) *Travel Agency Law,* Pitman Publishing.

French, T. (1997) Global Trends in Airline Alliances, Travel and Tourism Analyst No. 4, *Travel and Tourism Intelligence.*

Frew, E. (1994) International charter travel – a new opportunity for Australian tourism, in Seaton, A.V. *et al.* (eds) *Tourism: The State of the Art,* Wiley.

Graham, B. (1995) *Geography and Air Transport,* Wiley.

Hanlon, P. (1999) *Global Airlines – competition in a transnational industry,* 2 ed., Butterworth Heinemann.

Holloway, J.C. (1994) *The Business of Tourism,* 4 ed., Pitman Publishing.

Holloway, S. (1997) *Straight and Level: practical airline economics,* Ashgate Publishing Ltd.

Holloway, J.C. and Robinson, C. (1995) *Marketing for Travel and Tourism,* Pitman, 4 ed.

Horner, P. (1996) *Travel Agency Practice,* Addison-Wesley Longman.

Humphreys, B. (1994) European Air Transport: The Views of the "Wise Men," English Tourist Board Insights, Tourism Intelligence Papers.

Inkpen, G. (1998) *Information Technology for Travel and Tourism,* 2 ed., Longman.

Key Note Market Review (1998) *Travel Agents and Overseas Tour Operators.*

Krippendorf, J. (1987) *The Holiday Makers,* Heinemann.

Laws, E. (1997) *Managing Packaged Tourism - relationships, responsibilities and service quality in the inclusive holiday industry,* International Thomson Press.

Lickorish, L.J. and Jenkins, C.L. (eds) (1997) *An Introduction to Tourism,* Butterworth Heinemann.

Middleton, V.T.C. (1991) 'Whither the Package Tour?', *Tourism Management*, Vol. 12, No. 3, pp. 185–92.

Mintel (1999) Coach Holidays, Leisure Intelligence, January.

Mintel (1999) Crossing the Channel, Leisure Intelligence, July.

Mintel (1999) Cruises, Leisure Intelligence, January.

Mintel (1999) Fly-drive Holidays, Leisure Intelligence, April.

Mintel (1998) Inclusive Tours, Leisure Intelligence, March.

Mintel (1999) Long Haul Holidays, Leisure Intelligence, March.

Mintel (1999) No-Frills/Low-Cost Airlines, Leisure Intelligence, February.

Mintel (1999) Rail Travel, Leisure Intelligence, September.

Mintel (1998) Travel Agents, Retail Intelligence, January.

Mintel (1999) Travel Incentives and Promotions, Leisure Intelligence, November.

Morell, P. (1997) *Airline Finance*, Ashgate Publishing Ltd.

Page, S. (1999) *Transport for Tourism*, Routledge, 2 ed.

Pender, L. (1999) European Aviation: the emergence of franchised airline operations, *Tourism Management*, 20(5), October.

Pender, L. (1999) *Marketing Management for Travel and Tourism*, Stanley Thornes.

Pender, L. (2000) Travel trade and transport, in Lashley, C. and Morrison, A., *Franchising Hospitality Services*, Butterworth Heinemann.

Pender, L. and Baum, V. (2000) Have the frills really left the European airline industry? *International Journal of Tourism Research*, 2(6).

Poon, A. (1993) *Tourism, Technology and Competitive Strategies*, CAB International.

Renshaw, M.B. (1997) *The Travel Agent*, 2 ed., Business Education Publishers Ltd.

Shaw, S. (1987) *Airline Marketing and Management*, Pitman, 2 ed.

Towner, J. (1985) The history of the Grand Tour, *Annals of Tourism Research*, Vol. 12, No. 3, pp. 301–16.

Vellas, F. and Becherel, L. (1995) *International Tourism*, Macmillan Business.

Williams, G. (1993) *The Airline Industry and the Impact of Deregulation*, Ashgate.

Yale, P. (1995) *The Business of Tour Operations*, Addison Wesley Longman.

Journals

Annals of Tourism Research
The Journal of Air Transport Management
The International Journal of Tourism Research
Tourism Management
Travel and Tourism Analyst

Index

In this index, bold type refers to main coverage of the topic within the given page references, *t* refers to tables and *f* to figures. Tables and figures are only indexed where they are not covered by another term on the same page or in the same section.